China Academic Library

For further volumes:
http://www.springer.com/series/11562

Yining Li

Chinese Economy in Disequilibrium

Sponsored by Chinese Fund for the Humanities and Social Sciences
(本书获中华社会科学基金资助)

外语教学与研究出版社
FOREIGN LANGUAGE TEACHING AND RESEARCH PRESS

Springer

Yining Li
Guanghua School of Management
Peking University
Beijing
People's Republic of China

ISSN 2195-1853 ISSN 2195-1861 (electronic)
ISBN 978-3-642-39557-4 ISBN 978-3-642-39558-1 (eBook)
DOI 10.1007/978-3-642-39558-1
Springer Heidelberg New York Dordrecht London

Library of Congress Control Number: 2013954927
Sponsored by Chinese Fund for the Humanities and Social Sciences (本书获中华社会科学基金资助)

Preface to the Chinese Edition

"Among all your publications on current Chinese economy, which one is most representative of your academic viewpoints?" If this is the question someone asks me, "it is the book right in front of us, *Chinese Economy in Disequilibrium*," I would answer. Why do I have this answer? I have my own reasons.

Among my publications, *Institutions, Goals and People—Challenges to Economics* (Heilongjiang People's Press, 1986) studied comparative economics. Many of its chapters discussed Chinese economic issues. It also proposed a methodology for studying socialist economic theories. Nevertheless, it is not a book on current Chinese economy.

Socialist Political Economics (The Commercial Press, 1986) is a textbook which described the framework of my economic theories, but barely discussed real economic issues. Moreover, it is a book on socialist political economy intended for beginners. Therefore, it is unlikely to include in-depth discussions and analyses of certain economic theories. Nonetheless, I believe it is the most comprehensive and systematic publication on my own economic theories.

Exploring Reforms of Economic Institutions (The People's Daily Press, 1987) specifically discussed issues associated with the shareholding system, controlling shareholder system and conglomerates in the public ownership system. It did not further discuss any other issues.

Management of National Economy (Hebei People's Press, 1988) is also a textbook, primarily discussing the principles and policies for managing the national economy from short-term, mid-term, and long-term perspectives. Due to the requirements of a textbook, it is difficult to fully discuss in-depth issues related to economic disequilibrium.

Perspectives on Chinese Economic Reforms (China Prospect Press, 1989) summarized the general economic reform plan that I proposed for China, including the main reform directions and corresponding reform measures and execution processes. But it is not a book on disequilibrium.

Where is Chinese Economy Heading (The Commercial Press, Hong Kong, 1989) is a collection of my speeches delivered in Hong Kong at the beginning of 1989. It is intended to address a few specific issues encountered during Chinese economic reforms. Such topics as how to switch from the subcontracting system to the shareholding system, why it is not possible to privatize large and medium state-owned enterprises, and how to manage state assets were elaborated fairly thoroughly in the book. But it did not give a systematic analysis of the disequilibrium conditions prevalent in the Chinese economy.

Compared with the above-mentioned publications, *Chinese Economy in Disequilibrium* is different in three aspects. First of all, it is academic research, not a textbook for college students. Although my analysis herein is based on the principles stated in the books of *Socialist Political Economics* and *Management of National Economy*, the theoretical study on economic disequilibrium is far more detailed than that in those two books. Secondly, it focuses on current Chinese economy, unlike the book of *Institutions, Goals and People—Challenges to Economics*, which focused on comparative economics. Thirdly, it features theories, primarily analyzing the characteristics of economic disequilibrium in an attempt to discover the underlying reasons for resource misallocation, distorted industrial structures, and institutional innovation variation. The book does not designate economic disequilibrium as a prerequisite, as did the books of *Exploring Reforms of Economic Institutions*, *Perspectives on Chinese Economic Reforms*, and *Where is Chinese Economy Heading*, but directly discusses specific policies for Chinese economic reforms. With these thoughts, I believe *Chinese Economy in Disequilibrium* is the book that most fully presents my academic views on current Chinese economy.

In my opinion, the book provides featured analyses in the following eight aspects:

1. There are two types of economic disequilibrium. Type I disequilibrium refers to the disequilibrium condition under which the market has not been fully developed. Type II disequilibrium refers to the disequilibrium condition under which the market is not fully developed and enterprises lack profit maximization mechanisms and budget constraints. Current Chinese economy belongs to type II disequilibrium. We should do our utmost to first and foremost transit the economy from type II disequilibrium to type I disequilibrium, followed by gradually shrinking the magnitude of imbalance inherent under type I economic disequilibrium condition.
2. The socialist economy is susceptible to stagflation in economic disequilibrium. There are two types of inflation, open inflation and hidden inflation, the latter referring to an unchanging price level at which commodities are actually out of stock. There are open and hidden stagnation as well, with the latter referring to the situation of superficial growth in aggregate output with effective supply actually remaining unchanged. Therefore, stagflation has four potential forms of combinations. Any measure to prevent and tackle stagflation must be properly adopted according to the specific situation.
3. The impact of structural factors on current economic imbalances in China cannot be ignored. Difficulties in industrial restructuring are associated with the defects of enterprise operation mechanism, and the short-sightedness of corporate behavior as well as societal behavior. Therefore, the rationalization of industrial structure can only be achieved by accelerating the reconstruction

of enterprise operation mechanism and by actively leveraging the leadership of the central government in quota adjustment in the commodity market and the establishment of order in the socialist commodity economy.

4. Economic fluctuations are common in a disequilibrium economy. People tend to ask when an economy will come out of recession. It should be noted that it is relatively easy to pull the economy out of recession that is calculated based on the growth rate of output, for direct government spending or corporate spending with credit support will generate higher output growth. Nevertheless, it is far more difficult for the economy to come out of recession calculated based on the growth rate of enterprise profitability or the growth rate of actual fiscal revenues (i.e., excluding borrowings and net of inflation rate). We need to reform the enterprise operation mechanism, which is critical to actually pulling the national economy out of recession.
5. There are various rigidities under the economic disequilibrium conditions. In addition to many known rigidities, such as wage rigidity, employment rigidity, and welfare rigidity, there is a unique type of rigidity under current disequilibrium conditions (type II disequilibrium) in the Chinese economy, one called "enterprise rigidity." It refers to the situation in which an enterprise is not actually responsible for its own profits and losses or only responsible when it is profitable. Thus bankruptcy is almost out of the question. Without resolving the "enterprise rigidity," China will have to remain in type II economic disequilibrium for a long time.
6. If commodity shortages are prevalent, a dual-track price mechanism applicable to shortage commodities cannot be terminated if there are relatively severe resource constraints. Otherwise, even when the gap between the dual prices, i.e., planned and non-planned price, is eliminated, a gap between two new prices, i.e., open price and underground price, will appear. Therefore, a full price decontrol before all other conditions are ready will only lead to social turmoil and unjustified profits taken by certain people who can take advantage of the gap between open price and underground price.
7. Scarcity of certain resources, as well as the exclusivity stemming from such scarcity, may persist for a long time in the socialist commodity economy. The government has to make necessary adjustments, such as levying resource taxes on the producers of exclusive scarce resources. The government, however, should also be careful not to completely seize everything above normal profits, but only a portion. Otherwise, it won't help improve resource utilization efficiency.
8. It is essential to further push economic reforms under current economic disequilibrium conditions. We are often confronted with this challenge: A new institution or policy tends to deviate from its original plan (hereinafter referred to as "institutional variation"). This is mainly attributable to such issues as non-standardized institutional innovation, changes in enterprise expectations and personal expectations, and market imperfection. Institutional variation can only be addressed by making appropriate adjustments in these areas.

Preface to the English Edition

The Chinese language edition of *Chinese Economy in Disequilibrium* was first published in 1990, but the manuscript was finished toward the end of 1988. To explain why I wanted to write such a book at that time, I must start from the conditions of the development of the Chinese economic reform in the 1980s.

The Chinese economic reform started from the introduction of the Agricultural Contract System in 1979. Farmers in Anhui, Sichuan, and some other provinces spontaneously divided their lands and fixed farm output quotas on a household basis. This innovation greatly motivated farmers and boosted output. The state government closely monitored this change, sent out investigation teams to Anhui and Sichuan to learn from the farmers' experience, and eventually decided to promulgate their practice of the Agricultural Contract System to the whole country. This is deemed "the first spring thunder" of the Chinese economic reform. A few years later, farmers' markets flourished and the phenomenon of food shortage gradually disappeared. Another few years later, the urban food rationing system, which had been there for many years, was also abolished.

And then came the rise of township and village enterprises. These enterprises relied on funds raised by farmers: they needed no government investment and their products did not rely on government allocation. Consequently, the 1980s witnessed a unique phenomenon: Sales persons of these township and village enterprises traveled everywhere around the country, carrying samples of their products and seeking markets for them. The monopoly of planned economy was broken: a product market for township and village enterprise products emerged beside the planned economic system.

At the same time, a special economic zone was established in 1980 in Shenzhen of Guangdong, an area close to Hong Kong. There, resources were allocated by the market mechanism and economic growth accelerated in such speed known as "Shenzhen Speed." There is one thing people learned from this experience: The market mechanism in China is not only viable but also necessary.

The promulgation of the Agricultural Contract System, the rise of township and village enterprises, and the establishment of special economic zones were like 3 stones thrown into water that stirred waves—the Chinese economy was no longer a pool of quiet water. In the mid-1980s, the focus of the Chinese economic reform turned to cities. Concerning the questions of how to reform the urban system, and how to gradually transit from planned economy to market economy, Chinese economists saw a dispute between two ideas about the reform.

The dominant idea at that moment suggested "price decontrol" as the major route of reforms. Proponents of this idea believed that the experience of West Germany was applicable in China. They asked: West Germany did this, why can't China? Their opinion received attention from the central government. In 1988, the State Council decided to implement a reform scheme that was centered on price reform.

At this critical moment, in late April 1986, I gave a long speech at Peking University on the topic of "principal ideas of reform," where I pointed out that the Chinese economic reform should not be centered on price reform. Rather, it should be on ownership reform. I also pointed out in this speech that if the Chinese economic reform fails, it might be because of failures of the price reform. But the success of the Chinese economic reform must depend on ownership reform, that is, the success of enterprise reform.

This speech caught the attention of both domestic and foreign media. The Chinese State Council also took my advice seriously and postponed the announcing of the price reform scheme.

To get my ideas across to more people who are concerned of the Chinese economic reform, starting from that moment, I began to write this book in front of you, *Chinese Economy in Disequilibrium*. After 3 years' work and rounds of revisions, the manuscript was eventually submitted to the publisher at the end of 1988 and the book was officially published in 1990.

Such is the background of the writing and publishing of this book. 1988 was a critical year, because it was in this year that the Chinese government returned to the price reform scheme and was preparing to copy the "shock therapy" of West Germany, hoping to smooth the institutional transformation by way of price reform. I did not agree with this policy because in China under the planned economy regime, enterprises are not truly market players, instead, they are more like government affiliations. Thus, price stimulation could neither help sort out winner and loser enterprises in the market nor promote industrial restructuring. Thus, in China, the most suitable route for the reform could only be ownership reform and letting enterprises become genuine market players. My book *Chinese Economy in Disequilibrium* was written to clarify this principal logic for the Chinese economic reform.

Reforming practice in the 1980s and the 1990s proved my assessment of the conditions. As expected, a surge of panic purchasing out of peoples' expectation of price rise forced the 1988 price reform to a halt. In the 1990s, China gradually transformed state-owned enterprises into shareholding corporations, and thus eventually led the Chinese economic reform out of its dilemma.

Now at the time when the English edition of *Chinese Economy in Disequilibrium* is about to be published, I recall the conditions and history of the Chinese economic reform at the time when I started this book and write this preface specifically for the reference of my readers of the English edition.

Beijing, People's Republic of China Yining Li
21st September 2012

Acknowledgments

I express my sincere gratitude to Chen Shulang, who did an excellent job translating this book from Chinese into English; Dr. Niels Peter Thomas, Ms. Leana Li and Mr. Toby Chai from Springer Science and Business Media; Mr. Cai Jianfeng, Mr. Xu Jianzhong, Mr. Wu Hao, Ms. Deng Xiaojing, Ms. Yi Lu, Ms. Zhao Yaru, and Ms. Hu Yuyan from Foreign Language Teaching and Research Press; Mr. Cai Hongbin, Mr. Zhou Li'an, and Mr. Yan Se from Guanghua School of Management, Peking University; and Mr. Laixiang Sun from the University of London, UK. This book would not be with you so quickly without their generous help.

Contents

Chapter 1
Exploring the Issues in Resource Allocation

1.1 Resource Allocation in the Socialist Economy: From the Perspective of Disequilibrium

1.1.1 Disequilibrium Defined

In economics, disequilibrium is defined relative to Walrasian equilibrium, which is achieved under the assumption of a fully developed market and a flexible price mechanism. Disequilibrium refers to a balance condition under which there is neither a fully developed market nor a flexible price mechanism. In this sense, disequilibrium is also called non-Walrasian equilibrium.

According to the Walrasian theory, given that the market is fully developed and the price mechanism flexible, given also that every market participant possesses perfect information about current and future prices as well as a full understanding of current and future demand and supply, and that prices adjust instantaneously with changes in demand and supply, then, at any price level, aggregate demand is always equal to aggregate supply, and there is no excess demand or excess supply. All transactions are settled at equilibrium prices. If the equilibrium price is not reached, a transaction will not be concluded. Only when price is in equilibrium can a transaction be concluded. According to this theory, excess production, sluggish merchandise sales, chronic unemployment, and inflation due to excess demand will not occur.

The impractical Walrasian equilibrium has long drawn harsh criticism from some dissenting Western economists. Keynes discussed the issue of chronic unemployment in the capitalist society in his book titled *The General Theory of Employment, Interest and Money* published in 1936. Until the early 1960s, however, research on disequilibrium by economists remained limited and sporadic. Even their interpretations of the Keynesian economic theory were drastically divided. Orthodox Keynesian economists believed that Keynesian economic theory belonged to the economics of equilibrium and that Keynes himself did not deny Walrasian

Y. Li, *Chinese Economy in Disequilibrium*, China Academic Library,
DOI 10.1007/978-3-642-39558-1_1, © Foreign Language Teaching and Research
Publishing Co., Ltd and Springer-Verlag Berlin Heidelberg 2014

equilibrium but simply made some modifications. Other Keynesian economists, however, believed that the Keynesian theory had gone beyond the limit of equilibrium theory by providing an initial and systemic review on disequilibrium theory, as was demonstrated by Keynes' belief that market mechanism was not always fully effective in coordinating various transactions and that production, employment, and investment would fluctuate, often leading to overproduction, unemployment, and insufficient demand for investment in the capitalist society.

Since the late 1960s, the disequilibrium theory has made noticeable progress. Studies on disequilibrium have demonstrated that when a market is not fully developed and prices fail to function and adjust supply and demand, every economic factor will work its way to a point where they are mutually adaptable according to their respective situations to reach equilibrium. Obviously, the equilibrium under disequilibrium conditions is not one in a fully developed market, but one in a market that is not fully developed. It is not an equilibrium accompanied by zero unemployment or inflation rate, but one with certain unemployment rate and inflation rate. In other words, disequilibrium is actually a type of equilibrium, but unlike the equilibrium described in the Walrasian theory, it is real in daily life. This is the definition of disequilibrium in economics.

1.1.2 Resource Allocation Defined

Resource allocation refers to the allocation of various economic resources, i.e., labor, materials, and capital according to different uses. When resource supplies are limited, it is necessary to work out an efficient way to allocate various economic resources to meet various needs in order to maximize the output of products and services in demand. Any society, including socialist society, can only be considered to have achieved effective resource allocation when every person's talent has been fully employed, every product's utility has been maximized, and every inch of land has been fully utilized. If there are labor, materials, and capital left idle or wasted, the allocation of resources is considered problematic. One of the most important issues that economists study is how to achieve effective allocation of resources in order to fully utilize existing resources and discover potential resources.

Resource allocation can be viewed in two different tiers. The higher tier refers to the allocation of resources among various sectors, regions, and production units. Whether the allocation is effective or not depends on whether each resource is effectively allocated to its best place. The lower tier refers to the organization and utilization of pre-allocated resources by a production unit, a region, or a sector. The effectiveness of the allocation depends on whether or not these resources are utilized to their fullest potential.

These two tiers of resource allocation have certain connections as well as differences. From the perspective of overall society, allocations of existing resources in different areas undoubtedly impact resource utilization efficiency at each economic unit as the total quantity of existing resources is limited, and ineffective resource allocation in the macroeconomy will certainly lead to low utilization efficiency at some production units. On the other hand, if most production units are able to raise resource utilization efficiency to a higher level, the supply of resources in the economy will increase. Compared with unchanged quantity of resources, higher supply of resources is more favorable to adjusting resource allocation in various areas and more conducive to allocating resources effectively. This is the connection between the two tiers of resource allocation. Their differences, however, are represented by different goals and ways of execution. The goal of the lower tier resource allocation is to raise resource utilization efficiency at a production unit so as to increase total output with fixed amount of input, while that of the higher tier resource allocation is to effectively put every resource to its best use and allow factors of production to regroup to maximize their utility. The two tiers of resource allocation also vary in terms of way of execution, with the lower tier increasing resource utilization efficiency by using production or managerial techniques inside the production unit without transferring production factors. The higher tier resource allocation achieves its goal via rearranging the combination of production factors, regulating property rights, transferring fixed assets, making macroeconomic adjustments, as well as reforming macroeconomic management system.

Realizing effective resource allocation, either at the higher tier or at the lower tier, requires a long process. There is no absolute standard for effective resource allocation, nor is there a limit for how effective resource allocation can be. We can only say that whether resource allocation of this tier or that tier is more effective after certain adjustments or reforms, whether there is some improvement, or how much of an improvement. One of the important topics in the socialist political economics is to study how to manage the economy so as to improve resource allocation and increase effectiveness in the socialist economy, which will lead to higher effectiveness of both the higher tier and the lower tier resource allocation.

1.1.3 The Features of Socialist Economic System and Resource Allocation

Before studying resource allocation in the socialist economy, we must understand the socialist economic system as well as its impact on resource allocation. As various socialist economic systems can be categorized into several forms, resource allocation in the socialist economy can also be grouped accordingly. Each form of resource allocation has its own features associated with its economic system.

There are three types of economic systems categorized based on Chinese economic realities. The first type is the traditional economic system. The second type is the dual-track economic system whereby the traditional economic system is gradually giving in to the new economic system. The third type is the new economic system. The economic system from the late 1950s to the late 1970s was the traditional economic system, while that since the 1980s is the dual-track economic system, which we are currently under. The new economic system is the system we are aiming to establish through economic reform after breaking away from the dual-track economic system. It is still an economic system under planning and has not yet become reality.

The features of resource allocation under these three economic systems are as follows:

In the traditional economic system, mandatory planning is considered either the only form of economic planning in the socialist economy, i.e., the socialist economy is equivalent to a mandatorily planned economy, or the primary form of the socialist economy in which mandatory allocation is the primary method to allocate resources in the economy. In this economic system, the market does not play any role at all or has a very limited impact on resource allocation. Moreover, as the system does not recognize enterprises as goods producers, business operators, or decision-makers, disregards their private economic interests, and restricts the transfer of production factors, resource allocation at the higher tier is extremely ineffective, causing not only severe imbalances in industrial structure, technological structure, regional economic structure, and employment structure but also tremendous waste and destruction of resources. In terms of the lower tier resource allocation, enterprises have no incentive or possibility to utilize resources effectively, as their production and management decisions are constantly interfered by government agencies, resulting in low productivity as well as low resource utilization efficiency. These are the main features of resource allocation in the traditional socialist economic system. Therefore, reforming the traditional economic system is a necessary step toward more effective resource allocation.

The dual-track economic system is a system that exists during the transitional period between the traditional and the new economic system. As defects of the traditional economic system become more and more prominent, the economy will have to undergo a systemic reform and a series of new economic issues are likely to emerge afterward. The reason is that the new economic system can only be established on a gradual basis as the old economic system fades away and the transition process from the old system to the new one is relatively long. During this process, some economic activities may still be carried out according to the traditional economic system, while other activities are conducted according to the new economic system. In addition, there are potential scenarios where economic activities are restricted by both the traditional and new economic systems, as the traditional economic system has not been completely terminated while the new economic system has started to play certain roles in the economy, and there may also be gaps where both the traditional and new economic system fail to function, resulting in economic turmoil. It is necessary to point out here that the dual-track economic system is transitional in itself and resource allocation in the system is relatively complicated. More specifically, the industrial structure is getting more effective, idle or wasted resources are decreasing, and resource utilization efficiency is increasing; on the other hand, infrastructure construction projects are expanding irrationally, and the number of redundant construction projects is still on the rise, straining the supply of raw materials and leading to rampant inflation driven by both higher demand and cost. Under such complex circumstances, even though resource allocation may be better overall than that in the traditional economic system, it is quite possible that the allocation of resources in certain areas is even worse than that in the traditional economic system. Economic reforms have thus encountered unexpected obstacles. Some people who were optimistic about economic reforms in the first place lose confidence in economic reforms after witnessing chaos during the transitional period between the old and new economic systems. Some even think the traditional economic system has certain merits, for at least it steered clear of the chaos during the transitional period. These are the features of resource allocation in the dual-track economic system. They are also commonly referred to as "transitional symptoms," which are inevitable during the transitional period between the old and new systems, namely, pains brought by the birth of a new economic system.

The new economic system is the target system to be established after socialist economic reforms. It will be an economic system in which enterprises are highly motivated and factors of production can be freely transferred and recombined. The internal operation mechanism of enterprises would be fundamentally different from that under the traditional economic system. The lower tier resource allocation would become more effective as enterprises are more motivated by their economic interests. Because of the normalization of property rights and the possible rearrangement of production factors in the economy, effective allocation of resources among various areas in the economy would likely come true, thus realizing the goal of achieving the effectiveness of the higher tier resource allocation. It is obvious that the new economic system to be established is one that facilitates effective allocation of resources.

1.1.4 Economic Disequilibrium and Socialist Resource Allocation

Analyzing the features of resource allocation in the socialist economy from the economic system perspective helps understand the significance and tasks of economic reforms and economic regulations during the current period as well as in the future. However, simply analyzing the features based on various socialist economic systems is not enough. It is necessary to take the analysis of resource allocation one step further by incorporating the disequilibrium conditions China's economy is currently under. This way, we can better understand the features of resource allocation in the socialist economy.

According to the above discussions on disequilibrium, we can clearly understand that the disequilibrium theory studies the operation process of the economy under the circumstances that the market is underdeveloped and price signals are ineffective in automatically adjusting supply and demand. In terms of China, the economy under the traditional economic system was no doubt in a state of disequilibrium, while the economy under the current dual-track economic system is still in a state of disequilibrium. For a relatively long period of time in the future, the economy will continue to remain in a state of disequilibrium for reasons including sustained constraints on resources, even after the new economic system has been established and functioning. It may be a little different compared to the past, as the severity of disequilibrium is lower. These are the realities in current Chinese economy and we must not avoid them.

Now, let us focus on resource allocation under the dual-track economic system. The fundamental characteristics of a disequilibrium economy, such as underdeveloped market, unreasonable prices of comparable commodities, distorted price signals, severe constraints on resource supply, and an excess of aggregate demand over aggregate supply, all exist in the current dual-track economic system. More importantly, behind the operation of the economy lies such a fact: Enterprises, especially state-owned enterprises in the dual-track economic system, have not completely steered clear of their affiliation with government administrative agencies or become goods producers with decision-making authorities and responsibilities for their own profits or losses. Their investment and transaction activities are distorted to a large extent. Even when price signals are accurate, they cannot serve as an instrument for those enterprises to adjust demand and supply accordingly. Therefore, only after we have a relatively thorough understanding of current Chinese economic realities can we naturally reach the following conclusions based on the view of disequilibrium economy: It is necessary to reform the economic system in order to enhance the effectiveness of resource allocation; among various economic system reforms, the price reform is neither the only important reform nor can it become a breakthrough point of all economic reforms. The key is ownership reform or the reform of enterprise institution. The breakthrough point of economic reforms is first and foremost the vitalization of enterprises by recognizing them as goods producers who make their own decisions, take responsibility for their own profits and losses, and react to price signals to make necessary adjustments to supply and demand.

It is worth noting that since the purpose of economic reforms is to enhance the effectiveness of resource allocation, the mechanism of resource allocation and the mechanism of the operation of the economy need to be reformed. In terms of the reform of enterprise institution, it is the mechanism governing how enterprises themselves operate as well as how factors of production flow and combine that needs to be changed, not administrative affiliation or management scope (e.g., changing from vertical affiliation to horizontal affiliation or vice versa). In terms of price reform, it is the mechanism of price movement and price determination that needs to be changed, not the ratios of prices. As long as enterprises are still affiliated with administrative agencies, they will not be able to operate independently or take responsibility for their own profits and losses. In this case, the only thing reformed with regard to price is the ratio of prices, not the price setting mechanism. Such a price reform can only lead to reverted price ratios, i.e., the ratios of prices will soon return to the unreasonable level the same as before the reform, but with an even higher price level. This will do no good to the improvement of resource allocation.

If the reform of enterprise institution, or the reform of ownership, is set as the top priority, which reaffirms enterprises as goods producers, identifies investors and investees, separates enterprises from government agencies, and develops as well as improves the market system, investment principals will be identified, markets will be established and improved, price will be determined by market, and the issues related to resource allocation will naturally disappear. Hence, in a disequilibrium economy, it would be a mistake to attempt market establishment and price decontrol in the first place without tackling the fundamental obstacles to resource allocation that hinder market perfection and price signaling or without developing an effective resource allocation mechanism by allowing goods producers to become independent decision-makers responsible for their own profits and losses. If that direction is followed, unending inflation will follow, the ratios of merchandise prices will remain irregular, the market will unlikely be fully developed due to absence of decision-making and profit-driven enterprises, price signals will still be distorted, and effective resource allocation mechanism will be nothing but a dream. These analyses on disequilibrium are sure to reach this conclusion.

1.2 Resource Misallocation and Potential Stagflation in the Socialist Economy

1.2.1 The Cause of Stagnation and Inflation in the Socialist Economy

Stagnation refers to economic slowdown, which is characterized by lowering economic growth with growth rate hovering at a low level. Inflation refers to higher price level, characterized by rising prices. Stagflation refers to the phenomenon where stagnation and inflation exist simultaneously.

Stagnation and inflation may occur one at a time or at the same time in the socialist economy, a point I have discussed in *Socialist Political Economics.*[1] What is the root cause of stagnation, inflation, and stagflation in the socialist economy? Can we simply consider them the fallout from administrative mistakes or some coincidental events? The above analyses on economic disequilibrium and the impact on resource allocation from socialist economic system have revealed the fundamental root causes of stagnation, inflation, or stagflation. Administrative mistakes or coincidental events, even though having certain connections with stagnation, inflation, or stagflation, only make situations worse or are factors that induce them.

Current Chinese economy runs in a state of disequilibrium. Both aggregate imbalance and structural imbalance are probable. The former is demonstrated by

[1]Li Yining [1].

a mismatch between aggregate supply and aggregate demand, resulting in either economic slowdown or inflation, while the latter manifests as a mismatch between the demand and supply of key products, causing either economic slowdown or inflation. Thus, stagnation or inflation, due to either aggregate or structural factors, will normally occur separately. If aggregate imbalance and structural imbalance occur simultaneously, there will be four possible scenarios:

1. Stagnation due to aggregate factors and structural factors
2. Inflation due to aggregate factors and structural factors
3. Stagnation due to aggregate factors and inflation due to structural factors
4. Inflation due to aggregate factors and stagnation due to structural factors

Stagnation and inflation occur separately in the first two scenarios and simultaneously in the latter two scenarios, i.e., stagflation. These four scenarios are all probable in a disequilibrium economy. They are relatively easy to understand in the traditional economic system and the dual-track economic system. If we established the new economic system in the future, could we possibly prevent stagnation, inflation, or stagflation? Not necessarily. As mentioned above, in the new economic system, enterprises will have become goods producers that operate independently and are responsible for their own profits and losses. The market will have become relatively fully developed, if not completely fully. Prices can function normally as signals to adjust demand and supply. However, as long as resource constraints (and possibly demand constraints) persist, the socialist economy in the new economic system will remain a disequilibrium economy or an economy with a relatively low degree of disequilibrium. That being said, stagnation, inflation, or stagflation is still possible.

The above analysis has demonstrated that the root cause of stagnation, inflation, or stagflation in the socialist economy is not the socialist system itself, but aggregate imbalance and structural imbalance during the operation of a disequilibrium economy. Having said that, what is the cause of aggregate imbalance and structural imbalance? To answer this question, we have to look at potential macroeconomic and microeconomic mismatch in an economy.

1.2.2 The Cause of Macroeconomic and Microeconomic Mismatch

There are circumstances in which macroeconomic and microeconomic mismatch occurs, which is not entirely attributable to the traditional socialist economic system or the dual-track economic system. Let us assume that we have established the new economic system, where enterprises and individuals conduct economic activities independently and make their own decisions based on their best economic interests and intentions. This makes it impossible for them to automatically synchronize their activities with the national economy, hence leading to macroeconomic or microeconomic mismatch. More specifically, in the new economic system, enterprises make their own decisions with regard to the level of inventory and borrowings based on their own expectations of price level, interest rate, or supply and demand in the marketplace. So do individuals, who adjust their personal stock of consumer goods, cash holdings, and form of assets in accordance with their own expectations of price level, interest rate, or supply and demand in the marketplace. These activities will impact the demand and supply of both merchandise and capital in the marketplace. We understand from the changes of enterprise and individual behavior that the fluctuations of inventory in the market will cause abnormal inventory in the economy or excessive money in circulation, which will naturally lead to macroeconomic or microeconomic mismatch. Therefore, it is obvious that any macroeconomic or microeconomic mismatch in the socialist economy as well as the resulting aggregate imbalance and structural imbalance (manifested as stagnation, inflation, or stagflation) will not disappear even after the new economic system is established. However, whenever macroeconomic and microeconomic mismatch occurs, the new economic system is more effective in releasing the power inherent in the economy to offset such mismatch than the traditional economic system or the dual-track economic system, and the influences of government's actions to reduce or eliminate such mismatch are also more far-reaching in the new economic system than in the traditional economic system or the dual-track economic system. If we conclude that we will always see macroeconomic and microeconomic mismatch and aggregate and structural imbalances in the form of stagnation, inflation, or stagflation in any type of socialist economic system, the traditional economic system or the dual-track economic system will experience more severe mismatch or imbalance than the new economic system, and the cost to the economy to correct such mismatch will also be much larger. If we can summarize the process of socialist economic activities as one that gradually changes from macroeconomic and microeconomic mismatch to moderate match and then to a new level of macroeconomic and microeconomic mismatch, the traditional economic system and the dual-track economic system, in comparison to the new economic system, will need a longer period of time migrating from macroeconomic and microeconomic mismatch to moderate match, face more obstacles down the road, and pay a higher price. They, however, need a relatively short period of time transiting from moderate macroeconomic and microeconomic match to the new macroeconomic and microeconomic mismatch, which tend to develop fairly quickly.

Now, let us go back to disequilibrium economy. It is clear that if the socialist economy turned out to be in the equilibrium described by Walras, excess supply and demand would not exist and aggregate imbalance or structural imbalance would not occur either. It will be impossible to see macroeconomic and microeconomic mismatch, thus eliminating such phenomena as stagnation, inflation, and stagflation. However, the equilibrium economy that Walras described is not real. Disequilibrium is the reality for any economy. Therefore, we may conclude that any imbalance in the socialist economy or any macroeconomic and microeconomic mismatch is a result of the imbalances of economic activities, not administrative mistakes or coincidental events.

1.2.3 Stagflation and Resource Misallocation

Economic slowdown or inflation in the socialist economy represents resource misallocation. It is easier to understand that economic slowdown, as there are bound to be considerable idle resources during economic slowdown. In terms of the production process, idle resources include excess production capacity, idle labor, as well as raw material overstock. In terms of the circulation process, idle resources result from the sluggish sales of manufactured products and abnormal inventory in the marketplace. Of course, serious shortages of certain key products, such as energy, major raw materials, major equipment, and services by the transportation sector, can also cause economic slowdown, which is also a reflection of resource misallocation. Resource misallocation in this scenario manifests as a distorted industrial structure that throws resource allocation out of balance, causing severe product shortages, eventually causing an economic slowdown.

What is the relationship between inflation and resource misallocation in the socialist economy? Why can we say that inflation reflects resource misallocation in the same way as economic slowdown? We can answer these questions by analyzing three different types of inflation:

1. Inflation due to excessive aggregate demand, commonly known as demand-driven inflation

Excessive demand is either caused by escalating investment or rapidly increasing consumption, or both. The reason why demand exceeds supply by a large extent has something to do with resource misallocation, because the participants of resource allocation (i.e., enterprises, individuals, and government) allocate excessive resources to areas whose needs are not justified. In this case, excessive money in circulation is only a phenomenon. The truth behind it is excessive investment or consumption due to resource misallocation.

2. Inflation due to excessively rising cost, commonly known as cost-driven inflation

Excessively rising cost is ultimately determined by excessively rising prices of production factors, which is in turn caused by excessive demand or severe shortages of the supplies of relevant production factors. Severe shortages of the supplies of certain production factors can be attributed to a distorted industrial structure, constraints on the mobility of production factors, or lack of investment by the producers of production factors. After all, they are all associated with resource misallocation.

3. Inflation due to mismatch between the structures of supply and demand, commonly known as structural inflation

This type of inflation can be found with regard to certain key products when supply fails to meet demand. When certain key products experience excessive demand and shortages of supply, prices will jump and money in circulation will rise, giving rise to inflation. The reason why there is excessive demand for or shortage of supply of key products is still linked to resource misallocation and consequential product structure mismatch or industrial structure mismatch.

Therefore, any type of inflation is associated with resource misallocation. We can conclude that economic slowdown, inflation, and stagflation are all reflective of resource misallocation. In our research on the socialist economy, we must realize that stagnation, inflation, and stagflation are all linked to resource misallocation. With this in mind, we must concentrate on exploring methods that can eliminate resource misallocation, and search for effective resource allocation that can prevent stagnation, inflation, or stagflation.

1.2.4 *The Possibility and Prevention of Stagflation*

When an economy encounters structural imbalance, simply suppressing aggregate demand will cause excessive economic contraction. At the same time, rising price level due to structural imbalance will remain unchecked. As a result, stagflation will likely occur. This is a serious issue that we must face in managing the national economy. We must also note that the possibility of stagflation in the economy does not necessarily mean that it will turn into reality. It will require societal purchasing power to turn the possibility of stagflation into reality. It should be noted that even though structural imbalance likely leads to a higher price level, any rise in price level is also related to societal purchasing power. If purchasing power is not strong enough, it will be difficult for the price of shortage merchandise to rise, in spite of structural imbalance between supply and demand. Therefore, if suppressing aggregate demand (e.g., suppressing infrastructure investment, business spending, or residents' disposable income) still leaves us with relatively strong sequential societal purchasing power, which can in turn drive price level higher, we will have to understand the origin of societal purchasing power.

Can it originate from government spending? In other words, can a portion of government spending be diverted toward purchasing shortage commodities? Generally speaking, the possibility does not exist during an excessively contractive period, as suppressing aggregate demand first and foremost entail reducing government spending.

Can it originate from credit expenditures? In other words, can a portion of credit expenditures be diverted toward purchasing shortage commodities? The probability is normally minimal. Suppressing aggregate demand undoubtedly entails reducing credit expenditures.

Can it originate from exports, remittances from expatriates, spending by foreigners within the country (or tourism revenues), or foreign direct investments? All these revenues are likely to become purchasing power for shortage commodities in the domestic market. Suppressing domestic aggregate demand can proceed simultaneously with increasing exports, expatriates' remittances, tourism revenues, and foreign direct investments. Under such circumstance, however, we can prevent price level from rising, in spite of increasing domestic demand for shortage commodities, as long as rising foreign exchange revenues are appropriately utilized to increase supplies of shortage commodities, such as directly increasing the import of shortage commodities or raw materials for the production of shortage commodities.

Now we have a problem: Since rising purchasing power during the economic contractive period is not caused by government spending, credit expenditures, or foreign exchange revenues, where does it come from?

There are three potential sources:

1. Personal savings. During the period of economic contraction, residents may withdraw personal savings due to changing expectations and turn them into purchasing power for shortage commodities, thus pushing price level higher.
2. Personal cash on hand. Cash on hand, considered either pocket money or cash withheld to be spent, will likely be spent and drive price level up when there is change in people's expectations.
3. Corporate after-tax earnings. Businesses can utilize after-tax earnings to cover corporate expenditures or reward their employees, turning after-tax earnings into personal consumption by employees who purchase shortage commodities and pushing price level higher. But it should be noted that if businesses are driven by profitability and governed by long-term growth strategies, they will, during economic contraction, constrain the spending of after-tax earnings, reduce corporate expenditures and employee compensation, and pay more attention to increasing productivity, lowering cost, and preserving capital. On the contrary, if businesses are not driven by profitability and are shortsighted, they will likely ignore economic contraction and use up all after-tax earnings, thus driving price level higher.

Therefore, if the government adopts measures at time of structural imbalance to reduce aggregate demand without mitigating the impact on the market from personal savings and cash on hand, potential stagflation will turn into reality. Likewise, if the government fails to reform enterprise operation mechanism while reducing aggregate demand, businesses will lack the mechanism to pursue profitability as well as corporate governance for distributing after-tax earnings, business behavior will remain shortsighted, and potential stagflation will likely turn into reality.

Stagflation is very harmful to the economy. It is not comparable to stable economic growth and even worse than inflation during economic growth. As for current Chinese economy, it is imperative to reduce aggregate demand. Our research will be focused on preventing stagflation while reducing aggregate demand. Of course, we also have to stress the importance of lowering economic imbalance by increasing effective aggregate supply. If excessive reduction of aggregate demand leads to lower effective aggregate supply, the purpose of reducing aggregate demand to balance supply shortage will unlikely be fulfilled. In addition, we must also further analyze the abovementioned issues including personal savings, cash on hand, and enterprise operation mechanism in search of an effective solution to stagflation.

1. Personal savings

   In order to avoid run on the bank prompted by changing personal expectations at time of lower aggregate demand, we can raise interest rate as necessary and employ tools such as inflation-protected savings and savings for forward purchases to stabilize personal savings. Meanwhile, the government should divert a portion of personal savings to purchasing houses and financial instruments. Investments in housing and financial instruments are protected against inflation and are able to turn short-term capital into long-term capital or changing consumption funds into production capital. This is an effective method of redistributing personal savings.

2. Cash on hand

   Cash on hand is primarily treated the same way as personal savings. The government should turn cash on hand into personal savings and purchasing power for housing and financial instruments. Meanwhile, the government should also encourage small business owners and peasants to turn their cash on hand into production capital so as to increase the supply of capital and avoid exorbitant and extravagant consumption.

3. Corporate operation mechanism

   Increasing supply relies on deepening enterprise reforms, which, for example, includes motivating enterprises and their employees to facilitate the recombination of production factors and accelerating the adjustment of the industrial structure. Suppressing demand also relies on deepening enterprise reforms. We will discuss later on in the book that reforming enterprises is nothing but reforming corporate operation mechanism and that only when driven by economic interests can an enterprise care about how to use retained earnings, thus preventing corporate shortsightedness. Having said that, how do we reform corporate operation mechanism? Obviously, the subcontracting system is not sufficient, because it does not sever the relationship between enterprises and their administrative agencies. Enterprises under the subcontracting system have not been goods producers with decision-making authorities and financial responsibilities. The subcontracting system should gradually migrate to the shareholding system.[2] Economic activities under the shareholding system are driven by investors' interests. Macroeconomic regulatory plans can be drafted in accordance with the long-term interests of enterprises structured under the shareholding system. Driven by long-term economic interests, investors will voluntarily control their utilization of after-tax earnings to avoid shortsightedness, i.e., maximizing short-term interests by sacrificing long-term interests. Hence, corporate myopia, i.e., depleting retained earnings, can potentially be prevented.

The above discussions allow us to draw the following conclusion: Stagflation cannot be completely ruled out if there is structural imbalance. Stagflation can be prevented, as long as we devote to increasing effective supply while suppressing demand, take necessary measures to stabilize personal savings, try our best to divert deposits and cash on hand toward purchasing houses and securities, and deepen enterprise reforms by establishing the enterprise mechanism following the principle of maximizing economic interests. In other words, when these conditions are met, the economy will not be expected to experience stagflation. Instead, the economy will see medium economic growth and declining inflation rate.

---

[2]Li Yining [2].

This section describes stagflation in the socialist economy through a brief analysis. The following sections will present a detailed analysis of issues related to government regulation and enterprise reforms under the coexistence of commodity supply gap and demand shortfall.

1.2.5 The Need to Reconsider Resource Allocation

One of the purposes of studying economics is to find a satisfactory system or mechanism that facilitates efficient utilization of natural resources and effective resource allocation, which contributes not only to increasing national wealth but also to fair distribution of wealth or income. Ignoring resource allocation is actually forgetting the purpose of economics as a science. Existing research on resource allocation since the inception of classical political economics has revealed two trends. One believes that the market is the only effective mechanism that can perfectly and effectively allocate various limited resources in a society. Resource allocation is no more than the automatic regulation of the economy by the market. The other trend believes that the market mechanism is fairly limited in terms of resource allocation processes and results. The limitation of market regulation reflects either inefficient utilization of societal resources, which causes idling or waste of resources, or a mismatch between resource allocation and income distribution, which leads to wider income gaps despite relatively effective resource allocation and higher national wealth under the market mechanism. Such circumstance calls for government regulation or planned mechanism in replacement of the market mechanism so as to overcome its limitation.

In our study of resource allocation in current Chinese economy, it is not difficult to find that various schools of thoughts on resource allocation, despite the fact that many are useful, are not applicable to the realities of the Chinese economy. Given the Chinese economic disequilibrium, the belief that the market is the only effective mechanism to allocate resources is apparently incomplete. If the market pricing mechanism is selected as a starting point to resolve resource allocation issues, we will likely see considerable economic chaos. This is because in an economic environment where the market has not been fully developed and enterprises have not become independent decision-makers and often face noneconomic obstacles, to realize efficient utilization and effective allocation of resources first and foremost requires that enterprises be goods producers that are financially independent and responsible for their own investment and operations and that the market continues to perfect. Even after enterprises are motivated, endowed with decision-making authorities, full reliance upon price regulation is not sufficient to achieve efficient utilization and effective allocation of resources if constraints on resources are not removed. All these points demonstrate the complexity of resource allocation under disequilibrium conditions, which is why we have to come back and reconsider the issue of resource allocation according to current economic realities in China.

The fact that the Chinese economy is susceptible to stagnation, inflation, or stagflation, which is related to resource misallocation, clearly demonstrates the complexity of resource allocation in the current economy as well as the difficulty to find a viable solution. In other words, neither the model of resolving resource allocation issues by solely using the market mechanism nor one that replaces the market mechanism with the planned mechanism is able to reveal the true root cause of the problems and to provide a real solution. Our emphasis on "realistically describing the Chinese economy only by understanding China in the first place" does not mean we can look down on economic theories that provide appropriate guidance. Without economic theories and the analysis conducted according to these theories, we will be inundated with piles of tedious and unsystematic details or descriptions. Therefore, we value the guiding role of economic theories. But it does not mean we are able to draw an easy conclusion on resource allocation simply according to some superficial phenomena of economic activities. Instead, it requires us to look for economic theories that can be applied to resolve resource allocation issues in China. Even though there are many difficulties down the road, we will succeed eventually as long as we follow the research path that is consistent with Chinese realities.

As it is necessary to reconsider resource allocation issues, we can naturally reach the following conclusion: A theory on resource allocation applicable to China must follow real Chinese situations. In order to meet this requirement, the theory on economic disequilibrium is hereby proposed as an economic theory that is conducive to resolving resource allocation issues in socialist society.

References

1. Li, Yining. (1986). *Socialist political economics* (pp. 297–298). The Commercial Press, Beijing, China.
2. Li, Yining. (1989). *Perspectives on Chinese economic reforms* (pp. 31–34). China Prospect Press, Beijing, China.

Chapter 2
Market Regulation and Resource Allocation

2.1 Market Selection and Market Guidance

2.1.1 Market Selection

Any merchandise for sale is composed of at least two factors of production. For any natural resource to be merchandise, it requires the input of human labor. Therefore, merchandise in a society means a combination of resources. Studying resource allocation in the socialist society must start with the combination of resources in the form of merchandise.

The reason why one form of resource combination is preferred over another during a certain period of time in a society is ultimately determined by the needs and wants of human beings for particular merchandise. The way in which certain merchandise is supplied becomes a form of resource combination. This is a normal way of allocating resources. That is, demand guides supply as well as the combination of resources, which impacts resource allocation in a society and allows resources to be properly utilized. If the path is reversed, in which resource combination is determined in the first place, not only any product from the combinations of resources will fail to meet people's needs, resources will also be underutilized. As a result, resources will be utilized inappropriately as well as with low efficiency, and people's demand will be artificially suppressed.

This gives us a first look at the role of the market in resource allocation. That is, the market is an agent who determines resource combination. In research on resource allocation, market selection refers to the combination of various resources to produce various products to meet certain needs in a normal situation of resource allocation, in which the market serves as an agent to determine resource combination and functions as a bridge between demand and supply. For example, if the total quantity of overall resources is limited, there will be multiple ways of combining resources to produce different merchandise to meet various needs. If the market

Y. Li, *Chinese Economy in Disequilibrium*, China Academic Library,
DOI 10.1007/978-3-642-39558-1_2, © Foreign Language Teaching and Research
Publishing Co., Ltd and Springer-Verlag Berlin Heidelberg 2014

determines the combination of resources for production of merchandise to meet people's needs, ineffective usage or squandering of resources can be prevented, avoiding low utilization efficiency or suppressing demand.

2.1.2 Resource Combination

As an agent that selects resource combinations, the market functions as if it were a large mixer, which constantly mixes various resources and churns out required combination (products). The mixing process is the determination of resource combination.

Of course, this is just a metaphor. In real life, certain amount of sand, stones, and cement in a mixer will gradually reach a state of even distribution during the mixing process. Comparing the market to a large mixer allows us to get a better understanding of resource allocation. As different resources are put into the large mixer and being constantly mixed, the mixer executes appropriate combination and produces all sorts of merchandise that meets various needs. The result of the mixing not only meets people's needs but also realizes effective resource allocation.[1]

Market selection can be seen during the constant movement process as if the market were a large mixer. Market selection activities include economic activities such as market input decision, market output decision, and market distribution decision. Each and every decision is associated with the selection of resource combination. The activities of the market as a large mixer can be divided into three steps: production, sales, and distribution. These three steps happen to match market input decision, market output decision, and market distribution decision.

Market input decision refers to the decision of each market participant in terms of which resource is used in production, as well as its quantity, input ratio, and way of combination. Therefore, market input decision is a decision on the selection by each market participant of particular resource inputs and resource combination.

Market output decision refers to the decision made by each market participant with respect to where and how to produce certain outputs with certain inputs of resources. The output here mentioned refers to not only how each resource input can be turned into a physical product but also how a physical product can be exchanged for monetary income. Only after resource inputs are turned into monetary income through the production and sales processes can market conclude its input and output processes. Therefore, market output decision is a decision on how to turn a physical product into monetary income with certain combination of resources.

Market distribution decision refers to the decision on the distribution and usage of the monetary income generated from selling physical products. If such income is considered a resource, the next question is how to utilize it. If production, sales, and distribution are considered a continuous economic process, i.e., market input

[1] Li Yining [1].

decision, market output decision, and market distribution decision are continuous decisions in a series of economic activities, then the distribution and usage of monetary income is as a matter of fact the initial allocation and usage of resource inputs.

Production is a continuous process. Monetary income will turn into consumption, savings, or investment via the market distribution decision. Each item of monetary expenditures is associated with the selection of resource combination. Consumption is associated with sales activities in the marketplace, which concerns market output decision. Savings and investment are associated with production activities in the marketplace, which concerns market input decision. All these expenditures are integral parts of market selection, which completes the selection process in the "large mixer," the market.

2.1.3 The Dispersion of Market Decision

Market decision is made by each and every market participant, business, or individual, according to their own economic interests. Dispersion is an immanent feature of market decision. More specifically, every business or individual decides on the quantity of resource inputs, how resources are combined, what physical products are produced, how products are sold to generate income, how income from selling products is distributed, and how many resources are redistributed as inputs. In terms of decisions on market input, market output, and market distribution, each separate decision made by each business and individual jointly forms the market decision on or the market selection of resource combination as well as the direction of resource allocation.

The dispersion of market decision indicates that market decision or market selection is composed of each and every unique decision or selection and there is not a predetermined market decision or market selection that leads to a decision for each business or individual. We should note that businesses and individuals have different goals and preferences. Their expectations of the market and profitability in the future also vary. Therefore, the selection or decision of the overall market is determined by the selection or decision made by the majority of businesses and individuals. When the majority of businesses and individuals have similar goals and preferences, with optimistic expectations of the market and profitability in the future and favoring higher input of resources, the selection or decision of the overall market will be expansionary or aggressive. As a result, the economy will grow. On the contrary, when the majority of businesses and individuals have similar goals and preferences, with pessimistic expectations of the market and profitability in the future and favoring lower input of resources, the selection or decision of the overall market will be contractive and conservative. Economic slowdown and recession will follow.

In an economic environment that is characterized by disperse market decisions, complete and free flow of information not only ensures every market participant is able to make decisions to the best of its interests but is also important in facilitating coordinated market activities. Complete information means that every business and individual has access to information on current resource combination and utilization available in society, which is equivalent to having full knowledge of the decisions or selections made by other businesses and individuals. Free flow of information means that access to information is prompt, fast, and inexpensive. If these conditions are met, different market decisions, in spite of being disperse, are still able to meet the requirement of realizing relatively effective resource allocation. If these conditions are met, disperse decisions will optimize the allocation of resources to the largest extent possible via the interplay between prices and supply and demand, even though there are constraints on supply (or resource supply constraints) or constraints on demand (or market constraints) which cause insufficient supply or demand.

2.1.4 Market Guidance

That supply and demand in the marketplace influence price and price influences supply and demand demonstrates the function of the market in guiding the allocation of resources.

Market guidance is seen from the perspective of a dynamic equilibrium. The economic activities of the overall market can be divided into several stages. Supply and demand in the earlier stage not only determines the price in the current stage but also uses the price as an indicator to influence supply and demand in the next stage, signaling potential price changes as well as the magnitude of such changes. Potential price changes will in turn influence supply and demand as well as the price in the next stage. Various stages will go on and on, with the market providing guidance on resource utilization and combination in society as well as the possibility and method of turning potential resources into utilizable ones. We can come to the conclusion that what the market guides is the decision or selection of market participants.

Why does demand for certain resources gradually decrease while that for other resources gradually increases? Why is one form of resource combination gradually replaced by another one? Why do resource inputs in one sector gradually transfer to another one? These questions can be illustrated by the dynamic role of market guidance.

When looking at the role of market guidance, should we emphasize absolute price level or relative price level? Both are important. The absolute price of certain resources determines the quantity of aggregate demand and supply; the ratios of the prices of various resources, or relative price levels, determine the combination of resources, the distribution of resources in different areas, and resource utilization efficiency.

Looking at market selection and market guidance mentioned above, we treat businesses and individuals as if they were the same. In reality, businesses and individuals often appear as opposite sides of the supply and demand relationship. When individuals provide businesses with resources, individuals are resource suppliers and businesses are resource recipients. When businesses provide individuals with resource combinations in the form of physical merchandise, businesses are resource suppliers and individuals are resource recipients. Therefore, we must analyze two types of market behavior, investment and consumption.

2.2 Investment Principal, Investment Behavior, and Resource Allocation

2.2.1 Investment Principal

When analyzing the role of the market in allocating resources, we can identify two types of investment principal, business and individual. For now, we do not analyze government as one type of investment principal.

In order to be investment principal, a business must have resources to invest and the right to make investment decisions on its own. The motive for businesses to invest is to pursue value appreciation or profitability. There may be motives other than profitability. One of the following two scenarios will apply. In the first scenario, the ultimate motive for businesses to invest is profitability, although they invest due to reasons other than profitability. This is an indirect way for businesses to pursue profitability to ensure that investments will increase total profits. In the second scenario, businesses have other goals besides profitability. Businesses make investments in order to reach those goals. The second scenario does exist, but accounts for a small portion of overall investments. We can ignore this scenario when we study business investments.

Similar to businesses, individuals must also have resources to invest and the right to make investment decisions on their own before they are qualified as investment principal. The motive of investments by individuals is also to pursue value appreciation in order to increase personal income. This does not exclude individuals from having other motives when they invest. These scenarios are insignificant and can be ignored when we analyze investments by individuals.

If both businesses and individuals have the same investment motive, i.e., pursuit of profit or higher income, they will need to estimate opportunity cost in every scenario, even when there is only one investment opportunity. Estimating opportunity cost is to select the direction of use and the combination of resources. Businesses and individuals will naturally select the direction of use and the combination of resources that are in their best interests before they decide on whether to invest, how to invest, and how much to invest.

2.2.2 The General Principles of Investment Behavior

If a business or individual decides to invest after estimating the opportunity cost of an investment, the investment activities are generally only influenced by price or by market competition. The general principles of investment behavior hereby referred to are applicable to the investment activities under the Walrasian equilibrium condition.

Investment activities consist of a series of transactions. As investment principal, businesses and individuals must have sufficient monetary capital to invest, with some utilized to purchase production materials and some to pay salaries and rents. If they do not have enough monetary capital on hand, they will need to borrow from the capital market and pay interest. Purchasing production materials, paying salaries and rents, raising capital, and paying interest are all transactions. Under the Walrasian equilibrium condition, total demand is always equal to total supply at any price level. No excess demand or supply exists in the economy, and every transaction is conducted at the equilibrium price. Hence, business or personal investors are always able to borrow sufficient capital, if needed, at the equilibrium interest rate determined by the demand and supply of the capital market. If they need to purchase production materials, they will be able to secure the needed quantity at the equilibrium price in the production materials market. If they need labor, they will be able to find sufficient labor to meet production needs at the equilibrium salary level set by the supply and demand of the labor market. In summary, all these meet the investors' needs, as well as their economic interests.

Likewise, business and personal investors do not have to worry about the sales of the products produced by their investments under the Walrasian equilibrium condition. As the market does not have excess demand and supply, every product they produce will be sold at an equilibrium price. These situations are also consistent with investors' economic interests.

Investment decisions in such economic environment are actually very simple. As investment principal, businesses and individuals simply follow the principles of market competition, which states that the market determines everything and investors do not have to worry about their investments. This is because market information is complete and information flows freely. As a result, investors have a full understanding of the current market as well as the market in the future. There are no unknown uncertainties. As long as investors have enough information, they can proceed with investments, allocating resources, organizing production and sales without concerning about uncertainties, or taking precautionary measures. It is not necessary to reserve excess cash to cope with business uncertainties or to purchase additional inventory. Completely following market arrangement will bring satisfactory results to investors. This is the general investment principle, even though it only exists theoretically under the Walrasian equilibrium condition.

2.2.3 Business and Personal Investment Behavior Under Disequilibrium Conditions

As pointed out in Chap. 1 of this book, disequilibrium but not Walrasian equilibrium exists in real life. In the current socialist economy, the market is not fully developed, information is neither complete nor does it flow freely, and price does not function to adjust demand and supply as it is supposed to. These are the striking characteristics of economic disequilibrium, giving rise to a new requirement for the study of investments made by businesses and individuals.

Under disequilibrium conditions, business and personal investors must consider the constraints on resource supplies before making an investment decision. They include constraints on required capital, required production materials, and labor. If resource supplies are limited, the execution of investment plans will meet obstacles. In addition, current resource supplies as well as the prospect of future supplies are equally important to investors. The production capacity built through an investment requires continuing supplies of resources, particularly raw materials, energy, maintenance parts, and transportation capacity. Therefore, even though current resource supplies seem to have no or limited constraints, investments may still encounter obstacles if future supplies of resources are expected to be constrained.

As investment principal, businesses and individuals must also consider demand constraints, or market constraints, which actually exist under disequilibrium conditions. Market constraints refer to shortage of demand for the products produced by the new production capacity from an investment. If market is limited, fulfilling an investment plan is also not straightforward. Similar to resource supply constraints, current and future markets are equally important to investors. If products from an investment can only sell now, but demand in the future is uncertain, an investor will have to consider the feasibility of the investment.

Besides the constraints on resource supply and demand under disequilibrium conditions, businesses and individuals also have to consider various uncertainties. To ensure that the investment can proceed normally as well as the production capacity built through an investment can operate properly, investors will have to take various precautionary actions, such as raising additional capital to meet overspending and keeping extra cash on hand. Investors may also purchase additional inventory to guard against the potential interruption to raw material supplies or shortage of raw materials, thus resulting in abnormal inventories of raw materials, energy, equipment, and maintenance parts and greater use of working capital. To prevent market shares from shrinking or to avoid heightened sales competition, investors may have to adopt unusual measures to protect or increase their market shares, which also requires additional working capital. These situations require higher inputs of capital than those without uncertainties.

In addition, in a disequilibrium economy, investors feel compelled to find necessary information themselves, since information is neither complete nor flowing freely in the market, which is one of the characteristics of disequilibrium. These efforts also require additional investments. Marginal benefits from the additional investments in pursuit of information will outweigh potential losses due to incomplete or delayed information, and hence investors are willing to commit these additional investments.

Let us set aside discussions on the gap between the price level under equilibrium conditions and that under disequilibrium conditions. Compared with equilibrium conditions, the need for businesses to stock up abnormal inventory and hold additional capital to protect and increase market share as well as obtain relevant information under disequilibrium conditions requires more capital investment to install the same amount of new production capacity. The price level needs to be considered as well. If funding capital is constrained and the capital market is not fully developed, the interest rate required will be higher than the equilibrium interest rate. If supplies of production materials are constrained and the production materials market is not fully developed, the price of production materials under these conditions will be higher than the equilibrium price. If investors adopt noncompetitive measures to protect their market shares, merchandise selling prices under these conditions will exceed the equilibrium price formed through normal market competition under equilibrium conditions. Higher interest rate and production material prices require higher capital investment. In this circumstance, the same production capacity under disequilibrium conditions requires higher capital investment than that under equilibrium conditions. Higher merchandise selling prices in turn justify higher capital investment. That is, after factoring in the higher selling prices in the future market, investors would consider additional investment not only indispensable but also rewarding. Thus, extra capital investment is justified.

The above analyses clearly demonstrate that disequilibrium conditions require businesses and individuals to invest more capital to build the same production capacity than equilibrium conditions do. In other words, the total investment to build the same production capacity under disequilibrium conditions will always exceed that under equilibrium conditions. This is the characteristic of business and personal investment behavior under disequilibrium conditions.

2.2.4 The Relationship Between Investment Behavior and Resource Allocation Under Disequilibrium Conditions

Committing additional investment requires not only additional cash but also additional supply of production materials. It is relatively easy to understand additional cash, as the initial form of additional investment is always monetary capital. Additional investment in the form of supply of production materials (i.e., raw materials, energy, equipment, and parts) is reflected in abnormal inventory. Besides, additional costs to protect or increase market share or to obtain information are also partially reflected in the cost of purchasing production materials.

Hence, business and personal investment under disequilibrium conditions, including additional investment, will surely lead to resource allocations that are rather different from those under equilibrium conditions. Under equilibrium conditions, the market plays its roles to ensure resources automatically flow to sectors and regions where they are most profitable, and the changes of supply and demand in the market as well as subsequent price changes will place various resources in appropriate areas. There may be some cases of local or structural idling or waste of resources during the transfer between various sectors, regions, and investment principals, which normally are unable to be avoided. However, generally speaking, as excess demand and excess supply are equal to zero, resources can be effectively combined and efficiently utilized. However, it is quite different under disequilibrium conditions.

For example, due to resource supply constraints, business and personal investors often commit additional capital investment in excess inventory to protect against supply shortages or interruption, or other uncertainties in the economy, which further widens the existing shortages of resource supply. As a result, the existing imbalance between supply and demand will deteriorate, causing resource misallocation. The phenomenon of stagflation in the socialist economy mentioned earlier is to a certain extent related to the excess inventory that most businesses and individuals build up as a precaution.

Another example can be seen from the impacts of businesses and individuals on the capital market due to their needs for additional investment. Economic disequilibrium indicates that the demand for capital in the capital market probably exceeds the supply of capital during that period. The need for additional investments intensifies capital shortages.

In terms of resource allocation, it is very difficult to allocate resources in a way that contributes to increasing utilization efficiency if there are constraints on supply in the economy. The form of resource combination will have to adjust to the situation of supply shortages. If this situation happens, a portion of resources will remain idle in the economy. If we want to utilize that portion of resources in case of resource supply shortages, we will likely sacrifice the efficiency of resource allocation. Both scenarios are reflective of resource misallocation.

2.3 Consumption Principal, Consumption Behavior, and Resource Allocation

2.3.1 Consumption Principal

Consumption principal is analyzed in the same way as investment principal. Consumption principal is divided into business and individual from the perspective of the role of the market in allocating resources. For the time being, we do not analyze government as one type of consumption principal.

The prerequisite for a business to become consumption principal is that the business must have the resources for consumption as well as the right to make independent decisions on consumption. The purpose of business consumption is to cover businesses' public expenses, which are intended to increase employee benefits and fulfill corporate social responsibilities.

The prerequisite for an individual to become consumption principal is no different. That is, individuals must have the resources for consumption as well as the right to make independent decisions on consumption. Personal consumption mainly includes living expenses to meet physical, psychological, and social needs.

As consumption principal, businesses set aside a portion of earnings as public consumption reserves and use them to fund expenditures on public consumption, while individuals pay for consumption using personal disposable income.

2.3.2 The General Principles of Consumption Behavior

Without considering consumption preferences, business and personal consumption under the Walrasian equilibrium condition is normally influenced by prices or by market competition. This is the general principle of consumption behavior.

Consumption behavior, similar to investment behavior, consists of a series of transactional behavior. Business and personal investors use cash to pay for consumer goods. If consumption is funded by consumers' borrowings, they will also need to pay interest. In addition, they may also need to use some of the borrowings to pay for services. All these activities are transactions. Under the Walrasian equilibrium condition, every transaction, including consumption, is done at the equilibrium price. Excess demand for and supply of consumer goods are equal to zero. The market allows every business and individual to purchase the consumer goods they need. Meanwhile, there are no uncertainties in the current market and the market in the future. Business and personal consumers do not have to worry about whether they will be able to purchase the consumer goods they need, which will avoid building up excess consumer goods inventory. Everything in the market is reasonable and satisfies all consumers' needs.

Of course, any new consumer goods or consumption activity due to changing consumer preferences may cause temporary or local mismatch. Even so, the situation does not mean mismatch across the overall consumer goods market.

2.3.3 Business and Personal Consumption Behavior Under Disequilibrium Conditions

Business consumption behavior is somewhat different from personal consumption behavior under disequilibrium conditions, due to resource supply constraints, demand constraints, and uncertainties.

If resource supply is constrained, business and individual consumption will be influenced by theses constraints. Resource supply constraints are seen when there are shortages of certain consumer goods that are in demand. Under such circumstance, consumers' wishes to purchase these goods will not be fulfilled.

If consumers are not willing to purchase different goods that are not in shortage or these goods are also more or less in short supply, nonvoluntary savings will arise. In the case of nonvoluntary savings, consumers increase either bank savings or cash on hand.

If demand is constrained and the constraints on demand are characterized by the oversupply of certain consumer goods, business and personal producers of such goods will have difficulties selling these goods. In this case, if consumer income and preferences remain unchanged, the price of those consumer goods will fall because of restriction on sales, or if the price remains unchanged, production will contract and supply will fall. These situations will not have much influence on consumer behavior. If consumer income remains unchanged and consumer preferences change during this period, consumers will change consumption paradigm, as the price of those consumer goods with sales restrictions will fall, influencing the sales volume of other consumer goods.

Besides resource supply constraints and demand constraints under disequilibrium conditions, businesses and individuals also have to consider various economic uncertainties. To prevent supply shortages or interruptions, consumers may want to take precautionary measures, such as storing excess goods and adjusting the ratio of consumption to savings and consumption to investment, i.e., reducing savings or investment and increasing consumption.

Let us disregard the differences between the price under equilibrium conditions and that under disequilibrium conditions for the moment. Under disequilibrium conditions, consumers build up excess inventories of consumer goods and satisfy higher consumption needs by cutting back on savings or investment to meet any economic uncertainty. Therefore, spending on consumer goods, if physically comparable, is higher under disequilibrium conditions than that under equilibrium conditions. Yet we cannot ignore the price level, for as long as resource supply is constrained and the consumer goods market is not fully developed, consumer goods prices will be higher than under equilibrium conditions. Excess inventories and additional spending on consumer goods also push prices higher. Higher prices in turn lead to higher spending on consumer goods under disequilibrium conditions than under equilibrium conditions, thus maintaining comparable consumption level. This is the characteristic of business and personal consumption behavior under disequilibrium conditions.

2.3.4 *The Relationship Between Consumption Behavior and Resource Allocation Under Disequilibrium Conditions*

The impact of business and personal consumption behavior on resource allocation under disequilibrium conditions is in certain ways similar to that of business and personal investment behavior on resource allocation.

We know that under equilibrium conditions, the market mechanism works perfectly. Resources are allocated to sectors, regions, and businesses as needed during the production of consumer goods. There is neither production excess nor shortage, at least not from the perspective of the overall production of consumer goods. However, under disequilibrium conditions, constraints on resource supply and excess inventories of consumer goods further widen the existing gap between resource supply and demand and cause the supply and demand imbalance to deteriorate.

The relationship between consumption behavior and resource allocation under disequilibrium conditions is similar to that between investment behavior and resource allocation. When resource supply constraints or excess inventories of consumer goods emerge, the existing gap between supply and demand will widen, and it will be more difficult for resources to combine in the most efficient way. The way of resource combination will have to adjust to resource supply shortages, keeping a portion of resources in the economy idle or forcing resources to combine with low efficiency.

Moreover, excess inventories of consumer goods and resource allocation with relatively low efficiency will certainly influence the distribution of consumer goods between consumer goods producers and production material producers. The production of consumer goods will certainly reduce the availability of resources used in the production of production materials, thus hurting economic growth. This is also one of the potential consequences from resource supply constraints.

2.4 Market Self-Regulation During Resource Allocation

2.4.1 The Definition of Market Self-Regulation During Resource Allocation

Market self-regulation during resource allocation refers to the self-regulation function that the market performs without interference from noneconomic factors. The market prevents the economy either from overheating beyond control or from an excessive contraction that will paralyze the economy. The self-regulation function that the market performs in maintaining economic order is very important.

Why does the market have the self-regulation function? To answer this question, we have to look at the characteristics of economic activities by microeconomic units (i.e., businesses and individuals) who participate in transactions in the marketplace. Without interference from noneconomic factors, economic activities will be spontaneously carried out by separate microeconomic units (i.e., businesses and individuals), who are decision-makers themselves and fully motivated to operate their businesses autonomously to the best of their interests. Their economic activities and vitality are reflected in every transaction that is to pursue their best interests, which is seen in the market. The economic interests of microeconomic units are not all aligned. In terms of relationship in the market, they may be suppliers at one time and buyers at another time and realize their economic interests by way of business transaction. Therefore, for any microeconomic unit, its counterparty is both a partner and a competitor. They have common interests but also conflicts of interest. Therefore, microeconomic units have similarities as well as differences.

If the majority of microeconomic units engage in aggressive and expansionary activities, the economy will tend to be expansionary. Meanwhile, there must also be a small number of microeconomic units who engage in conservative and contractive activities, which to some extent mitigate or slow down the economic expansion. Moreover, when the majority of microeconomic units engage in expansionary activities, aggregate demand will rise and so will prices, forcing those who engage in expansionary activities in the first place to reconsider their economic interests. Under such circumstance, economic expansion will stop after reaching a certain level. This is a sign of market self-regulation. On the contrary, if the majority of microeconomic units engage in conservative and contractive activities, the economy will slow down and contract. There must also be a small number of microeconomic units who engage in aggressive and expansionary activities at the same time, which to some extent mitigate or slow down the economic recession or contraction. In addition, when the majority of microeconomic units engage in conservative activities, aggregate demand will decline, and so will prices, forcing those who engage in conservative activities in the first place to reconsider their interests. Under such circumstance, economic contraction will stop after reaching a certain level. This is also a sign of market self-regulation.[2]

2.4.2 Market Self-Regulation and Resource Allocation Under Equilibrium Conditions

If the economy is in Walrasian equilibrium, the self-regulating function of the market will be noticeable. The market performs such a function by enabling each microeconomic unit to balance internal and external cost–benefit relationships.

In terms of internal cost–benefit relationship, every microeconomic unit who faces the decision of whether to commit additional resources must consider the changes in its average cost, marginal cost, average return, and marginal return. If internal benefit increases and internal cost decreases with additional resources, it indicates higher efficiency and these additional resources are beneficial to the microeconomic unit itself as well as to the overall resource allocation in society. If, on the contrary, additional resources cause internal benefit to decrease and internal cost to increase, the microeconomic unit who makes the investment decision will learn that incremental resources are not cost-effective and hence stop committing more resources. From the perspective of overall resource allocation in society, that incremental resources cause internal benefit to decrease and internal cost to increase

---

[2]Li Yining [2].

indicates lower efficiency or ineffectiveness. Therefore, when a microeconomic unit realizes that additional input of resources is not beneficial and decides to stop committing more resources, it is making a decision in compliance with the efficiency standard of resource allocation. That is, "ineffective and inefficient resource allocation shall be stopped, and effective and efficient resource allocation shall continue."

In terms of external cost–benefit relationship, every microeconomic unit who faces the decision of whether to commit additional resources must consider changing external cost–benefit relationship due to the impacts of additional resources on overall sector capacity or production capacity in the economy. Changing external cost–benefit relationship affects average cost, marginal cost, average return, and marginal return of those microeconomic units, allowing them to learn whether their benefits increase or decrease. They will naturally pursue benefits and minimize costs. From the perspective of resource allocation in the economy, if additional resources lead to higher external costs and lower external benefits, the input of resources is ineffective and inefficient. Therefore, when the majority of microeconomic units find resource input to be uneconomical and decide to stop committing additional resources, their decision is also consistent with the efficiency principle of resource allocation in a society.

The above discussions reveal that under equilibrium conditions where the market is fully developed and pricing is flexible, and resource input by microeconomic units is driven by their own economic benefit, then resource allocation will surely be influenced by market price, and resources will be invested in effective sectors, regions, and enterprises and withdrawn from ineffective sectors, regions, and enterprises. The function of market self-regulation during resource allocation is demonstrated by the fact that the market does not allow sustained ineffective input of resources, and resource allocation will automatically follow the efficiency principle under market regulation.

2.4.3 Two Different Types of Microeconomic Units and Disequilibrium

The above analysis of market self-regulation during resource allocation reveals that the reason why the market can self-regulate excessive economic expansion and contraction is closely related to the strong motivation of market participants. The state of economic equilibrium is arrived at under the assumption of a fully developed market and flexible prices. But a more important or fundamental precondition is the presence of fully motivated microeconomic units.

We can therefore divide microeconomic units into two types, one with full motivation and one lacking sufficient motivation (or totally without motivation). The reason why microeconomic units are fully motivated is that they are responsible for business operations and their profits or losses and are able to select various investment opportunities and mode of operation in accordance with the best of their interests, distribute after-tax earnings according to their economic interests, and bear investment and operational risks. Such an enterprise is an independent goods producer and operator. Such an individual, in economic terms, is an independent market participant. If microeconomic units do not meet these standards, they must lack full motivation or end up without any motivation.

Under equilibrium conditions, microeconomic units are undoubtedly fully motivated, which has been mentioned in the previous discussions. We need to analyze whether they are fully motivated under disequilibrium conditions. In order to answer this question, we need to divide economic disequilibrium into two types.

Type I economic disequilibrium refers to a disequilibrium condition under which the market is not fully developed, pricing is not flexible, and there are excess demand and supply as well as constraints on demand and constraints on supply, but microeconomic units who participate in market activities are independent and responsible for their own profits and losses, investment opportunities, and business operations and bear investment and operational risks.

Type II economic disequilibrium refers to a disequilibrium condition under which the market is not fully developed, pricing is not flexible, and there are excess demand and supply as well as constraints on demand and constraints on supply, but microeconomic units who participate in market activities are not independent or responsible for their own profits and losses. They lack the authority to make any decision on investment opportunities and business operations and do not bear investment and operational risks. Such a microeconomic unit has not severed its affiliation with government agencies.

If economic disequilibrium can be categorized into these two types, we can conclude that disequilibrium in a capitalist economy is considered type I disequilibrium, while that in a socialist economy varies. Disequilibrium under the traditional economic system and the dual-track economic system is type II disequilibrium, because enterprises are affiliated with government agencies. Economic reforms will establish the new economic system, under which enterprises are independent goods producers who are in charge of operations, responsible for profits and losses, granted with operating authorities, and accordingly liable for investment and operational risks. The economic disequilibrium in this case is considered type I disequilibrium.

Microeconomic units existing under type II disequilibrium condition clearly lack sufficient motivation or even have no motivation at all.

Under type I disequilibrium condition, a microeconomic unit itself is fully motivated. However, as they face disequilibrium conditions, they conduct business transactions in an underdeveloped market and with inflexible prices and incomplete and inaccessible market information. In this case, although they are fully motivated, such motivations are constrained by external factors. For example, rigid prices are not necessarily capable of functioning as signals to adjust production, and rigid wages are not necessarily capable of functioning in allocating and combining resources in a way that optimizes resource allocation. Of course, that a microeconomic unit is fully motivated yet such motivations are constrained is quite different from a microeconomic unit that has insufficient motivation. This is the difference between type I disequilibrium and type II disequilibrium.

2.4.4 Market Self-Regulation Under Type I Disequilibrium Condition

As discussed earlier, the market performs self-regulation effectively under equilibrium conditions, i.e., the market will not allow ineffective resource input to exist for a prolonged period of time, due to the following two conditions. First, the market is fully developed and pricing is flexible. Second, microeconomic units are fully motivated and able to produce, operate, and transact in their own interests. However, type I disequilibrium condition only meets one of the two conditions. That is, microeconomic units are fully motivated, but the market is underdeveloped, pricing is inflexible, and there are either resource supply constraints or demand constraints, or both in the economy. How does the market perform self-regulation under such circumstances? How effective is market self-regulation?

The condition that microeconomic units are fully motivated should be considered more important than that the market is fully developed. The reason is that a fully developed market and flexible prices primarily create a benign environment for the development of the commodity economy, but the condition that microeconomic units are fully motivated resolves the issues related to the economic interests, responsibilities, incentives, and motivations of market participants. If microeconomic units do not take advantage of a fully developed market, in spite of its availability, or flexible prices, and have neither motivation to combine resources effectively or increase utilization efficiency nor any responsibility for economic losses due to resource misallocation, the function of market self-regulation in resource allocation will be discounted. If microeconomic units have no motivations, they are neither sensitive to nor care about economic profits or losses resulting from market activities. The market in this scenario will not be fully developed. A fully developed market exists only when market participants are fully motivated, not vice versa.

The above analyses indicate that the more important condition of those two has existed in an economy in type I disequilibrium. That condition is that microeconomic units are fully motivated. This condition facilitates the function of market self-regulation in resource allocation. Even though the market is not fully developed, pricing is not flexible, and there are resource supply constraints and demand constraints, microeconomic units are able to conduct business transactions in their best interests and intuitively avoid ineffective input of resources or refuse ineffective and inefficient resource combinations and utilization. Therefore, the market can still regulate input and combination of resources in accordance with the efficiency principle during the process of resource allocation, avoiding prolonged ineffective input of resources.

Nevertheless, type I disequilibrium still belongs to the category of disequilibrium. Input of resources in this scenario is after all different from that under equilibrium conditions. The influences of type I disequilibrium on microeconomic business activities are seen in the following three aspects:

1. When the market is not fully developed and information is not complete or freely accessible, microeconomic units cannot collect sufficient timely market information, much of which is even misleading. They are forced to make decisions on input of resources and resource combination with limited or even erroneous information. As a result, the economy will likely suffer from low efficiency, and resource allocation in society will be inconsistent with the efficiency principle.
2. When pricing is inflexible, or in the case of price rigidity, microeconomic units are not free to allocate resources. The reason is that price rigidity does not indicate resource scarcity or reveal the result of resource input and it is not possible for microeconomic units to select required resources optimally during the course of resource combination. If some microeconomic units are unable to optimally select the combination of resources due to price rigidity, it is inevitable to find idle or wasted resources in the economy.
3. Due to resource supply constraints and demand constraints, the allocation of resources will be short term whenever there is imbalance between supply and demand. As a matter of fact, this situation means microeconomic units face heightened competition. When under supply constraints, a microeconomic unit as a resource buyer is challenged by limited supply of resources and is forced to make extra efforts to secure supplies. When under demand constraints, a microeconomic unit as a seller is challenged by a limited market and is forced to make extra efforts to sell its products. These extra efforts by microeconomic units to secure supplies or to sell products in the case of constraints on supply and constraints on demand excessively drain societal resources from an overall societal perspective, which is one form of resource misallocation.

The analysis above shows the influences of type I disequilibrium on the business activities and ways of resource utilization of microeconomic units, demonstrating that market self-regulation is functional but constrained under type I disequilibrium condition.

2.4.5 Market Self-Regulation Under Type II Disequilibrium Condition

Neither of the two conditions (i.e., fully developed market and flexible prices and fully motivated microeconomic units) required of market self-regulation to function during resource allocation exists under type II disequilibrium condition. Thus market self-regulation plays a limited role during the process of resource allocation.

As discussed earlier, market self-regulation is constrained under type I disequilibrium condition due to underdeveloped market and incomplete and inaccessible market information, together with price rigidity and resource supply constraints and demand constraints. These situations also apply to type II disequilibrium condition. More importantly, as microeconomic units are not fully motivated or even totally lack motivation, constraints on market self-regulation are even more obvious. We will analyze that from the following two perspectives.

The reason that microeconomic units lack motivation is because they are not real economic entities with self-interest that is not directly tied to their operational results. They are not responsible for economic losses resulting from faulty operations or bad investment decisions. As a result, they lack not only motivation and incentive but also pressure and responsibility. They may see no value in pursuing any business that brings in additional profits and contributes to higher resource utilization efficiency for the economy. Meanwhile, they may continue doing whatever may reduce their profits and contribute to lowering resource allocation efficiency for the economy. Market self-regulation appears powerless because of the indifferent attitude of microeconomic units, let alone discussing how to control input of resources and resource utilization following the efficiency principle.

On the other hand, the reason why microeconomic units lack motivation is not only because they do not care about or pay enough attention to operational profits and losses but also because government agencies interfere with their operational decisions and they have to obey orders from government agencies. Therefore, even though some microeconomic units care for their profits and losses and wish to adjust input of resources and resource utilization in their own economic interests, the affiliation with government agencies makes it difficult for them to do so. Hence market self-regulation cannot function during the allocation of resources.

These two aspects clearly demonstrate that the market cannot actually perform the self-regulation function during resource allocation under type II disequilibrium condition. This is in sharp contrast to type I disequilibrium condition. If we say the function of market self-regulation still exists during the course of resource allocation, although restricted to some extent, under type I disequilibrium condition, it barely functions under type II disequilibrium condition.

The following situations are often seen under type II disequilibrium condition. When input of resources is executed or resources are combined or utilized inappropriately and inefficiently, the market is unable to correct the situation. When the market signals some alerts (such as widening gap between the supply and demand of certain resources, lowering economic efficiency, and increasing price volatilities), microeconomic units cannot gain access to those alerts or fail to make adjustments to input of resources and resource combination after they receive the alerts. They are even reluctant to make any change. Resource misallocation continues or deteriorates, which will give rise to one of the following three scenarios:

The first scenario: Deteriorating resource misallocation causes an economic downturn, forcing the government to intervene using noneconomic measures to tackle resource misallocation. The intervention, or called rectification or policy adjustment, is not done via the market, which is often seen under type II disequilibrium condition. It is necessary to point out that the government hereby mentioned refers to the highest authority. Only after the highest authority detects the severity of resource misallocation and decides to apply rectification or policy adjustment can those nonmarket measures take effect to tackle resource misallocation. There must be a considerable time lag between when the issue is detected and the decision of rectification or policy adjustment is made, which inevitably brings considerable damage to the economy.

The core issue is how the highest authority rectifies resource misallocation. Only after the highest authority truly understands that the cause and deterioration of resource misallocation is due to type II disequilibrium condition (i.e., underdeveloped market, inflexible prices, and microeconomic units' lack of motivation) and takes actions to resolve type II disequilibrium condition can such rectification measures be truly effective. If the highest authority only plans to use some nonmarket measures to correct resource misallocation while maintaining type II disequilibrium condition, the imbalance between resource supply and resource demand can only be temporarily alleviated. The resource misallocation problem will persist and become complicated and eventually lead to re-rectification or policy readjustment after a certain period of time. In addition, final consequences must be unsolved problems one after another, greater obstacles, more difficult rectification, and worsening rectification results.

The second scenario: Under the circumstance of worsening resource misallocation and resulting economic downturn, the government does not intervene using nonmarket measures. In this case, the government does not intend to correct resource misallocation. The persistence of the situation may lead to numerous unsolved problems. As unsolved problems keep piling up, conflicts between resource supply and resource demand will be fully exposed, and the economy will suffer from stagnation, inflation, or stagflation. Severe stagnation, inflation, or stagflation may even paralyze the economy. Only under that circumstance can we clearly see the market self-regulation function. This is because economic chaos and paralyzed economy will force microeconomic units to find their own way out. Faced with extreme difficulties and almost despair, they will have to pursue business transactions in their own interests (or in the interests of their employees) in order to survive.

Under type II disequilibrium condition, some of the business transactions conducted by some microeconomic units in pursuit of their own interests are underground. In other words, underground markets quickly develop at this time. These emerging underground markets may cost certain microeconomic units dearly to pursue transactions in their own interests, which are likely to further exacerbate resource misallocation. However, an underground market is after all one kind of market. In this market, counterparties in a transaction may set aside noneconomic interference and allow the scarcity of commodities to determine the price (similar to prices in imperfect competition). Instead, market self-regulation during resource allocation is seen in this kind of market, allowing transactions to be concluded at conditions satisfactory to both counterparties. Underground market activities will more or less alleviate economic hardship and to some extent prevent resource misallocation from devastating the overall economy. As ironic as these phenomena may look, they are likely to occur under type II disequilibrium condition.

The third scenario: Deteriorating resource misallocation and consequential economic downturn allow the government to recognize the root cause of the issue, i.e., worsening economic disequilibrium, as well as the fact that economic disequilibrium is demonstrated not only by underdeveloped markets but more importantly by microeconomic units' lack of motivation. Therefore, the government decides to reform the economic system, adopt appropriate measures to motivate microeconomic units, and gradually develop the market. Meanwhile, the government also introduces some macroeconomic regulations during economic reforms, appropriately coordinating government regulation and market regulation to alleviate conflicting allocation of resources and gradually rationalizing input of resources and resource combination in society.

Undoubtedly, the third scenario is not easy to come by. When the economy is in the midst of type II disequilibrium, it normally follows its trajectory and ultimately ends up in a scenario more similar to the first one. The second scenario is usually the result of natural economic consequences from ineffective government intervention or ineffective policies that are intended to tackle economic chaos, rather than what the government has hoped for under type II disequilibrium condition. If the economy turns out to be close to the second scenario, it is very likely that the government is incapable of correcting resource misallocation as well as regulating underground business activities. But the occurrence of the third scenario needs a series of premises.

First of all, severe resource misallocation and economic downturn have forced the government to recognize the necessity of economic reforms, especially the necessity of endowing microeconomic units with motivation via reforming the economic system.

Secondly, the government has adopted effective measures to reform the economic system, which gradually separate microeconomic units from their affiliation with government agencies, give them internal motivation and external pressures, and prompt them to care for their profits and losses.

Thirdly, the government simultaneously adopts appropriate macroeconomic regulatory measures to alleviate resource misallocation and to allow market self-regulation to function.

Lastly, as reforms on the economic system and government economic regulation make progress, a dual mechanism that consists of market regulation and government regulation gradually comes into being. As the dual mechanism takes effect, resource allocation gradually improves.

It can be seen that any one of these conditions cannot be easily met. If resource misallocation under type II disequilibrium condition has three possible outcomes, only the third scenario is worth pursuing. If the third scenario became a reality, type II economic disequilibrium would become type I economic disequilibrium. If we say that economic equilibrium is not realistic, type I disequilibrium is the second best choice available.

Of course, under type I disequilibrium condition, the magnitude of disequilibrium varies due to different degree of market underdevelopment, price inflexibility, market information imperfection and inaccessibility, and resource supply constraints and demand constraints. The purpose of research on resource allocation in the socialist society is to understand how the government applies market mechanism and government regulation to facilitate the transition of resource allocation from ineffectiveness to effectiveness under various disequilibrium conditions.

References

1. Li, Yining. (1988). *Management of national economy* (pp. 418–424). Hebei People's Press, Shijiazhuang, Hebei, China.
2. Li, Yining. (1986). *Socialist political economics* (pp. 322–323). The Commercial Press, Beijing, China.

Chapter 3
Government Regulation and Resource Allocation

3.1 The Meaning of Government Regulation

3.1.1 Government Regulation and Government Planning

Government regulation means the government adopts certain measures in accordance with market situations to regulate the economy and direct the operation of the economy and economic growth toward a specific goal.

The scope of government regulation is wider than what is known as planned regulation, which is a form of government regulation. Generally speaking, planned regulation falls into the category of economic regulation. It refers to the regulation of the economy by the government using plans (including mandatory and nonmandatory plans) and is therefore characterized by "planning." Government regulation is not limited to planning or economic regulation. When necessary, the government may carry out regulation using administrative, legal, and economic measures. When it comes to the economy, the government may regulate it by planned or non-planned measures. Government regulation is not necessarily predetermined or planned ahead of time. If necessary, the government may carry out contingency regulation by taking interim abnormal emergency measures.

The government may adopt the following measures of planned regulation: planned price regulation, planned fiscal and credit regulation, planned income regulation, and planned exchange rate regulation. These measures are explained in detail as follows:

Under planned price regulation, the government, in accordance with market situation, sets planned price or uses planned price to directly or indirectly influence market price. Planned price regulation can also be executed by using a sole unified price set by the government.

Under planned credit regulation, the government, in accordance with market situation, sets planned interest rate to influence market interest rate or stipulates a planned credit quota as the basis for adjusting credit. Planned credit regulation can

Y. Li, *Chinese Economy in Disequilibrium*, China Academic Library,
DOI 10.1007/978-3-642-39558-1_3, © Foreign Language Teaching and Research
Publishing Co., Ltd and Springer-Verlag Berlin Heidelberg 2014

be executed by a sole interest rate approved by the government, which is planned interest rate, or by a sole credit mechanism approved by the government, which is planned credit quota.

Under planned fiscal regulation, the government uses fiscal revenue and spending to regulate the economy. The feature of planned fiscal regulation is reflected in the execution of a proposed fiscal budget. The government takes current and future market situations into consideration and uses tax revenues (including tax category and tax rate), other national income, and changing fiscal spending as regulatory tools to influence the market.

Under planned income regulation, the government uses fiscal, credit, and price measures to make planned adjustments to personal income according to its current situation and potential changes so that personal income level, distribution of personal income, and personal income gap are consistent with planned targets.

Under planned exchange rate regulation, the government makes planned adjustments to exchange rate or exchange rate regime according to current balance of payments and potential changes so that foreign exchange inflow and outflow are consistent with predetermined economic targets.

Therefore, as a measure adopted by the government to regulate the economy, planned regulation is characterized by planning. Government regulation, which has a wider scope than planned regulation, includes not only all of the abovementioned planned regulatory measures but also non-planned regulation and noneconomic regulation. Regulation of price, credit, fiscal spending, revenue, and exchange rate mentioned above can be executed by the government using administrative and legal measures according to the specific situation, which may even include the eventual freezing of price, credit, or income. The government may also use non-planned emergency regulatory measures, such as levying temporary taxes or planning certain special expenditures to meet specific fiscal needs and taking expedient measures to regulate price and exchange rate. It is obviously incorrect to equate government regulation with planned regulation.

3.1.2 The Government Serving as Market Administrator

We have used a large mixer as metaphor for the market during resource combination. The mixing process is to select resource combination. The activities of the market as a large mixer are broken into three stages, production, sales, and distribution. These three stages correspond to market input decision, market output decision, and market distribution decision. Inside this large mixer, the market constantly makes various selections so that resource combination and resource utilization meet the efficiency standard of resource allocation.

If a large mixer is used as metaphor for market, it needs an administrator in the same way as a mixer needs an operator. The function of the government in resource allocation to some extent is similar to the operator of the large mixer. In the case of insufficient resource supply or demand, the government can adjust resource supply and demand by allocating limited resources to where they are needed or by allocating limited demand to different suppliers. The government can be a direct supplier or buyer itself. Perhaps more importantly, the government as the market administrator is responsible for maintaining market order and ensuring orderly market activities, the same as a mixer operator is responsible for troubleshooting problems in order to maintain the normal operation of the mixer.[1]

As market administrator, the government can be a direct supplier or buyer when necessary and has a clear understanding of its roles in resource allocation. It is necessary to further clarify the role that the government plays in resource allocation as a force that influences market selection, i.e., one that influences the behavior of market participant with regard to input, output, and distribution. What is the relationship between the influence of the government and the operation of the market as a large mixer? To answer this question, we need to look at market selection first.

Market selection is all about the selection of input, output, and distribution, all of which can be considered the selection of resource combination. If resources in an economy are limited and the scarcity of various resources varies, government regulation is to influence the selection of input, output, and distribution by microeconomic units. That is, the government adopts certain measures to direct microeconomic units toward selecting one form of resource allocation over the other in accordance with their economic interests, which leads to a result that fulfills the government's purpose. The role of the government in economic regulation is not to force every microeconomic unit to accept its plan, but jump-starts a microeconomic unit's inherent power so that it can pursue its own economic interests. Government regulation is not to lower microeconomic units' motivation or enthusiasm. Even if microeconomic units realize that some government measures discourage a form of resource combination that they initially chose and decide to abandon it, they are still motivated decision-makers on resource combination. The decision to abandon the form of resource combination is made based on their own interests, not because of administrative pressures from the government.

Let us continue with the mixer metaphor. The market keeps running like a large mixer with inputs of various resources. Its operational power originates from inside. That is, the power of market operations comes from the motivation of microeconomic units to conduct various business transactions. Government regulation measures cannot curb such motivation. The stronger motivation microeconomic units have, the more smoothly the market operates, and the more free and efficient combination of resources the market can achieve with various inputs. On the contrary, if government regulation curbs microeconomic units' motivation, making them dumb and insensitive, the mixer will not operate easily or operates very slowly, unable to fulfill the goal of allocating resources effectively.

---

[1]Li Yining [1].

3.1.3 Rational Government Regulation

Government regulation should be rational and realistic. Irrational government regulation is very harmful to resource allocation. Under the dual-track economic mechanism, if government regulation works together with the market mechanism, it is rational government regulation. We can explain this issue from the following three aspects.

The first aspect is input. Without government regulation, microeconomic units, in the case of being solely regulated by the market, will decide on the variety and quantity of input factors according to the assessment of the market. If the variety and quantity of various factors decided by microeconomic units are not consistent with demand in the market, the market will change its assessment on the various factors. When microeconomic units learn that the market has changed, they will in turn adjust their factor inputs accordingly. This process will go on and on, bringing the factor inputs by microeconomic units closer to demand in the market in terms of variety and quantity. If at this time the government unreasonably intervenes, distorting market assessment of factor inputs, the market or the government will deliver a distorted message to microeconomic units. As a result, the gap between microeconomic units' inputs and demand in the market will not shrink but widen.

The second aspect is output. Without government regulation, microeconomic units are solely regulated by the market. Every microeconomic unit as a seller will have to decide on its output in response to the buyer's request, which is made known to the seller primarily via the market. Sellers make constant adjustments to output varieties and quantities to satisfy the changing demand. If the government unreasonably intervenes at this time, sellers will not be able to receive relatively accurate information either from the market or directly from buyers. As a result, the gap between output varieties and quantities and demand in the market will also widen.

The third aspect is distribution. Without government regulation, microeconomic units are solely regulated by the market. Every microeconomic unit will distribute its income among consumption, savings, and investment according to its own situation and market expectations. The comparison of economic interests plays a primary role in each microeconomic unit's decision on how income is distributed. Although the distribution of income decided by each microeconomic unit in its own interests may not be able to satisfy the requirement of resource allocation for the economy, market regulation will induce constant changes in the current and expected interests of microeconomic units. As a result, their distribution of income will change accordingly and toward a closer alignment with the overall resource allocation in the economy. If the government unreasonably intervenes at this time, which causes resource allocation in society to deviate from the efficiency standard and misleads microeconomic units to inappropriately distribute their income when they receive somewhat erroneous market information, the distribution of income by microeconomic units among consumption, savings, and investment will further deviate from the requirement of resource allocation for society.

The above analysis is based on the perspective that the government indirectly influences market selection. Nevertheless, we have clearly seen serious consequences of irrational government regulation. If the government enforces irrational regulation as a direct supplier or buyer, or directly interferes with input, output, and distribution decisions in an irrational way, or makes wrong decisions that prohibit the market from functioning, the potential losses from resource misallocation due to irrational government regulation will be much larger than what has been discussed in the above analysis.

3.2 Nonidealized Government Behavior and Its Impact on Resource Allocation

3.2.1 *The Meaning of Nonidealized Government Behavior*

The criterion of rational or irrational government regulation resides in whether or not the government regulation follows objective economic principles or whether it is consistent with the reality. Yet we cannot neglect the difference between understanding objective economic principles and utilizing these economic principles. The government may try its best to regulate the economy by following objective economic principles. However, it may fail to meet its goals due to various constraints. Therefore, there arises the problem of nonidealized government behavior

The difference between idealized government behavior and nonidealized government behavior is not because of different government regulation results, but the fact that they represent two different viewpoints. Idealized government behavior is based on the assumption that an ideal government, as the monitor of economic activities, is able to adopt any kind of measure, has access to every piece of information, is capable of thoroughly considering and accurately predicting every ongoing issue and policy execution results using various analytical methods, and can take appropriate measures according to each and every potential event. Such a government is an "almighty" government: As long as it has decided on how to regulate the economy, it will be able to proactively take regulatory measures as planned, which will definitely meet the goals once executed. Therefore, the assumption of idealized government behavior is based on the belief that the government is endowed with supernatural and almighty power. Nonidealized government behavior, on the other hand, refers to the action of the government who is subject to various subjective and objective constraints and who is not necessarily able to fully satisfy its policy goals. Nonidealized government behavior is based on a belief different from that of idealized government behavior.

This means that an idealized government, the same as an idealized person, only exists in books or the mind of some scholars. It does not exist in reality. Any government, regardless of how experienced or capable its members are, is subject to various subjective or objective constraints. It is impossible for the government to have access to every piece of information or only make decisions after gaining access to every piece of information. Moreover, even if it is possible for the government to use all necessary measures in making a decision, the execution of these measures may be time-consuming and costly and thus practically unworthy. By the same token, it is not possible either for the government to accurately know the economic outlook or the result from executing a policy, most of which is beyond the expectation and control of the government. In a world of uncertainty, the government cannot decide everything, as it is constrained by many factors. Idealizing government behavior is neglecting the complexity and variability of economic activities and overestimating the role of the government in economic activities. Only by assuming nonidealized government behavior can we draw a practical conclusion on the role of government regulation.

3.2.2 *The Lag in Policy Effect*

In order to further analyze nonidealized government behavior, we need to firstly discuss the lag in policy effect.

Let us assume that the government plays its role in regulating the economy using certain economic policies. For now, let us refrain from discussing some other lag effects, i.e., the lag in recognition by the government of a certain economic phenomenon, the lag in deciding whether the government needs to take regulatory measures, and the lag in selecting regulatory plans or measures. The recognition lag refers to the time delay between the development of an economic problem and the government's recognition of the problem, as there is normally a period of time before the government can understand the problem. The decision lag refers to the time delay between the government's recognition of a problem and its decision to take action. After the government has a better understanding of an economic problem, it will consider whether it is necessary to use any regulatory measure. There is a period of time before the government can reach a conclusion. If the government believes regulation is not necessary, it will not take action, even after it has recognized and understood the problem. Only after the government has understood the problem and believes that regulation is necessary will it decide to take certain regulatory measures. As for the selection lag, the government must select a regulatory plan or certain regulatory measures after it decides to take action. In this case, it is unlikely that there is an existing plan applicable to the situation or an existing regulatory measure that fully addresses the need. Hence, the government needs a certain period of time to formulate a new plan or a new regulatory measure. Therefore, the time period from when the government decides to carry out regulation till when a regulatory plan or measure is ready for execution is referred to as the selection lag. The fact that policy effect will lag during as well as after the execution of the policy has clearly revealed the limitation of government behavior.

The lag in policy effect refers to the lag in the execution of a certain regulatory measure after the government makes a decision to take such action. As the nature and enforcement of regulatory measures vary, the timing for each measure to take effect will also vary. Therefore, the timing of policy effect will vary. The time period from when government regulatory measures are executed till when they take effect is called the lag in policy effect. Two commonly seen economic regulatory policies, tax policy and interest rate policy, are used here as examples to explain the lag effect. If the government wants to control personal consumption and decides to raise income tax rate, this policy will work to reduce personal consumption because higher income tax rate reduces personal disposable income. In addition, if the ratio of personal spending to total income remains unchanged and personal preferences may change to a certain degree, reduced personal after-tax income will correspondingly reduce personal consumption. Nevertheless, there is a relatively long time lapse between when the regulatory measure is implemented and when the consumption in the economy starts to contract. The contraction of consumption is not instantly seen as soon as personal income tax rate is raised. In terms of interest rate policy, if the government wants to increase investment and decides to lower the discount rate charged by the central bank, the policy will function to stimulate investment because businesses believe that a lower interest rate will generate higher investment returns. If the expected profitability remains unchanged, the gap between the expected rate of return and the interest rate will widen, hence attracting more investment. There is, however, a relatively long period of time from the start of the regulation till more businesses are interested in applying for loans and increasing investment. The increase in investment in the economy is not instantly seen as soon as the central bank lowers the discount rate.

Other government regulatory measures, such as adjusting exchange rate, changing balance of payments, adjusting planned price, and changing the relationship between aggregate demand and aggregate supply, will also reveal the lag in policy effect. The reason is because economic activities are done in markets and market participants are separate microeconomic units, each of whom has its own economic interests. Whether regulatory measures are effective or not will need to be seen from whether or not microeconomic units will change their economic activities. From the onset of a regulatory measure until every microeconomic unit is influenced by economic activities under the regulatory measure and adjusts its own economic activities accordingly, the length of this process varies, but the lag in policy effect cannot be averted.

It is necessary to note that the lag in policy effect, as analyzed above, is not directly associated with the rationality of government regulation. Under bad government regulation, policy effect should lag to some extent. Under good government regulation, policy effect will also lag. The difference is not whether policy effect will lag or not, but whether policy effect will benefit the economy and facilitate the realization of economic growth target. Of course, if government regulation is good and its policies have thoroughly compared various regulatory plans or measures as well as considered potential new situations during execution, the execution process will be relatively easy and the lag in policy effect can be shortened. However, it does not mean the lag will disappear.

3.2.3 The Imbalance of Policy Effect

The lag in policy effect reflects certain limits of government regulation. However, government regulation is subject to more restrictions. The effect of various policies also varies. The variance of policy effect reflects the complexity of economic activities as well as the fact that policy effects are subject to restrictions.

Many economic issues can be viewed from opposite sides based on different perspectives. For example, price, wage, profit, tax, interest, benefit, and enterprise, of which some rise, some fall, some grow, and some decline. For another example, income can be broken down into consumption and savings and expenditures into consumption and investment. If the proportion of consumption to income rises, the proportion of savings to income will fall, provided that income is the same. Here is another example that reveals opposite relations. If the proportion of consumption to expenditures rises, the proportion of investment to expenditures will fall, provided that expenditures are the same. As one more example, if a specific resource is used in A, it cannot be used in an area other than A, provided that the total amount of the resource is fixed. If A uses more of the resource, less will be available for areas other than A. The imbalance in policy effect refers to an unequal impact of a policy, if effective on economic activities, on the opposite sides in the same area. For example, there are many economic phenomena such as price rigidity, wage rigidity, welfare rigidity, and employment rigidity. Any regulatory measure that influences price, wage, welfare, and employment will have unequal impacts on a different area. As price, wage, welfare, and employment are easier to rise than fall, price policy, wage policy, welfare policy, or employment policy tends to be more effective in stimulating growth in price, wage, welfare, or employment than in controlling the rise of price, wage, welfare, or employment and is especially ineffective in lowering price, wage, welfare, or employment. This demonstrates the imbalance in policy effect.

Let us look at income as consumption and savings or expenditures as consumption and investment. The same regulatory measure will have different impacts on these two opposite perspectives. For example, if the proportion of consumption to income is relatively high and that of savings to income is relatively low, any fiscal regulatory measure will likely have a larger impact on consumption, but little impact on savings. Any credit regulatory measure, on the contrary, is likely to have a larger impact on savings, but little impact on consumption. Another example is the switch of savings to investments. The effect of various government regulatory measures can be generally summarized as follows: It is more difficult to accelerate the switch from savings to investments and it is easier to slow the switch from savings to investments. More specifically, if the government raises either taxes on businesses or interest rates on commercial loans, the switch from savings to investments will slow down. On the contrary, if the government lowers taxes on businesses or interest rates on commercial loans, savings will be switched to investments, but the switch is not that easy. Perhaps the government must work harder or adopt more powerful measures to reach its goal. Why? This has something to do with the difference between business motivation and personal motivation.

It is necessary to know that businesses have motivations different from that of individuals, even though they are both agents of economic activities and subject to government regulatory measures. Business motivations can be summarized as the drive to maximize profit, or at least the primary motivation is to maximize profit, while personal motivations are more complicated. To maximize personal income is just one of the many personal motivations. Besides maximizing income, there are some other motivations that are not necessarily less important. As personal income rises, other motivations will become more important. Businesses are the main conduits of investment, while individuals are the main providers of savings. This means that investment activities are mainly influenced by profit maximization, while saving activities are not necessarily mainly influenced by personal income maximization. The government normally takes the maximization of profit or personal income into consideration when adopting regulatory measures. In particular, the government hopes that the stakeholders of investment or saving activities will be driven by profit or income maximization, which will enable a government regulatory measure to accomplish its mission. Since individuals who provide the majority of savings tend to deviate further away from the focus of maximizing profit or income than businesses who are main participants of investment activities, it will be more difficult for the government to enforce a regulatory measure that targets savings to achieve its anticipated results.

3.2.4 The Decrease of Policy Effect

During our discussions on nonidealized government behavior, we must also pay attention to the decrease of policy effect. The decrease of policy effect refers to a diminishing effect as time elapses after the execution of a government regulatory measure. It may even end up having little impact at all in the end even if it still exists.

We can analyze this situation from four different perspectives.

First, situations change or a new situation appears.

When the government begins to draft a policy or a regulatory measure, it may fail to anticipate future changes or a new situation, or it may underestimate the development of the situation due to subjective restrictions. Therefore, as the policy or the regulatory measure comes across a new unanticipated situation after its execution, the original policy or the original regulatory measure will become less effective. As thorough as the original decision may be, such situational changes will always happen. It reflects the limitation of government behavior.

Second, a government policy or a regulatory measure has some side effects.

Any policy or any regulatory measure may have some side effects. For example, while a policy or a regulatory measure may facilitate the accomplishment of one goal, it may harm another. The latter is referred to as side effect, or negative impact. This side effect may have existed at the beginning of a policy or a regulatory measure and is simply hard to detect. It is gradually seen as time goes by. This side effect may also appear some time after the execution of a policy or a regulatory measure. Anyway, the longer after the execution of a policy or a regulatory measure, the more obvious the side effect will be, the more powerful it will become in reducing policy effect.

Third, microeconomic units adopt counter policies in response to a government policy or a regulatory measure.

Assume that a policy or a regulatory measure places some restrictions on the economic activities of a microeconomic unit or discourages some profit-seeking activities of a microeconomic unit. The microeconomic unit will adopt certain counter policies out of its own economic interests to lower the effect of the policy or the regulatory measure so that its economic interests will not be harmed.

It is necessary to point out that the counter policy employed by a microeconomic unit is normally legal. Of course, there are always some microeconomic units who ignore the regulation and engage in illegal activities. If this situation occurs, policy effect will definitely decrease. However, such a situation cannot be taken as evidence of nonidealized government behavior. So long as the government strictly abides by the law and vigorously punishes illegal activities, it will have the capability to reduce illegal activities committed by microeconomic units. As for legal counter policies, they are directly associated with nonidealized government behavior. This means that once a microeconomic unit finds its economic interests are harmed by a government policy or a regulatory measure, it may try its best to circumvent the restrictions placed by the government regulation and seek on its own a way to gain profits. Or it may take advantage of the market mechanism to flexibly adjust in the relatively familiar economic environment in pursuit of its economic interests. Or it may look for any policy loophole or any ambiguous explanations of a policy or a regulatory measure to support its decisions. All these actions are legal. As no government policy or regulatory measure is ever perfect, it is very possible for a microeconomic unit to legally lower policy effect.

Fourth, microeconomic units take precautionary actions in anticipation of a policy or a regulatory measure.

A microeconomic unit with independent economic interests will collect information from various sources and analyze the information available to forecast subsequent government policies. After the analysis, if the microeconomic unit is able to forecast the next government regulation and anticipate the potential negative impacts these future regulatory measures may bring, it may take precautionary actions so that the policy will be less effective or even ineffective at all. The precautionary actions by microeconomic units can also be taken legally. Of course, just as microeconomic units take precautionary actions in anticipation of government behavior, the government can also take actions to offset these precautionary actions in anticipation of microeconomic units' reactions. Theoretically, the government has every reason and possibility to do so. In reality, the government is always in a reactive position. The reason is because the government is not as prompt and nimble as a microeconomic unit in the process of making decisions. There is only one government in a country, yet there are numerous businesses and individuals. Numerous businesses and individuals focus their attention on the government, yet the government cannot keep an eye on each and every business and individual. Government activities are easily recognized by the public, yet the government cannot easily understand the action of each business or individual, nor their next action plan. This is the limitation of government behavior.

3.2.5 Resource Allocation Under the Condition of Nonidealized Government Behavior

The above paragraphs discussed the lag in policy effect, the unbalance of policy effect, and the decrease of policy effect. All these issues demonstrate that government behavior is not ideal. If government decisions are relatively consistent with objective economic principles and made on the basis of democracy and science, there will be less nonidealized government behavior. Otherwise, nonidealized government behavior will intensify. In general, nonidealized government behavior is common.

Now let us analyze resource allocation under the condition of nonidealized government behavior. First of all, we will have to analyze resource combination with the government as a direct resource investor and producer. As a direct investor, the government can add to insufficient investment in the market or fill in the gap if microeconomic units do not come up with sufficient investment. As a direct producer, the government can bring additional output to the market or meet any deficiency of output from microeconomic units. In the case of insufficient input or output in the market, it is critical to have input or output from the government. But the input or output from the government must follow economic rules as well as the efficiency principle of resource allocation.

It is more common to see the government use various regulatory measures to influence resource allocation. In this circumstance, the government uses fiscal, monetary, price, or exchange rate regulatory measures to influence either input or output decisions made by the market. These decisions are not exempt from the lag in policy effect, the variance of policy effect, and the decrease of policy effect that we discussed earlier. Nonidealized government behavior will surely be seen more or less, resulting in a gap between actual and expected government regulation effects.

Due to the lag in policy effect, there is a time period before regulatory measures implemented by the government to influence resource allocation can take effect. Of course, theoretically, if the government knows that regulatory measures take effect with a time lag, it will adopt certain regulatory measures beforehand so that the time lag between the start and the functioning of those regulatory measures can be minimized or eliminated. In reality, however, this is not practical. It is nearly impossible that the government can adopt regulatory measures in advance, as it is unlikely for the government to take appropriate regulatory measures before the problem of resource allocation fully emerges. The government is more likely an ex post rather than ex ante regulator of resource allocation. Therefore, it is inevitable to have the lag before regulatory measures take effect, which will certainly reduce the effect of such measures. Moreover, situations may change during the period from the onset of a regulatory measure till when it takes effect. It is even possible that the second round of regulatory measures is needed due to situational changes before the first round takes effect, or the third round of regulatory measures is called for before the second round becomes effective. Although it is premature to reach a conclusion that government regulation is ineffective, we can at least draw the following two conclusions: (1) it is normally difficult for government regulation to reach resource allocation target; (2) the government is normally in a reactive position during resource allocation or normally ends up trying to come up with ex post remedies.

Let us look at the imbalance of regulation effect as well as its impacts on resource allocation. The imbalance of policy effect demonstrates that government regulatory measures are not very flexible when the government takes certain measures to influence resource allocation to reach its target, despite its wishes to influence input or output decisions by microeconomic units. Due to price rigidity, wage rigidity, employment rigidity, and welfare rigidity, the government can only reach or approach one regulation target while unable to reach another simultaneously. For example, in spite of great efforts, it is not easy for the government to lower price level, wage level, the number of people employed, or expenditures on welfare. In other words, if under certain circumstances effective resource allocation can be only realized by means of lowering price, wage, employment rate, or the percentage of welfare expenditures to national income or fiscal expenditures, the power of the government will be rather limited. In addition, as we discussed earlier, businesses are the primary source of investments and individuals are the primary source of savings and they have different motivations. The motivation of personal savings is more complicated than that of business investment. Therefore, a regulatory measure is more effective on investment than on savings. This means that under certain circumstances, if the only way to achieve effective resource allocation is to turn savings into investment or lower the switch from savings to investment, the power of the government will be limited.

Lastly, we should also consider the impact of the decrease of policy effect on resource allocation in the economy. This impact perhaps more clearly demonstrates the limitation of government regulation. It should be noted that microeconomic units make decisions on input and output for the market. Their preference for one form of resource allocation over another is more or less associated with their expected economic interests. Government regulation is nothing but a plan to change the expectations of microeconomic unit's economic interests via fiscal, monetary, price, and exchange rate measures so that the government can alter the resource combination originally decided by microeconomic units toward a closer alignment with the government's preset goals. Whether the government can realize its plan or not is not dependent upon its own wishes, but the following three points.

First, are government regulatory measures powerful enough? Are they able to alter microeconomic units' decisions on resource combination?

Based on the discussions on the decrease of policy effect, it is inevitable to have some doubts about this point. Government regulation is not necessarily powerful enough to change the decisions on resource combination made by microeconomic units. Moreover, it may be powerful enough to change resource combination at the beginning when it is executed, but it will gradually become less effective as time passes, reducing the power of the government to alter resource combination decisions.

Second, will a microeconomic unit accept government regulation and alter its original decisions on resource combination after considering cost and benefit?

Although government regulation benefits a microeconomic unit in a certain way, a microeconomic unit may choose to resist the pressure from government regulation and avoid altering its original resource combination decision if either the original resource combination brings more benefits or abandoning the original resource combination incurs higher losses than the losses from rejecting the government regulation. With the decrease of policy effect, microeconomic units tend to maintain their original resource combination. This exactly demonstrates the limitation of policy effect.

Third, do microeconomic units adopt counter policies or precautionary measures?

If microeconomic units consider a counter policy in response to certain government regulatory measures or precautionary measures in anticipation of government behavior, it will not be easy to guide the input and output decisions made by microeconomic units to be consistent with government's predetermined targets.

These three points generally illustrate that government regulation, in spite of some impacts on resource allocation, is subject to various limitations due to nonidealized government behavior, which makes it very difficult for the government to reach its preset goal for resource allocation.

3.3 The Appropriateness and Optimization of Government Behavior During Resource Allocation

3.3.1 Government's Dilemma in Regulating Resource Allocation Under Type II Disequilibrium Condition

All discussions above on nonidealized government behavior are not based on type II disequilibrium condition. In other words, the issues of lagging, unbalanced, and decreasing policy effect are independent of whether or not enterprises are able to make their own decisions and responsible for their own profits or losses. We may say that even if enterprises are no longer affiliated with administrative institutions and have become microeconomic units that are able to make decisions on production and operation in accordance with their own economic interests, the effect of government policies will still be lagging, disparate, and diminishing.

The lag, disparity, and decrease of policy effect are the inherent limitations of government behavior. Even after the market is fully developed and price signals fully function, the limitation of government behavior will continue to exist. The reason why nonidealized government behavior is prevalent is because it does not disappear after enterprises are fully motivated and the market is fully developed.

Having said that, how effective are government regulatory measures under type II disequilibrium condition where enterprises are not fully motivated and the market is not fully developed? Can we conclude that nonidealized government behavior is no different with or without motivated enterprises and a fully developed market? We are certain that such a conclusion cannot be drawn. Rather, the effect of government regulatory measures will change gradually, which will lead to more inefficient resource allocation. Let us analyze this issue from the following two aspects:

First, while the market has not been fully developed and information is not complete or timely, prices can still function to flexibly adjust supply and demand.

Under this circumstance, the lag, imbalance, and decrease of policy effect are even more obvious. This is because a policy itself is probably stipulated on the basis of an underdeveloped market and incomplete and untimely information. In addition, during the execution of the policy, the government is unlikely to collect sufficient information on the result of the policy due to the underdeveloped market and incomplete and untimely information. As a result, the gap between the predetermined goals set by the government and the actual policy results will likely get larger. On the other hand, as microeconomic units adopt counter policies based on their own expectations of government behavior, which is also based on an underdeveloped market and incomplete and untimely information, their expectations and counter policies may be excessive, even likely to bring more abnormal interference to government behavior. This will cause the actual policy results to further deviate from the predetermined goals set by the government.

Second, enterprises are not fully motivated and thus unable to pursue their economic interests as independent goods producers.

Compared with the situations of the first aspect, the interference to government regulation by unmotivated enterprises is more severe. The reason is very clear: When the government detects ineffective resource allocation in the economy, it will propose and execute appropriate measures to adjust resource allocation, believing that the measures will motivate microeconomic units to act according to their own economic interests and adopt new forms of resource combination that are consistent with the intention of the government's regulatory measures. However, that belief is contingent upon whether enterprises are fully motivated or whether enterprises are able to pursue their economic interests as independent goods producers. If this condition is not met, the issue is no longer only lagging or unbalanced policy effect, nor decreasing policy effect, but more of policy ineffectiveness or policy failure.

As far as precautionary measures or counter policies adopted by enterprises are concerned, they should follow certain paths or abide by certain rules as long as enterprises are independent goods producers following economic principles. In other words, enterprises are rational entities following normal rules. Therefore, even if government regulatory measures cannot easily attain the planned results, resource allocation in the economy, in spite of deviation from the government's intention, will still follow certain rules, i.e., the quantity of each entity's marginal benefit, because enterprises pursue resource combination in their own economic interests. If the condition that enterprises follow economic principles is not real or possible, coupled with nonidealized government behavior, resource allocation in society will be in chaos. It will ignore the marginal benefit for society, nor follow the rule of marginal benefit for each entity. We can conclude that this case is the most ineffective resource allocation for an economy. It is very likely to see this scenario under type II disequilibrium condition.

Based on the analysis, we can further understand that resource allocation under type II disequilibrium condition is the worst case among all possible scenarios. That is, enterprises act irrationally and resource allocation is getting much more ineffective.

3.3.2 The Appropriateness of Government Behavior During Resource Allocation

To study the appropriateness of government behavior during resource allocation is to find optimal government behavior during resource allocation. Appropriateness is a prerequisite for optimization. This is a point that must be stressed in our research on government regulation.

The appropriateness of government behavior during resource allocation means that the government should not try to do everything and should not do those things that should be done by the market and that the market is known to be good at. This point is consistent with the analogy of the market as a large mixer for resource combination and the government is the administrator of the mixer. Just as the administrator of a mixer who is unable to replace the mixer itself, the government cannot replace the market. This explains the appropriateness of government behavior.

From the government perspective, an important issue is whether the government is able to understand its mandatory and potential roles during resource allocation. The government has a mandatory role during resource allocation because microeconomic units, due to various limitations of market regulation, are only concerned about their own marginal benefits, not the marginal benefit for society. The potential role of the government during resource allocation means that the government should be down to earth, regulate the economy according to realistic conditions, and refrain from setting excessively high expectations for regulatory measures, because of nonidealized government behavior as well as lagging, unbalanced, and diminishing policy effect. That the government has to understand its roles is the prerequisite for the appropriateness of government regulation. Otherwise, the government is not only unable to suitably arrange its regulation activities, but may even go overboard. That is, the government undertakes a task that should never or can never be done by the government.

If we analyze the issue from the perspective of type II disequilibrium condition, we will get a better understanding. Type II disequilibrium has two features. One, the market is not fully developed. Two, enterprises are not independent goods producers. Given the first feature, i.e., an underdeveloped market, together with incomplete and untimely information, if government regulation is inappropriate or excessive, how much reliable information can the government rely on to regulate the economy? This means that government behavior must be appropriate in an economic environment in which the market is underdeveloped and information is incomplete and untimely, and the government should not try to do anything that should never or can never be done by the government.

Another feature of type II disequilibrium is that enterprises are not independent goods producers. It appears that the government should do much more as a direct investor and direct producer. But the critical issue in this case is that the relationship between government and enterprise has been reversed. We should first ask the question why enterprises are not independent goods producers. Then we should ask how large of an impact excessive government regulation of resource combination can have on increasing the effectiveness of resource combination under the assumption that enterprises are not independent goods producers.

The above two questions can be answered as follows:

As an enterprise, it should become an independent goods producer and should be responsible for its own operation as well as its profits and losses. If so far enterprises have still been unable to act as independent goods producers and still been distorted as affiliates of administrative agencies, it is not enterprises themselves but the economic system that is responsible for the issue. The reform of the economic system has not been deep enough to change enterprises' affiliation with administrative agencies. In this case, if the government wants to use excessive regulation of resource combination to make up for the deficiency of enterprise motivation, it will be impossible to fundamentally resolve the issue of ineffective resource combination.

Furthermore, as enterprises have not been able to make their own decisions and been held responsible for their own profits and losses, they do not follow the principle of self-interest in determining profitable resource combination. In that case, even if governments carry out excessive regulation of resource allocation, it will possibly further lower enterprise motivation. This will not do any good to enhancing the effectiveness of resource allocation in society.

Therefore, under the circumstance that enterprises are not independent goods producers, if the goal of government regulation is to promote effective resource allocation in society, the first thing that the government needs to do is to allow enterprises to become independent goods producers who can make their own decisions and are liable for their own profits and losses, rather than excessively regulate resource allocation. Otherwise, the situation of ineffective resource allocation will get worse.

3.3.3 Setting a Security Line and Reserving the Measures of Last Resort

The government cannot ignore two issues during resource allocation or economic regulation, regardless of whether or not the economy is in disequilibrium or whether the disequilibrium is type I or type II as defined earlier. One is to set a security line for the economy and the other is to reserve the economic measures of last resort and get ready to use them when necessary. These two issues fully reveal the government's position and functions in the economy.

The security line for the economy hereby mentioned refers to the boundary, which, once crossed, will prompt the government to take regulatory measures in accordance with its predetermined goals and development plans in order to ensure economic stability and growth and social harmony. This means that if the economy is operating within the boundary, or the security line, the government will not carry out economic regulation, despite uncertainties in the economy, weaknesses exposed during economic growth, or some issues related to social harmony. The market will handle these economic issues without government intervention. If instead the operation of the economy crosses the boundary, or the security line, the government will assume the responsibility for regulating the economy so that it can operate within the security line.

The setting of the security line for the economy by the government actually allows the government to take a proactive position, i.e., it reserves the right to regulate the economy. The government will decide in accordance with the actual situations at different time on whether or not to use a regulatory measure, what kind of regulatory measures to adopt, the strength of these regulatory measures, or when to terminate the regulatory measures that have been in place. In other words, the government will not regulate the economy unless necessary and will decide according to specific conditions on whether or not to regulate the economy if regulation is optional. The government will regulate the economy only if it is necessary. These situations reflect the appropriateness of government behavior and the flexibility of government regulation.

The security line itself is not only variable but also flexible with certain upper and lower bounds. When the government decomposes its goal into a few specific parameters, the security line it draws is actually decomposed into specific security lines for each parameter. For example, there is an upper bound and a lower bound for economic parameters such as unemployment rate, inflation rate, the ratio of government deficit to national income, and the ratio of foreign debt to GDP. The government may or may not carry out regulation if parameters are within the upper and lower bounds of the security line. The specific upper and lower bounds for each specific security line will be determined according to the actual situation at certain point of time.

The government reserves the economic measures of last resort and is ready to use those measures whenever necessary, which means that the government can use all irregular measures available, together with regular measures, such as fiscal regulation, monetary regulation, price regulation, and exchange rate regulation, to regulate the economy. Such irregular measures include price and wage control, foreign trade and foreign exchange control, emergency taxes or special taxes, commodity rationing, and certain special controls on economic activities. Other irregular measures include freezing price, income, or foreign exchange. That the government reserves these irregular measures and is ready to use them whenever necessary does not mean it can use them without thorough consideration. It is necessary to know that these measures of last resort demonstrate the government's determination and power to regulate the economy, revealing that the government will not allow the economy to deteriorate while standing by. They are a powerful dose of medication. Yet they come with obvious side effects. Price and wage control and foreign trade and foreign exchange control are harmful to the normal operation of the economy and are detrimental to the market mechanism, especially freezing price, income, and foreign exchange, which may lead to social turmoil, damaging effective resource allocation. Therefore, using these regulatory measures carelessly will undoubtedly bring damage to the economy. Nevertheless, the government still needs to reserve these measures of last resort and gets ready to use them when necessary. This is based on the consideration that between two necessary evils, the lesser will be chosen.

Let us assume that an economy is in dire situation, close to collapse or chaos. Regular economic regulatory measures have basically proven relatively ineffective or no longer effective. At this critical moment, the government can choose to do one of the following: allowing the economic chaos to continue and the economy to suffer more severe damage or allowing the market mechanism to sustain some damage by enforcing irregular regulatory measures to regulate the economy so that the economy will benefit in the long run. The government must choose the latter instead of the former. In addition, economic problems usually come with social and political problems. High unemployment rate, hyperinflation, and severe shortages of living necessities are not only economic problems but also social and political problems. The government also reserves the measures of last resort for the benefit of society, which is consistent with the target of social and political stabilization.

Setting the security line and reserving the measures of last resort are consistent with the appropriateness of government behavior during resource allocation that we discussed earlier. To the government, the setting of the security line is comparable to the setting of a road sign. When an economy is operating on its normal track, the government does not have to replace the market, nor can it replace the market. As for the measures of last resort, it is an issue of getting ready without pulling the trigger from the government's perspective. The government has those measures of last resort, but refrains from using them under normal situations. This demonstrates that government regulation is a kind of high-level regulation, one that cannot be replaced by market regulation. Getting ready without pulling the trigger reveals that the government always has control of economic regulation.

3.3.4 The Seriousness of the Law and Government Behavior

Economic activities must follow the law. This is the prerequisite of orderly economic activities. The government is the lawmaker and enforcer. No economic activity can violate the law or cross the boundaries set by law. If we can use the analogy that all economic activities, including the action of the government itself and the economic activities of businesses and individuals, must occur inside a large cage, then the large cage will be the boundary of the law. Inside the boundary of the law, all economic activities are allowed. Any economic activity that violates the law shall be prohibited and prosecuted afterward. Everyone is equal before the law and no one is above the law. This ensures that orderly economic activities can be conducted.

Law is serious. A law that is not followed is equivalent to having no law or even worse than that. If the authority of law vanishes, the authority of government as the law enforcer will also vanish. Therefore, once a law is passed, the government must follow it by all means and defend the seriousness of the law. However, it should be noted that protecting the seriousness of the law is not an issue of the same level as the appropriateness of government behavior during resource allocation. Protecting the seriousness of the law is the prerequisite for government regulation behavior during resource allocation. The appropriateness of government behavior during resource allocation illustrates government behavior. The appropriateness of government behavior during resource allocation means that the government does not have to do whatever market regulation is capable of and instead should do whatever the market is incapable of. Regardless of whether market regulation does everything that government is capable of, or the government does everything the market is incapable of, the law should be followed. If government behavior during resource allocation is not to defend the seriousness of the law, the situation of ineffective resource allocation in society will get worse instead of better.

We have to clarify another issue. The government has the responsibility to maintain order in the economy and the marketplace. In order to do this, the government has to use any necessary measure, including legal measures. Legal measures and economic measures coexist. If under certain circumstance the government uses legal measures to regulate the economy and maintain economic order as needed, is this government behavior appropriate? As a matter of fact, there are two different scenarios.

In the first scenario, the government passes a new law and follows it to operate and regulate the economy in order to maintain economic order and promote economic growth. This scenario is not contradictory to the appropriateness of government regulation behavior. The passing of the new law is to standardize the behavior of economic entities, including government, enterprises, and individuals so that either economic regulation or no regulation at all by the government will follow the law. If the new law allows the government to adopt certain measures to regulate the economy, government regulation behavior has gained legal support and is appropriate.

In the second scenario, as situations change, the old law is no longer applicable and the government either revises it or abolishes it. This indicates that the economic activities of government, enterprises, and individuals are no longer able to follow the old law. Instead, they must follow the revised law or some other laws. That government regulation must follow the law will remain unchanged, which is not contradictory to the appropriateness of government regulation behavior.

The appropriateness of government regulation behavior can be very confusing. This is because people tend to mix government regulation behavior with the legality of the activities by economic entities, i.e., government, enterprises, and individuals. It is necessary to stress once again that protecting the seriousness of the law and how the government regulates the economy are two different issues and cannot be mixed. The government of a nation that has the law and abides by the law is one that can regulate the economy appropriately. A government that mandatorily regulates the economy in any area at any time can also be one without a sound legal system or even totally without the law or without following the law.

3.3.5 The Optimization of Government Behavior During Resource Allocation

The optimization of government behavior during resource allocation means that the government chooses the optimal timing, the optimal regulatory measures or the combination of regulatory measures, and the optimal regulation extensity in accordance with actual situations in order to achieve relatively good results. Just as the government can choose its regulation behavior only if the seriousness of the law is protected, the government can choose its optimal behavior only by following the principle of appropriate government behavior. In other words, the optimization of government behavior is impossible without the appropriateness of government behavior during resource allocation.

Earlier, we have discussed that regardless of whether an economy is under the condition of type II disequilibrium, government regulation behavior has to be appropriate during resource allocation. This is very clear. Whether government regulation behavior can be optimized during resource allocation is dependent upon the following four conditions.

Firstly, as we discussed previously, it depends on whether government regulation behavior is appropriate. If government regulation violates the principle of appropriate government behavior, either the government is seen undertaking many tasks that should not be done by the government or even that beyond its capability, or the government always tries to replace the market, the optimization of government behavior will be out of the question. Despite its best effort to optimize regulation behavior, the government will be unable to accomplish that.

Secondly, the optimization of government regulation behavior during resource allocation must follow the law and act under the premise of using the law as the criteria. This point has been addressed previously. We can conclude that any government regulation that crosses the boundary set by the law cannot be optimal. It is the same with any government behavior that does not seriously punish business and individual economic activities that cross the boundary set by the law.

Thirdly, the optimization of government regulation behavior should be based on the principle of target multiplicity, in other words, the principle of meeting various targets, because the target resource allocation varies during different periods of time. If government regulatory measures only benefit a single target while unable to balance the pros and cons of various other targets, the optimization of government regulation is not accomplished.

Fourthly, due to nonidealized government behavior, the optimization of government regulation behavior should be based on the principle of limiting the negative roles that the market plays in resource allocation and promoting the positive roles that the market plays in resource allocation. The reason is as follows: If the measures that the government takes during resource allocation influence direct input and direct output, they will reveal more nonidealized government behavior due to lagging, unbalanced, and decreasing policy effect. If regulation indirectly impacts input and output, which means the government limits some negative roles that the market plays in resource allocation and promotes some positive roles that the market plays in resource allocation, government regulatory measures, if planned systematically, will allow the government to accomplish to the largest extent possible the predetermined regulation targets during resource allocation, in spite of lagging, unbalanced, and decreasing policy effect. In summary, if government regulation behavior needs to be optimized, the government should execute regulation by means of its impact on the market. This is more consistent with the principle of optimizing government regulation behavior compared with government regulation by means of direct input and direct output. Of course, it does not mean that government direct input and direct output is unnecessary under certain circumstances or contradictory to the principle of optimizing government behavior during resource allocation in any scenario. Under certain circumstances, it is still necessary for the government to use direct input and direct output measures in order to achieve predetermined regulation results. We can only say that if policy goals can be achieved either by means of the direct input and direct output from the government or by means of government's impact on the market, the latter is more consistent with the principle of optimizing government regulation behavior.

Reference

1. Li Yining. (1988). *Management of national economy* (p. 424). Hebei People's Press, Shijiazhuang, Hebei, China.

Chapter 4
The Mechanism of the Operation of the Economy

4.1 Dual Mechanism of the Operation of the Economy

4.1.1 The Coverage of Government Regulation in the Operation of the Economy

We have clearly known from our discussions in Chaps. 2 and 3 that the operation of the socialist economy does not follow a sole mechanism, i.e., the market mechanism or the government regulation mechanism. The dual mechanism of the operation of the socialist economy, which refers to the coexistence of the market mechanism and the government regulation mechanism, has the following meanings.

First of all, the coexistence of the dual mechanism does not mean the economy can be separated into two groups, with one mechanism only good for one group and the other mechanism only good for the other group.

Secondly, the coexistence of the dual mechanism does not mean two mechanisms commingle with each other, with one mechanism primarily working in one area while infiltrating the other area or vice versa.

Thirdly, the coexistence of the dual mechanism does not mean two mechanisms are parallel, being equally important for the operation of the economy.

These clarifications are necessary. The understanding of the dual mechanism in this book focuses on the complementary relationship between these two mechanisms, of which market regulation works at first, followed by government regulation, which works at a higher level. The analyses on the functions of market regulation and government regulation in resource allocation in Chaps. 2 and 3 in this book have described the complementary relationship between these two mechanisms. It is now necessary for us to draw on prior discussions to further understand the dual mechanism of the operation of the economy.

We have often heard people mention market regulation and government regulation work together on the economy. More specifically, market regulation covers the whole economy and so does government regulation. Both forms of regulation

Y. Li, *Chinese Economy in Disequilibrium*, China Academic Library,
DOI 10.1007/978-3-642-39558-1_4,

work on the economy simultaneously. This understanding demonstrates some progress when compared with the Group Theory, the Penetration Theory, and the Parallelization Theory. These viewpoints can be summarized as the Coverage Theory. But this theory still has one shortfall, that is, it does not clearly describe the definition of the coverage.

We should note that the government regulation hereby mentioned refers to the regulation of resource allocation by the government as well as the regulation of the operation of the economy by the government. If government regulation is applicable to the law promulgated by government, it will undoubtedly cover the whole society, i.e., any economic activity in society cannot violate the law. If government regulation is applicable to the social and economic development targets set by the government, it will also cover the whole society, as every entity needs to work hard to realize those development targets. If government regulation is applicable to direct input and output, however, it is obvious that it will not be able to cover the whole society. Now the question is: If government regulation refers to various measures that impact market regulation, can we simply say it does or does not cover the whole society? Before answering this question, we have to do some detailed analysis.

First of all, in the socialist commodity economy, the impact of government regulation of resource allocation will certainly reflect the functions of government regulation in various areas in the economy by means of changing the balance of demand and supply in the marketplace. In this sense, government regulation covers the whole society. However, we cannot ignore the fact that the coverage of government regulation in society is a second layer of coverage. That is, this layer of coverage is on top of market regulation. This understanding is consistent with the argument that government regulation is to regulate the economy for the second time. First comes market regulation, which covers the economy for the first time. Government regulation comes next and covers the economy for the second time. Just as government regulation cannot function without the market, it is hard to understand that the coverage of government regulation over the economy for the second time can function without the coverage of market regulation in the economy.

In summary, the Coverage Theory is an opinion on the relationship between market regulation and government regulation. It is different from the Group Theory, the Penetration Theory, or the Parallelization Theory. Although the Coverage Theory is better than the Group Theory, the Penetration Theory, and the Parallelization Theory, we can correctly understand the dual mechanism of the operation of the economy only with the acknowledgement that the coverage that the Coverage Theory refers to is one for the second time.

4.1.2 The Relationship Between the Two Mechanisms

To further understand the dual mechanism of the operation of the economy, we will have to understand the complementary relationship between market regulation and government regulation. As discussed before, the imbalance between aggregate demand and aggregate supply under economic disequilibrium conditions is common, as there are resource supply constraints or resource demand constraints. From the structural perspective, resource supply constraints and resource demand constraints can happen simultaneously. Therefore, the function of market self-regulation during resource allocation will be restricted in that case. Here arises an important question under disequilibrium conditions: how to use limited resources to satisfy the needs of society and how to adjust limited demand to meet supply in the economy. This is the reason why the issue of rationing equilibrium discussed in the disequilibrium theory is applicable in a relatively wide range of areas. Because either using limited supply of resources to meet demand or adjusting limited demand to meet supply is accomplished through quantitative rationing.

Under the market mechanism in which resource supply constraints exist, the way to allocate limited resources is to follow either the priority principle or the monopoly principle. The priority principle hereby discussed refers to the principle of business transactions that are conducted on a first-come-first-served basis until all limited resources are sold out. The monopoly principle hereby discussed refers to the case in which the suppliers of limited resources are able to sell their commodities at prices higher than equilibrium prices as they enjoy the monopolistic position. Obviously, the monopoly principle is applicable to business transactions under imperfect competition. The priority principle is also applicable to business transactions under imperfect competition. This is because commodity supplies are limited under the circumstance of resource supply constraints. If transactions are done based on the principle of first-come, first-served, information on the timing and location for the sale of certain commodities will be critical. Whoever has access to the information will be the first to come and be served. Those who have no access to the information will actually be excluded from transactions. Therefore, both the priority principle and monopoly principle are transaction principles for imperfect competition. If there were any difference between them, the transactions conducted in accordance with the monopoly principle would be open transactions under imperfect competition, while those conducted in accordance with the priority principle would retain the form of perfect competition but actually take place under imperfect competition.

Under the market mechanism in which demand constraints exist, the priority principle and monopoly principle are also applicable to allocating limited market or limited demand. The priority principle refers to one that business conduct transactions based on first-come, first-served. The monopoly principle refers to one used by market leaders, who, once become a market monopoly, will squeeze out other competitors to protect their own market and economic interests. Apparently, the monopoly principle is one for transactions under imperfect competition. The priority principle is also related to the information on limited market or limited demand. Whoever has such information will be able to come first and sell first. Whoever has no access to such information will actually be shut out of transactions. By the same token, business transactions that follow the priority principle are transactions under imperfect competition, yet done in the name of perfect competition. Business transactions that follow the monopoly principle, however, are openly known as transactions under imperfect competition.

Therefore, as long as the economy is under disequilibrium conditions, the rationing equilibrium that is realized following either the priority principle or the monopoly principle is always linked to transactions under imperfect competition. If by any chance government regulation is needed, it will apply any one of the following three principles to realize rationing equilibrium and all business transactions that follow these principles will be carried out under imperfect competition. These principles are the equalization principle (i.e., allocating limited commodity supplies equally to each buyer or limited demand equally to each supplier), the target principle (i.e., allocating limited commodity supplies or limited demand in an order of target priority set in advance by the government), and history principle (i.e., allocating limited commodity supplies or limited demand by ration in accordance with historical records). The complementary relationship between government regulation and market regulation can be considered the complementary relationship between transactions under various forms of imperfect competition, rather than a supplementary relationship between various forms of imperfect competition or a relationship in which perfect competition supplements imperfect competition.

It is meaningful to describe such complementary nature or feature. We have to know that there is a popular belief as follows: Market regulation means that market transactions are conducted under perfect competition and the market will self-regulate until equilibrium is reached, whereas government regulation means that market transactions are conducted under imperfect competition and government interference will destroy perfect competition in the marketplace. Due to various defects of perfect competition, government regulation is justified and indispensable, even though it destroys perfect competition in the marketplace. This belief can lead to the following conclusion: Under a circumstance where market regulation and government regulation coexist, that market regulation and government regulation complement each other becomes perfect competition supplementing imperfect competition or imperfect competition supplementing perfect competition. This is not correct. The reasons are as follows:

First of all, market regulation is not necessarily the market regulation under perfect competition, and market regulation under imperfect competition is also a form of market regulation. Equating market regulation to perfect competition is not only a biased understanding of market regulation but also an incorrect understanding of perfect competition, because perfect competition is never universal as one form of market regulation. The theoretical meaning of perfect competition far exceeds its practical meaning.

Secondly, perfect competition only exists under equilibrium conditions, where neither excess demand nor excess supply exists and all transactions are concluded at the equilibrium price. In reality, however, disequilibrium is common, and so are resource supply constraints and resource demand constraints. As a result, there is a need for quantitative rationing, and equilibrium can be realized by using quotas. Under this circumstance, market regulation is executed under imperfect competition and so are transactions in the marketplace.

The above two points can lead to the following point.

Thirdly, if the economy is in equilibrium or under perfect competition, it will not be necessary to carry out government regulation, because the market has arranged everything perfectly. Since there is no need for government regulation, the so-called dual mechanism will be unnecessary, let alone two mechanisms complementing each other. If the economy is in disequilibrium, it is necessary to use quantitative quotas to reach ex post equilibrium. And, market regulation is conducted under imperfect competition. If government regulation is needed in this case, it must also be executed under imperfect competition. Therefore, that market regulation and government regulation complement each other indicates various transactions under imperfect competition are complementary. The purpose of such complementary relationship is to better regulate quantitative rationing to achieve equilibrium. As we pointed out earlier, that quota allocation under market regulation in the circumstance of resource supply constraints and demand constraints has to be executed following either the priority principle or the monopoly principle, whereas quota allocation under government regulation in the circumstance of resource supply constraints and demand constraints has to be executed in accordance with the equalization principle, the target principle, or the history principle, or certain combinations of these principles. Therefore, the complementary relationship between market regulation and government regulation actually reflects the complementary relationship between business principles or business transactions under imperfect competition following the priority principle and monopoly principle and those following the equalization principle, the target principle, and the history principle.

If we analyze the issue from the above perspective, we will have to answer this question: Under disequilibrium conditions, what kind of transaction is primary and what is secondary so that limited supplies can meet the needs of various buyers or that limited demand can adjust to the needs of various suppliers?

It seems that this question is related to the degree of economic disequilibrium or the severity of resource supply constraints or demand constraints. If resource supply constraints are relatively light (i.e., slight resource supply gap) or demand constraints are relatively light (i.e., slight demand shortfall), it will be more important to have the market coordinate business transactions, and hence it is less important to have the government regulate the economy. On the contrary, if resource supply constraints are relatively heavy (i.e., severe resource supply gap) or demand constraints are relatively heavy (i.e., severe demand shortfall), it will be less important to have the market coordinate business transactions, and it will be more important to have the government regulate the economy. The importance of market regulation and government regulation in regulating the economy will reverse when resource supply constraints and demand constraints reach a certain level (i.e., supply gap and demand shortfall reaching a certain limit). At that level, as market regulation becomes less important, government regulation becomes more important. All in all, everything will change according to various degrees of economic disequilibrium.

In other words, if we do our analyses on the basis of the complementary relationship, we can draw the following conclusion:

In an economy with both market regulation and government regulation, business transactions under imperfect competition that follow the priority principle and the monopoly principle of market regulation will become less important among all transactions in the economy as supply gap and demand shortfall increase; business transactions under imperfect transactions that follow the equalization principle, target principle, and history principle of government regulation will become more important among all transactions in the economy as supply gap and demand shortfall increase. If the economy operates toward the direction of lower supply gap and lower demand shortfall, market regulation will become more and more important. On the contrary, if the economy operates toward the direction of larger supply gap and larger demand shortfall, market regulation will become less important and government regulation will become important, regardless of whether you like it or not.

4.1.3 Government Hierarchy and Market Hierarchy

The hierarchy of government refers not only to the supervision and subordination relationship between government agencies or the hierarchy structure of various government institutions but more importantly to the hierarchy of government regulation, or how government regulation is executed by various levels of government institutions. As for the hierarchy of market, it primarily concerns the relationship between the whole and the parts. Just as any kind of market system is composed of a number of interrelated markets, any national market is composed of several regional markets. In addition, if we view the market from the structural perspective, it can be infinitely subdivided until reaching a market that includes only one specific commodity. Understanding the hierarchy of market is to find out how we can fully utilize market regulation functions when the market is continuously subdivided.

The general principle should be as follows: As far as government regulation is concerned, if a subordinate government institution is capable of accomplishing a mission on its own, it is not necessary for its superior to step in and do the job on its behalf. Government shall do whatever the market is incapable of, and a superior government institution shall do whatever its subordinate is incapable of. If both the superior and subordinate government institutions perform some functions for the second regulation, the regulation by the superior government institution is at a higher level than that by the subordinate government institution, even though they are both conducting the second regulation. Here is a simple example: If there is mismatch between supply and demand in the labor market or the resource market, it will be difficult for the market to resolve the supply constraints or demand constraints of labor or capital on its own, and hence it will be necessary to have the government step in as the organizer of the second regulation to take certain regulatory measures. In this case, if supply gap or demand shortfall has been alleviated by some measures adopted by the regulatory institutions of a town, there will be no need for further regulation by a city, assuming an administrative structure in which a town is governed by a city. If the economic regulatory institutions of a city can adopt effective measures to alleviate demand and supply mismatch, there will be no need for further regulation by the province. Only after provincial government institutions fail to accomplish regulation missions will it be necessary for the central government to function as the organization that performs the second regulation of the economy. This is the meaning of hierarchical government regulation. Every level of the government, from the central government to local governments, should be capable and effective and handle its own responsibilities. Superior government institutions should not take care of everything but instead should delegate those tasks that subordinate government institutions themselves are responsible for. The hierarchical management by various government institutions is not contradictory to government's role as an organization in charge of the second regulation and will even facilitate better government performance in the second regulation.

As of the hierarchy of market, the word "hierarchy" has a different meaning from the one used in hierarchical government regulation or the hierarchical management by government, both of which were discussed earlier. The hierarchy of market is an analytical method that continuously subdivides the market according to its structure. After all, the market is an integrated system. Various markets that form this system are closely connected. Various regional markets inside a market are also closely interconnected. Market regulation is, after all, a form of systematic regulation, which is very difficult to be separated into subcomponents. This is different from the hierarchical regulation or the hierarchical management by government. We can illustrate this point with a few simple examples:

1. If supply is less than demand in the consumer goods market, price will rise. Despite that supply and demand are balanced in the production materials market at the beginning, rising consumer goods prices will expand consumer goods production capacity, driving up the prices of production materials. Therefore, market regulation should not be limited to the consumer goods market, but should include the production materials market as well.
2. If supply is less than demand in the consumer goods market, causing price to rise and production capacity to increase, the supply and demand for capital in the money market will also change correspondingly. As a result, consumer expenditures will increase to accommodate rising consumer goods prices, and money supply (i.e., personal savings) will likely decrease. On the other hand, manufacturers of consumer goods will have higher demand for capital due to rising consumer goods production capacity. Therefore, market regulation should not be limited to the consumer goods market, but should include the money market as well.
3. As a matter of fact, changes of demand and supply, prices, and production capacity in the consumer goods market will to some extent change not only the production materials market and the money market but also the labor market and the technology market. Under such circumstance, it is impossible for market regulation to function only in one market. Instead, it will impact every relevant market.

Thus, we can give a brief illustration on the relationship between government hierarchy and market hierarchy. Government hierarchy represents an argument that supports the second regulation. That is, it indicates which scenario would require regulation by subordinate government institutions and which would require regulation by superior government institutions. Market hierarchy is an analytical method of analyzing markets, which clearly illustrates the relationship between various markets via continuously subdividing the market and therefore reveals the holistic feature of market regulation.

Can we draw the following conclusion: Local governments regulate local markets and the central government regulates national markets, which leads to government hierarchy that is in line with market hierarchy? This argument cannot illustrate the relationship between market regulation and government regulation. As long as the market can solve any problem on its own, neither the central government nor local governments should interfere, whether it is local markets or national markets. Although local governments are only authorized to regulate regional markets while the central government can regulate all regional markets, regulating the market is no equivalent to regulating the economy. Regulating the market can be done by following the law to maintain order in the marketplace and allowing markets to perform regulation functions, or regulating the market can be done by government taking certain regulatory measures to influence supply and demand in the market, which also serves the purpose of regulating the economy. The central government and local governments can use the former method or the latter method to regulate the market at the same time. Or the central government uses the former method while local governments use the latter method to regulate the market. It all depends. If the central government uses the latter method to regulate the market, it may apply to regional markets or national markets. Market hierarchy is not the reason to restrict government behavior. If a local government also uses the latter method to regulate the market, it will apply to the markets that are under its jurisdiction. As different regional markets are interconnected with one influencing another, a regulatory measure once adopted by a local government to adjust regional supply and demand will actually have far-reaching effects that are by no means limited to regional markets. This explains from a different perspective the complexity of the relationship between government hierarchy and market hierarchy.

4.1.4 The Difference Between Fully Developed Market and Complete Market System

Fully developed market and complete market system are different and cannot be misunderstood as one concept. Whether the market is fully developed or not is related to the degree of competitiveness and self-restraint of the market. The more competitive the market is, the better the market can perform its self-restraining function through market competition as well as changing supply and demand, and the more developed the market will be. On the other hand, the more constraints market competition is subject to, the weaker the market self-restraining function will be and the less developed the market will be. Whether the market system is complete or not refers to the market structure. In the socialist market system, the core of the market system is the commodity market. Labor market, capital market, real estate market, enterprise asset market, and technology information market are the components of the market system. Whether the market structure is balanced is linked to whether the market system is complete. The more complete the market system is and the more coordinated the market structure is, the better the market system will facilitate enterprise production and operation and the better the environment will be to generate economic growth.

When the economy is in equilibrium, not only the market is fully developed, but the market system is also complete and the market structure is balanced. If the economy is in disequilibrium, the market is not fully developed, neither can the market system be complete or the market structure be balanced. In this sense, the degree of market development is associated with how complete the market system is and how balanced the market structure is. Therefore, in order to develop the socialist market, it is critical to persistently increase the degree of market development and promote a balanced market structure and a complete market system. In reality, when the market is not fully developed, the market system is not complete, and the market structure is not balanced, we need to find out what is the start point of developing the socialist market. If this issue is not resolved, developing the market will not be a smooth process.

Establishing a fully developed market is a long process. This is because how market mechanism forms and works, how market competition proceeds, and how the market performs self-restraint are all dependent upon whether or not the operation mechanism of market participants (i.e., enterprises) is fully developed and functional. In other words, the market goes through a natural cultivation process. It is the same with any region, including special economic zones. Hence, it is hard for us to imagine that the market can be fully developed before enterprises become goods producers who make their own decisions and are responsible for their own profits and losses. However, complete market system can be established by government policies. This is because whether the market system is complete or not is associated with the progress of reforms on the planned mechanism. Under the traditional planned mechanism, only the consumer goods market exists in the socialist economy. There are no other markets. Hence, it is unnecessary to talk about market system. During the reforms of the planned mechanism, production materials market, capital market, labor market, and technology information market have emerged one after another. Eventually, real estate market and enterprise asset market will also appear. These are the results from the reforms of the planned mechanism initiated by the government. Therefore, even though the market cannot be quickly developed fully, it is absolutely possible for us to take one step ahead to complete the market system. Although emerging production materials market, capital market, labor market, technology information market, real estate market, and enterprise asset market are not fully developed at the beginning, having these markets is after all better than having nothing. Upon having established the socialist market system to a large extent, we can gradually proceed with coordinating the market structure while improving the market itself.

This is the market environment which Chinese enterprises are currently facing. Even the enterprises in special economic zones face similar market environment. Every enterprise, domestically oriented or internationally oriented, must understand the features of market environment. More specifically, the market system, with the reforms of the planned mechanism, has been largely established, but the market has not been fully developed because the reforms of enterprise operation mechanism are yet to be deepened further and interference with and restrictions on enterprises placed by administrative departments are yet to be removed. In this environment, the operation of enterprises compared to the past has its disadvantages and advantages. The disadvantages lie in the fact that enterprise operation is still subject to interference and restrictions and business profitability motivations are still weak. Enterprises do not compete with each other on the level play field in the marketplace. Fluctuations of market demand and supply do not necessarily effectively affect business operational decisions. It is not possible for enterprises to really pursue profitability and self-expansion through increasing efficiency and competitiveness. However, we have seen some advantages of how enterprises operate compared to the past: After all, there are more than just the consumer goods market. Enterprises are able to obtain resources they need, in spite of only a portion, through transactions in the production materials market, capital market, labor market, technology information market, and real estate market. The rise of the enterprise asset market provides businesses with an opportunity to increase production capacity as well as pursue mergers and acquisitions. This means that businesses operate in multiple markets at the same time and that the relatively complete market system has reduced some difficulties that businesses face due to relatively underdeveloped market. For businesses, it is more important that they take advantage of the progress of the market development that was nonexistent in the past to alleviate the conflicts arising from underdeveloped market so that they can survive and grow in a market that has not been fully developed. At the same time, as long as the market system is relatively complete, the more proactive businesses are in taking advantage of the existing market system, the faster the market will be fully developed.

4.2 Frictions in the Operation of the Economy

4.2.1 Frictions in the Operation of the Economy Under Type I Disequilibrium Condition

In the operation of the economy, there are some situations in which the market mechanism and the government regulation mechanism coexist and can work together. In other situations, however, these two mechanisms cannot work together.

Why is the coexistence of these two mechanisms likely to cause frictions during the operation of the economy? This issue is related to economic disequilibrium.

We know that economic disequilibrium can be divided into two types, type I disequilibrium and type II disequilibrium. Therefore, to analyze possible frictions that are brought about by the dual mechanisms, it is also necessary for us to start with the features of the two types of disequilibrium. First, let us look at type I disequilibrium.

Type I disequilibrium refers to an economic condition under which the market is not fully developed, information is incomplete, and price cannot function to adjust demand and supply, as well as the economy muddles along with supply constraints or demand constraints, i.e., resource supply gap and demand shortfall. In this case, the market mechanism and government regulation mechanism cannot work together, which is seen from the following two aspects:

First of all, when the market mechanism cannot fully function, any regulation by government will likely aggravate the situation of underdeveloped market and incomplete information, making it even harder for market participants to make any decision based on market information.

Under type I disequilibrium condition, the market has not been fully developed, and complete and timely information is unavailable. Therefore, price cannot function to fully adjust demand and supply. This is not hard to understand. If market regulation and government regulation are applied to the economy, with market regulation functioning as fundamental regulation and government regulation functioning as the higher-level regulation, these two mechanisms may have the following frictions: When supply is lower or higher than demand, supply gap or demand shortfall can only be temporarily alleviated after price rises or declines, because the market is not fully developed and price changes are not completely consistent with the requirements of market regulation. If at this time the government adopts regulatory measures, which might be contradictory to the intentions of market regulation, supply gap or demand shortfall can be eliminated. However, the market mechanism will be destroyed. In other words, in this situation, government regulation mechanism can only work by sacrificing the function of the market mechanism to some extent.

How do we evaluate the frictions between these two mechanisms? We can only look at it from the outcome of the regulation. Is it necessary to destroy the market mechanism, even if it is only to a certain degree? Is it worthwhile? Of course, it would be better that the market mechanism is not destroyed while government regulation resolves the issue of excess supply or excess demand. In that case, these two mechanisms can work together, and there will be no frictions between them. In reality, this is not necessarily always the case. Therefore, if we conclude that these two mechanisms cannot work together and as a result, government regulation brings some damage to the market mechanism, we can only judge whether the actions are justified or worthwhile on the basis of the outcome of the regulation.

Secondly, under type I disequilibrium condition, the market mechanism may potentially restrict the functions of government regulation.

That is also directly associated with underdeveloped market, incomplete and untimely information, the failure of prices to fully function in adjusting supply and demand, as well as resource supply constraints or demand constraints. For example, when it is necessary for the government to carry out regulation, the regulatory measures may not necessarily achieve anticipated results due to the fact that the market has not been fully developed and information has not been complete or timely. In this case, market regulation will restrict government regulation to some extent. Here is the reason: Government uses regulatory measures to send market participants a message on anticipated gains and losses from the regulatory measures and expect them to adjust resource combination and resource investment directions according to their own economic interests. Meanwhile, the market itself also delivers the information on the gains and losses from the regulatory measures to market participants. Because the information delivery channel is not the same and because information is incomplete and untimely, market mechanism may work with government regulation, which of course is ideal, or may interfere with government regulation, which becomes a hurdle to government regulation. This is also a kind of friction between these two mechanisms during resource combination or the operation of the economy.

In summary, under type I disequilibrium condition, as long as market regulation and government regulation coexist, these two mechanisms may or may not work together. It is possible that they have some frictions, and sometimes it is even unavoidable.

4.2.2 Frictions During the Operation of the Economy Under Type II Disequilibrium Condition

Type II disequilibrium condition is characterized not only by an underdeveloped market but also by enterprises who have not become independent goods producers. As enterprises lack not only the incentives to pursue economic interests but also the mechanism to make their own business decisions, economic disequilibrium is more severe under type II disequilibrium condition than under type I disequilibrium condition. Possible conflicts arising from the coexistence of market mechanism and government regulation mechanism may also be more severe or frequent. This issue can be illustrated from the following three aspects:

First of all, since enterprises are not independent goods producers, they have not been severed from affiliation with their administrative institutions. It is difficult for them to make decisions on business operations and investments on the basis of the profitability principle. There is a lack of market evaluation standards for good or bad business operational results. As a result, business productivity must be low. In this case, any measure that the government takes to regulate the economy will be unable to achieve anticipated regulation results. The primary reason is that enterprises lack the status of independent goods producers and the market mechanism itself is distorted. Conflicts between government regulation and the distorted market mechanism are inevitable.

Secondly, in addition, if enterprises have not been severed from affiliation with their administrative institutions and the government lacks information on business profits and losses, it is unlikely for the government to adopt reasonable economic regulatory measures. In this case, the measures that the government takes to regulate the economy may also be distorted and make it very difficult to work with the market mechanism.

Thirdly, if supply gap and demand shortfall due to resource supply constraints and demand constraints exist under type II disequilibrium condition, how different are they compared to type I disequilibrium condition? Under type I disequilibrium condition, they are resolved by rationing equilibrium through transactions under imperfect competition that either follow the priority principle and the monopoly principle applicable to market regulation or follow the equalization principle, the target principle, or the history principle that are applicable to government regulation. In spite of frictions between the market mechanism and the government regulation mechanism, rationing equilibrium can still be reached as long as people continue to do business transactions in the imperfect competition environment. Situations may be different under type II disequilibrium condition. This is because enterprises are not independent goods producers and are unable to decide on resource combination and investment according to their own economic interests. As a result, any distribution principle (including the priority principle and the monopoly principle for market regulation and the equalization principle, the target principle, and the history principle for government regulation) will not follow its original intention and will be distorted whenever enterprises lack independent economic interests and fail to conduct business transactions in their own economic interests. Transactions under imperfect competition will not necessarily lead to rationing equilibrium. Supply gap or demand shortfall will possibly deteriorate. Frictions between the market mechanism and the government regulation mechanism will be more severe than those under type I disequilibrium condition.

4.2.3 Understanding Frictions in the Operation of the Economy

Based on the above analysis, we have clearly understood that frictions in the operation of the economy between the market mechanism and the government regulation mechanism are inevitable in some cases, regardless of the type of disequilibrium. This issue can be considered the limitation of the dual-track mechanism.

The fact that different intensity of frictions exists between the two mechanisms in the operation of the economy only demonstrates the limitation of the dual-track mechanism, revealing that the operation of the economy under disequilibrium conditions is far from perfect. However, it cannot prove the dual mechanism is unjustified.

It should be noted that if an economy is in equilibrium, excess supply or excess demand will not exist, and there will be no need for the dual-track mechanism. Since economic equilibrium condition only exists in theory and disequilibrium condition is economic reality, the dual-track mechanism will exist in the operation of the economy whether you like it or not. Under disequilibrium conditions, in the case of resource supply constraints (supply gap) or resource demand constraints (demand shortfall), we can realize rationing equilibrium only by allowing the dual-track mechanism to fully function and supporting business transactions under imperfect competition.

Undoubtedly, frictions between the two mechanisms under type II disequilibrium condition are heightened. The lower the degree of economic disequilibrium, the less severe the frictions between these two mechanisms. This point further demonstrates the urgency to deepen the economic restructuring currently being carried out in China, especially the reforms of enterprises. Through deepening the reforms of enterprises, the Chinese economy will gradually transit from type I disequilibrium to type II disequilibrium, and frictions between the two mechanisms will also gradually abate. This will be beneficial to economic growth.

Chapter 5
Rationing Equilibrium of the Commodity Market

5.1 Commodity Market Equilibrium with Quantity–Price Adjustment

5.1.1 Commodity Supply Gap Under the Dual-Track Economic System

Current economic disequilibria in China have shown that the supply of commodities in the commodity market is limited. The supply gap is related to market underdevelopment as well as enterprises' lack of motivation.

Commodity supply gap will inevitably drive up prices of scarce commodities. If the government adopts compulsory measures to curb rising prices, either black-market activities will arise or there will a phenomenon where some commodities have listing prices, but they are actually out of stock.

If the scarce commodities are raw materials used in production, production costs will rise as prices rise, which will in turn push the overall price level higher. If the scarce commodities are consumer goods, the increase of commodity prices will either drive wages upward or lower real personal disposable income. The former situation occurs when wages are flexible, while the latter one emerges when wages are inflexible or the effect of wage adjustment is lagging. If the rising prices of scarce consumer goods drive wages higher, it means the cost of production will rise accordingly, and rising costs will contribute to higher price level. If the rising prices of scarce consumer goods cause real personal disposable income to fall, the commodity market will reach the ex post equilibrium in form. In other words, commodity supply gap will disappear. Obviously, this is done at the cost of allowing physical consumption to be insufficient, which means we choose depressing consumption as a viable solution to the commodity supply gap.

Now, the issue that we need to discuss is as follows: Under disequilibrium conditions, the rising prices of production materials or scarce consumer goods are unlikely to bring additional supplies because of resource supply constraints. The

Y. Li, *Chinese Economy in Disequilibrium*, China Academic Library,
DOI 10.1007/978-3-642-39558-1_5, © Foreign Language Teaching and Research
Publishing Co., Ltd and Springer-Verlag Berlin Heidelberg 2014

price elasticity of commodity supply is relatively low. Under such circumstances, if the price elasticity of demand for commodities is also relatively low, or even normal, the commodity supply gap after prices rise will not disappear. If, instead, the price elasticity of demand for commodities is fairly large, rising prices will likely lead to significantly lower demand for commodities. In other words, the alleviation or elimination of commodity supply gap still hinges on insufficient consumption of physical commodities.

Here is a process we need to pay attention to. That is, the shortage of commodities starts with excess demand. Regardless of whether wage rises in tandem with inflation or not, as long as there are resource supply constraints, the relatively low price elasticity of commodity supply will eventually end the entire process with insufficient consumption. That is, excess demand is unilaterally alleviated by existing insufficient consumption of physical commodities.

The issue does not end here. The existence of the dual-track economic system indicates the existence of type II disequilibrium conditions. The fact that enterprises have not become independent goods producers has significant implications for the supply gap in the commodity market. It should be noted that under the dual-track economic system, the price of some commodities is fixed while that of some other commodities is determined by the market. Or within the same category, some commodities are sold at fixed price while others are sold at market price. The profit margins are different among those commodities in the same category. In this case, if enterprises are goods producers who take responsibility for their own business decisions as well as profits and losses and carry out business activities in pursuit of their self-interest, they will be able to handle different profit margins under these two pricing mechanisms by adjusting their decisions on resource combination, despite the existence of two pricing mechanisms. For example, when enterprises are unable to secure raw material supplies at fixed price, they will try to make their own business decisions on the basis of profitability. Driven by the principle of profit maximization, enterprises will adjust their production volumes to meet demand shortfall in the commodity market. Even with resource supply constraints that result in almost zero or relatively low price elasticity of commodity supply, as was mentioned earlier, the adjustments to production volumes will to some extent ease the price rise and insufficient consumption of physical commodities that are brought about by commodity supply gap. Nonetheless, if enterprises are not goods producers who are responsible for their own business decisions as well as profits and losses and thus unable to conduct business activities according to their self-interest, the situation will be somewhat different.

In the latter scenario discussed above, once there is supply gap in the commodity market, price rise and insufficient consumption of physical commodities will become inevitable. Meanwhile, enterprises themselves have no incentive or capability to adjust resource combination or production volumes according to their self-interest. They simply follow the intention of administrative institutions and passively endure the losses due to rising production costs brought about by commodity shortages. If enterprises could purchase raw materials at fixed price and sell finished products at market price, they would make money. But such profitability does not come from higher operational efficiency due to their hard work. If enterprises were to purchase raw materials at market price and sell finished products at fixed price, they would incur losses. Yet such losses do not reflect their operational performance. Even if they could purchase raw materials and sell finished products at fixed price, as long as the fixed prices of raw materials and finished products were not properly set, the consequential profits or losses would not only affect operational performance but also become an important factor that dampens enterprises' motivation to pursue their self-interest. If enterprises lacked the motivation to pursue self-interest, it would be very difficult to reduce commodity supply gap and might even widen the gap. That explains why the commodity supply gap under type II disequilibrium conditions has been so persistent and so hard to alleviate.

5.1.2 The Coexistence of Commodity Supply Gap and Commodity Demand Shortfall Under the Dual-Track Economic System

The socialist economy may experience the coexistence of commodity supply gap and commodity demand shortfall. The former originates from limited supplies and the latter from a limited market. If the structure of commodities is taken into consideration, it won't be difficult to understand the coexistence of supply gap and demand shortfall. In Chap. 1 of this book, we discussed the issues of resource misallocation and stagflation in the socialist economy and analyzed the reasons for the simultaneous existence of stagnation and inflation. These analyses are also applicable to the coexistence of commodity supply gap and commodity demand shortfall. Next, instead of focusing on the reasons why supply gap and demand shortfall exist simultaneously, we will discuss how this coexistence impacts on the equilibrium in the commodity market, including the initial impact and the subsequent impact.

1. The Initial Impact of the Coexistence of Supply Gap and Demand Shortfall on Commodity Market Equilibrium

When supply gap and demand shortfall exist simultaneously, it is extremely rare to come across a situation where the volume of commodity supply gap exactly equals the volume of commodity demand shortfall in the case of commodity structural imbalance. Oftentimes, either the volume of commodity supply gap is larger than that of commodity demand shortfall, or vice versa. The former situation clearly indicates that commodity supply gap is dominant and commodity demand shortfall is secondary; the latter indicates that commodity demand shortfall is dominant while commodity supply gap is secondary.

Due to differences in commodity structure, commodities in oversupply cannot substitute for commodities in short supply. That is, commodity supply gap and demand shortfall cannot offset each other.

The coexistence of supply gap and demand shortfall has far more complicated implications for commodity market equilibrium than the existence of only one of them does. It is necessary to point out that under economic disequilibrium conditions, prices are not flexible, or at least the magnitude of price changes is asymmetric. In the case of commodity supply gap, prices will rise, whereas at time of commodity demand shortfall, prices will stay put or only decline slightly. Therefore, the price level under the coexistence of both supply gap and demand shortfall still tends to rise. From the perspective of the consumption of physical commodities, rising prices in the case of commodity supply gap will eventually lead to declining real income and insufficient consumption of physical commodities. Under the circumstance of commodity demand shortfall, although prices remain constant or decline slightly, economic slowdown (as demonstrated by the lower production volume of the commodities that see sluggish sales or a declining growth rate of production) will have the following three implications for the economy:

First, economic slowdown or a declining economic growth rate concurrent with a rising price level indicates that there will be inflation accompanied by higher unemployment or a slowing growth rate of employment.

Second, economic slowdown or a declining economic growth rate concurrent with rising prices indicates that there will be inflation accompanied by lower fiscal income or a slowing growth rate of fiscal income.

Third, higher unemployment or a slowing growth rate of employment, as well as lower fiscal income or a slowing growth rate of fiscal income, will likely lead to lower real income or lower consumption of physical commodities.

Therefore, the coexistence of supply gap and demand shortfall is more or less the same as the situation where only commodity supply gap exists. That is, under disequilibrium conditions, as the price elasticity of commodity supply is relatively low, prices will rise and the consumption of physical commodities will be insufficient, regardless of whether only commodity supply gap exists or it coexists with commodity demand shortfall, and commodity supply gap will be ultimately alleviated by the insufficient consumption of physical commodities. The process of alleviating commodity supply gap becomes much more complicated under the coexistence of commodity supply gap and commodity demand shortfall than under only commodity supply gap. This is related to the subsequent impact on commodity market equilibrium from the coexistence of supply gap and demand shortfall.

2. The Subsequent Impact of the Coexistence of Supply Gap and Demand Shortfall on Commodity Market Equilibrium

We can look at the subsequent impact from the following two perspectives:

First of all, commodity supply gap and commodity demand shortfall do not offset each other, but it is difficult to keep them from influencing each other. For example, the supply of production materials is insufficient, and the demand for consumer goods materials also becomes insufficient; or in another case, some production materials (such as raw materials) are in short supply, and the demand for other production materials (such as equipment) falters; or the supply of some consumer goods materials (such as food) is insufficient, and the demand for other consumer goods materials (such as consumption materials used in industrial production) also becomes insufficient. In these scenarios, the prices of those commodities with insufficient supply will rise, while the prices of those commodities with insufficient demand will remain where they are due to price rigidity, despite sluggish sales and inventory buildup. In addition, the rising prices of the commodities with insufficient supply will impact the prices of the commodities with insufficient demand. That is, either because the price of one commodity is a component of the cost of another commodity or because the price of one commodity is compared with that of another commodity, ultimately, the prices of the commodities with insufficient demand will rise. The commodities with insufficient demand will in turn influence the commodities with insufficient supply, possibly causing the prices of different commodities to rise one after another. This situation is particularly noticeable under type II disequilibrium conditions.

Secondly, if we ignore the price rigidity associated with the commodities with insufficient demand, their prices will fall once supply exceeds demand, which will cause the production volume of those commodities to fall. In a fully developed market, commodity manufacturers who cut their production volume can transfer resources to other commodity manufacturers with insufficient supply, which will slow down the rise of the prices of those commodities in short supply. Under disequilibrium conditions, however, those commodity manufacturers who cut their production volume are not able to easily transfer idle resources to those who have insufficient supply due to the underdeveloped market and the difficulties in transferring resources. In this case, it is hard to curb the rising prices of the commodities with insufficient supply. This is not the end of the story. The rise in price due to insufficient supply means a decline in real income, while the lowering of production volume due to insufficient demand means a decline in revenues. Hence, the subsequent production and sales volume of the commodities with either insufficient supply or insufficient demand will change due to changing personal disposable income. The disequilibrium conditions in the commodity market are unlikely to disappear during the transition period. It could get even worse. Therefore, we cannot ignore the subsequent impact, especially under type II disequilibrium conditions.

3. A Further Understanding of Stagflation in the Socialist Economy

The negative effects of commodity supply gap and commodity demand shortfall are normally ignored or underestimated. Similarly, people tend to ignore the likelihood of stagflation in the socialist economy.

The existence of commodity supply gap will drive prices higher. The existence of commodity demand shortfall will slow down commodity sales and lower economic growth. The coexistence of both supply gap and demand shortfall will drive economic growth rate lower (i.e., stagnation) and prices higher (i.e., inflation). In a disequilibrium economy, the following situation is possible: While economic growth rate declines, the slowdown is moderate and the economy continues to grow at a certain rate. While price rises, inflation is moderate and the price index rises slightly. This is seen as proof that stagflation has not developed yet. Underestimating stagflation will lead to erroneous decisions on economic policies and the postponement of the efforts to deal with stagflation that has actually developed.

It must be pointed out that there are two kinds of inflation under disequilibrium conditions, open inflation and hidden inflation. Open inflation refers to the situation where price rises, as shown by rising price index. Hidden inflation refers to the situation where price or price index appears to be unchanged, but commodities are actually out of stock, or people have to wait in a long queue to purchase the commodities they need (rationing in accordance with the priority principle), or commodities are sold in a fixed or limited quantity to each buyer (rationing according to the equalization principle, target principle, or history principle). From the commodity structure perspective, the prices of some scarce commodities appear in the form of open inflation, while the prices of others appear in the form of hidden inflation. Therefore, open inflation and hidden inflation coexist.

Stagnation in the socialist economy under disequilibrium conditions can also be classified as open stagnation and hidden stagnation. Open stagnation refers to the situation in which economic growth rate declines and hovers at a relatively low level, including almost zero growth rate or even negative growth rate. Hidden stagnation refers to the situation in which total output seems to continue growing, i.e., economic growth rate remains at a certain level, but effective supply has not actually grown. For example, economic growth rate remains at a certain level, but some commodities that have been produced are not really what society needs. Those commodities become inventories stored at factories and department stores, and their sales are slow. Because production continues to grow, people do not realize that this situation is a kind of stagnation—hidden stagnation.

Since there are two types of inflation and two types of stagnation, there are four possible combinations of stagflation. They are:

1. Stagflation due to open inflation and open stagnation
2. Stagflation due to open inflation and hidden stagnation
3. Stagflation due to hidden inflation and open stagnation
4. Stagflation due to hidden inflation and hidden stagnation

Some people do not know that inflation and stagnation can be divided into two different types, nor do they understand that hidden stagnation is also a form of stagnation and hidden inflation is also a form of inflation. Therefore, they have a different understanding of the above four combinations of stagflation. That is, they are of the opinion that only the first combination is stagflation, the second combination is not stagflation but inflation, the third combination is not stagflation but stagnation, and the fourth combination is not inflation, nor stagnation, nor stagflation. Obviously, the incorrect understanding of stagflation is a very unfavorable factor in the fight against stagflation, as the complexity of economic disequilibrium is underestimated.

As a matter of fact, these four combinations of stagflation are all reflections of the coexistence of commodity supply gap and commodity demand shortfall under disequilibrium conditions. To resolve stagflation in the socialist economy, we need not only take appropriate measures according to specific situations but, more importantly, also understand from a theoretical perspective the various combinations of stagnation and inflation as well as the possibility of stagflation and further study the approaches to achieving rationing equilibrium in the commodity market.

5.1.3 The Possibility of Gradually Achieving Rationing Equilibrium in the Commodity Market

Based on the above analysis, we can draw the following two conclusions. First, the existence of commodity supply gap under the dual-track economic system or the coexistence of commodity supply gap and commodity demand shortfall not only drives prices higher but also decreases personal disposable income, making it very difficult to restore equilibrium in the commodity market. Second, if the economy is under the dual-track system, it means that it has not yet broken away from type II disequilibrium, i.e., not only the market has not been fully developed, but enterprises also have not been able to make independent business decisions and take responsibility for their own profits and losses. Under such circumstances, if commodity supply gap (let alone the coexistence of commodity supply gap and commodity demand shortfall) emerges, it will be necessary to carry out rationing in the commodity market to achieve ex post equilibrium, i.e., rationing equilibrium. How can we achieve rationing equilibrium? This is a topic yet to be studied.

Of course, rationing equilibrium in the commodity market under the dual-track economic system is still doable. Theoretically, the following three different measures will be effective in gradually achieving rationing equilibrium in the commodity market under the dual-track economic system:

First of all, according to the abovementioned requirements of the transition from type II disequilibrium to type I disequilibrium, if the economy is under the dual-track system, the most important policy is to fully motivate microeconomic units so that they can change their status of having no authority over their own business decisions as well as no responsibility for operational profits and losses.

This is the prerequisite for any microeconomic unit to develop the internal mechanism to achieve organic growth and self-control. As long as microeconomic units can truly establish a profit-oriented mechanism to adjust their production and operation, despite insufficient supply of commodities or insufficient demand for commodities, they can at least adjust to the changing supply and demand in the marketplace so as to prevent commodity supply gap and commodity demand shortfall from deteriorating.

It should be pointed out that the frictions between the traditional economic mechanism and the new economic mechanism under the dual-track economic system do not primarily reflect the conflicts between the two types of prices or markets. Instead, they reflect the lack of motivation of microeconomic units and their inadaptability arising therefrom to the two types of prices or markets, as well as the distorted transactional behavior due to the lack of constraint on microeconomic units imposed by self-interest. We have to keep in mind that as long as the economy is under equilibrium conditions, i.e., perfect competition without excess demand or excess supply and with potentially only one price (market price under perfect competition) or one market (the perfectly competitive market). While under disequilibrium conditions, there are various cases of imperfect competition in the economy and both commodity supply gap and commodity demand shortfall exist. There are always two types of prices (i.e., a market price under perfect competition and one under imperfect competition) and two types of markets (i.e., perfectly competitive market and imperfectly competitive market). There are always situations that require the use of rationing to cope with limited supplies of resources or limited demand. Therefore, among all commodity market issues under the dual-track economic system, the top priority is to turn microeconomic units into goods producers who can make their own business decisions and take responsibility for their profits and losses and to enable them to adapt to the reality of two concurrent types of prices and markets so that they can perform self-adjustment and exercise self-restraint according to the profitability principle to reduce supply gap or demand shortfall in the commodity market.

Secondly, it is not realistic to postpone resolving the issue of supply gap or demand shortfall in the commodity market until after every microeconomic unit has become a goods producer who makes its own business decisions and is responsible for its profits and losses. Doing so will also bring unnecessary losses to the economy.

Under such circumstances, it is necessary to apply the following measures: In the process of turning microeconomic units into goods producers who make their own business decisions and take responsibility for profits and losses, we need to appropriately handle the relationship between government regulation and market regulation, allowing government regulation and market regulation to work together on supply gap and demand shortfall in the commodity market. With the joint efforts of government regulation and market regulation, rationing equilibrium in the commodity market can come true. The dual regulation is reflected in the process of reaching rationing equilibrium in the commodity market. This means that we shall try our best to allow market regulation to function in the process of realizing rationing equilibrium in the commodity market and let government regulation, which regulates the economy at a higher level and for the second time, work on any issue associated with rationing equilibrium in the commodity market that market regulation is unable to tackle until the eventual realization of rationing equilibrium. Here, we cannot reverse the roles of the first regulation and the second regulation. Otherwise, it will be difficult to realize rationing equilibrium in the commodity market. Even though rationing equilibrium has been barely realized at one time, it will be more difficult rather than easier to regain rationing equilibrium in the commodity market due to the persisting supply gap or demand shortfall in the commodity market if economic operations are viewed as a continuing process.

Thirdly, since the rationing equilibrium accomplished by means of government regulation and market regulation occurs during the process in which microeconomic units are gradually turned into goods producers that make their own business decisions and are responsible for their profits and losses, we should actively capitalize on the influences of government regulation to help alleviate disequilibrium conditions.

That is to say, we should keep in mind that when microeconomic units are not yet fully capable of making business decisions and taking responsibility for profits and losses, their reactions that interfere with government regulation and market regulation are equivalent to hindering rationing equilibrium in the commodity market. On the other hand, we should note that if we can correctly manage the relationship between government regulation and market regulation and come up with regulatory measures accordingly, we can shorten the process of turning microeconomic units into organizations that are responsible for their operational decisions as well as profits and losses while realizing rationing equilibrium in the commodity market. This is the positive impact of realizing rationing equilibrium on the transition from type II disequilibrium to type I disequilibrium.

5.2 Applying Quantity–Price Adjustment Measures in the Commodity Market

5.2.1 Quantity–Price Adjustment Measures in Broad Sense and Narrow Sense

If the economy only encounters commodity supply gap, it is necessary to apply quantity–price adjustment measures in order to achieve ex post equilibrium. It is also necessary to set the priority for quantity adjustment measures and price adjustment measures in the comprehensive adjustment package according to the scale of ex ante disequilibrium conditions in the commodity market so that ex post equilibrium in the commodity market can be realized. Simply put, the more severe the ex ante disequilibrium conditions, the more important the quantity adjustment measures, relatively speaking; the less severe the ex ante disequilibrium conditions in the commodity market, the less important the price adjustment measures, relatively speaking.

In our discussions on quantity adjustment measures and price adjustment measures, both price adjustment measures and quantity adjustment measures are discussed in their broad sense. The broad sense of price adjustment measures is different from their narrow sense. The narrow sense of price adjustment measures refers to the sole adjustment of commodity prices (including the prices of production materials and consumer goods). For example, lowering prices will lower production costs, causing supply to increase; raising prices will lower sales of finished goods and curb demand, both of which can serve the purpose of removing commodity supply gap. The broad sense of price adjustment measures broadens the scope of price adjustment related to the price of commodities to the adjustment of prices in other markets, such as adjusting interest rate in the money market, wages in the labor market, real estate prices or rental rates in the real estate market, and exchange rates in the foreign exchange market. They are all included in the broad sense of price adjustment measures. The broad sense of quantity adjustment measures is also different from the narrow sense. The narrow sense of quantity adjustment measures refers the sole adjustment of commodity quantities (including the quantities of production materials and consumer goods). For example, under certain circumstances, increasing or lowering the quantity of the commodities that are not subject to rationing and lowering or increasing the quantity of the commodities that are sold at fixed prices will help increase supply or curb demand, thus removing the commodity supply gap. The broad sense of quantity adjustment measures broadens the scope of quantity adjustment from commodity quantities to the quantity in every other market. Here are some examples:

Adjusting credit scale available for the money market is a form of quantity adjustment. Using a dual-credit mechanism (under which planned credit mechanism and market credit mechanism coexist) as well as adjusting the respective weights of planned credit scale and market credit scale in total credit scale are both quantity adjustment measures. Adjusting the required deposit reserve ratio, a tool used by the central bank, is also a quantity adjustment measure, not a price adjustment measure, in spite of some similarities between adjusting the required deposit reserve ratio and adjusting interest rate, because changes of the required deposit reserve ratio directly impact the credit scale of commercial banks.

In terms of the labor market, adjusting the size of employment, changing the structure of the labor force or retirement age, as well as using a dual employment mechanism (under which permanent jobs and contract jobs coexist) are some of the quantity adjustment measures.

In terms of the real estate market, controlling the volume of rental properties or properties available for sale is a quantity adjustment measure.

In terms of the foreign exchange market, using export subsidies and import and export quotas and controlling foreign exchange without adjusting foreign exchange rates are also some of the quantity adjustment measures.

Moreover, fiscal adjustment measures are primarily quantity adjustment measures in a broad sense. They are not price adjustment measures. It is relatively easy to understand the quantitative nature of fiscal expenditure regulation. How to understand the nature of fiscal income regulation? Selling government bonds primarily is a quantity adjustment measure, because the quantity of additional government proceeds is determined by the sale of government bonds. It is the same with the sale of state assets. Price is certainly a factor, but quantity adjustment should come first. As for tax regulation, we should look at it this way: Determining the total quantity of tax revenues and adjusting the tax structure are undoubtedly quantity adjustment measures, whereas determining and adjusting tax rates to a certain extent have some quantity adjustment features. The quantity of taxes is not necessarily related to the ratio of supply to demand on which price adjustment falls back. Some Western economic theories have also regarded taxes as the market price for public goods. We will not talk about to what extent this argument is right or wrong. If we look at the market of public goods, it is different, by nature, from the abovementioned commodity market, money market, real estate market, or foreign exchange market. This is because the most important public goods—national defense, justice, and police—representing security, righteousness, and order, have a sole provider, the government. Buyers have no alternatives, and the price of these most important public goods is determined by the supplier and is normally unrelated to whether or not supply and demand are balanced, nor is it related to the price elasticity of supply or the price elasticity of demand. Therefore, even though we know tax rate regulation to some extent share some of the features of price adjustment, it is quite different from the price adjustment in a normal market. By the same token, we believe that changing tax rates is to some extent a quantity adjustment measure.

5.2.2 *Quantity Adjustment and Price Adjustment Versus Market Regulation and Government Regulation*

As discussed above, when only commodity supply gap exists or supply gap and demand shortfall coexist, quantity adjustment measures are always applied in coordination with price adjustment measures. Before learning how quantity adjustment measures and price adjustment measures are coordinated, we have to analyze their relationship.

Can we simply think that price adjustment is primarily related to market regulation and quantity adjustment is primarily related to government regulation? We should admit that the argument has no theoretical grounds, nor is it consistent with the economic realities. Price adjustment can work either under market regulation or under government regulation. The situation where price adjustment works under market regulation refers to the following case: If supply exceeds demand or vice versa in the economy with no government intervention, changing demand or supply in the market will change prices, which will in turn change demand and supply until they reach a balance in the end. Such autonomous changes in prices are the price adjustment under market regulation. The price adjustment that works under government regulation refers to the following case: When supply exceeds demand or vice versa in the economy, the government intervenes by regulating prices to influence demand and supply using measures such as raising or lowering fixed prices, setting a price ceiling or floor on market prices and allowing market prices to fluctuate within a certain band. Therefore, the price adjustment under government regulation means that the government uses price as leverage to regulate demand and supply in the market. The above explanations of the price adjustment under market regulation and government regulation are applicable to price adjustment in both its narrow sense and broad sense.

Quantity adjustment is similar to price adjustment in that it is also linked to both market regulation and government regulation. The quantity adjustment under market regulation means that the government does not intervene and the market performs quantitative rationing regulation on its own. For example, when a commodity has supply gap, some of the commodity will be sold following the priority principle, or "first-come, first-buy," until it is sold out. When a commodity encounters demand shortfall, a portion of the demand will be met in accordance with the priority principle, or "first-come, first-sell," until all needs are met. These cases are quantity adjustment by the market. Here is another example. Under the circumstance of either commodity supply gap or demand shortfall, if some enterprises are in a monopolistic position in the market, the monopolies can employ quantity adjustment methods (such as divvying up market shares or sources of supply), which of course is not the quantity adjustment under government regulation, but the quantity adjustment in the monopolistic competition market or the monopoly market. The quantity adjustment under government regulation means that the government utilizes all sorts of quantity adjustment measures in various markets to regulate the economy to make up for the shortfalls of price adjustment.

Therefore, when we analyze the relationship between quantity adjustment and price adjustment, we have to first of all understand that either market regulation or government regulation can include price adjustment or quantity adjustment measures, and we cannot think that price adjustment is primarily linked to market regulation or that quantity adjustment is primarily linked to government regulation.

5.2.3 The Mutual Influence of Quantity Adjustment and Price Adjustment

Next, let us analyze the relationship between quantity adjustment and price adjustment in a different sense.

If quantity adjustment and price adjustment can be regarded as two adjustment methods that impact the business behavior of microeconomic units (i.e., enterprises and individuals), we can come to the conclusion that pure quantity adjustment or pure price adjustment does not exist and these two types of adjustment methods have a mutually influential relation when they work in the economy. That is, quantity adjustment, once executed, must create some price adjustment effects, and price adjustment, once executed, must also create some quantity adjustment effects. Any one of these two adjustment methods must rely on its own regulation effects as well as the effects of the other regulatory method to work on commodity supply gap or commodity demand shortfall. To better illustrate this point, we will discuss price adjustment method and quantity adjustment method separately.

A. Quantity Adjustment Effects in Price Adjustment

Based on our earlier discussions, we have known that any change of price, interest rate, wage, rent, foreign exchange rate, or tax rate is to some extent a way of price adjustment. The effects of price adjustment itself are manifested in these changes that influence the current and expected interests of microeconomic units in a way that can change their business behavior accordingly. However, after price adjustment is executed, the effects of quantity adjustment are gradually manifested.

(i) Commodity Market. If the commodity market performs autonomous price adjustment, the demand and supply of commodities will change as the price of commodities changes, and commodity supply gap or commodity demand will also change, and so does the quantitative rationing regulation that the market or monopolistic enterprises carry out. The quantity adjustment in the market (i.e., rationing regulation) following the price adjustment is done without government intervention. As a matter of fact, if price adjustment performed by the market causes commodity supply gap or commodity demand shortfall to shrink, we should consider the contraction the result of both price adjustment and quantity adjustment.

If in the commodity market, the government performs price adjustment on purpose, there will be price adjustment effects after the government raises or lowers fixed prices. Not only that, changes to fixed prices will certainly influence non-fixed prices, the ratio of fixed prices to non-fixed prices, and the sales volume of commodities that adopt fixed prices and non-fixed prices as well as their respective weights in total commodity sales. Hence, price adjustment influences government's rationing regulation. The government needs to adjust its future regulatory measures according to changes in demand and supply brought about by the price adjustment, including adjusting quantity adjustment measures. Therefore, if the government performs price adjustment that lessens commodity supply gap or commodity demand shortfall, the result should also be attributed to both price adjustment and quantity adjustment.

(ii) Other Markets. Other markets are similar to the commodity market. When the market performs autonomous regulation of interest rate, wage, or rent or the government regulates interest rate, wage, or rent on purpose, they adopt price adjustment measures. When supply gaps in these markets change with the implementation of price adjustment measures, the effects of quantity adjustment are manifested. For example, changing interest rate will impact the allocation of credit quota; changing wages will impact the quota of job openings; changing rent will impact the quota of rental properties. These examples demonstrate that the ultimate results obtained through regulating supply gap or demand shortfall are related not only to price adjustment but also to the joint effects of price adjustment and subsequent quantity adjustment.

The quantity adjustment effects arising from price adjustment are perhaps more obvious in other markets than that in the commodity market. This is because there are so many different commodities, and some commodities can be substituted by others. Buyers have many alternatives. If a commodity buyer is a person, he or she can also choose to postpone consumption to a later time, i.e., a decision on consumption and savings. These are the characteristics of the commodity market. Other markets do not necessarily have these characteristics. The reason is that there are relatively few different types of "commodities" in the money market, labor market, or real estate market, and substitutions between different "commodities" in these markets are relatively few and far between. Buyers also have relatively few alternatives. Therefore, when there is a supply gap or demand shortfall, quantity adjustment effects are very obvious. For example, if there is a surplus of capital in the money market, money suppliers will try their best to find a solution, or they will lose interest income. If instead money is tight in the money market, borrowers will try their best to find funds, or they will risk business shutdown. In this case, either surplus funds seeking solutions or shortage of funds forcing borrower to secure capital will quickly give rise to rationing by the money market (allocating surplus funds to meet limited demand) or the rationing of money itself (allocating scarce funds to meet excess demand). These quantity adjustment effects will be quickly reflected in the money market, regardless of whether or not there is coordinated price adjustment. As a matter of fact, once money supply gap or demand shortfall occurs, the market will start autonomous interest rate adjustment even though the government chooses not to. Autonomous market regulation will soon take effect, together with quantity adjustment effects. It is the same with the quantity adjustment effects in terms of the adjustment of employment and rent.

B. Price Adjustment Effects During Quantity Adjustment

Price adjustment effects during the execution of quantity adjustment further reveal the mutually influential relation between quantity adjustment and price adjustment. The autonomous quantity adjustment by the market or the planned quantity adjustment by the government must take advantage of rationing regulation to influence the current and expected interests of microeconomic units in a way that affects their business behavior. As long as quantity adjustment is launched, price adjustment effects will be gradually revealed. This situation is similar to quantity adjustment effects during price adjustment.

(i) Commodity Market. If the commodity market performs autonomous quantity adjustment, i.e., demand and supply are adjusted according to quantitative rationing so that limited supply can meet excess demand or limited demand can be allocated to excess supply, price will change accordingly. Because under the circumstance where supply gap or demand shortfall coexist, autonomous quantitative rationing regulation will surely entice the buyers whose needs are not met to raise their bid price or the suppliers whose needs are not met to lower their offer price. Therefore, price adjustment effects (even though price adjustment is autonomous) are reflected during quantity adjustment.

If quantity adjustment is executed by the government in the commodity market, price adjustment effects will also appear after the launch of quantity adjustment. For example, the government adopts some measures to adjust the scope of commodities that are sold at fixed prices. This will undoubtedly influence the prices of the commodities that are sold at non-fixed prices, driving them up or down, which will impact the demand and supply in the commodity market. For another example, the government can adopt measures to equally allocate the supply of commodities that have a supply gap or equally allocate the market of commodities that have a demand shortfall, which is also one way of quantity adjustment. Once again, the government can adopt measures to allocate the supply or demand of commodities that have supply gap or demand shortfall according to the target priority determined by the government. This method of quantity adjustment will also cause price to change. Overall, quantity adjustment measures adopted by the government, regardless of which method is used, will demonstrate price adjustment effects.

(ii) Other Markets. Price adjustment effects of the quantity adjustment carried out by the government are more obvious in other markets, such as the capital market, the labor market, the real estate market, and the foreign exchange market, than in the commodity market. This has something to do with the differences between the commodity market and other markets discussed in our analyses of quantitative adjustment effects during price adjustment.

For example, if the government sees money supply gap or demand shortfall in the money market and chooses quantity adjustment measures such as adjusting the credit scale, the ratio of planned credit scale to market credit scale, and the required deposit reserve ratio, the changes of money demand and supply in the money market will influence market interest rate by driving it upward or downward, even though the official interest rate may remain unchanged. Changing market interest rates will sooner or later influence the official interest rates. This is reflective of the price adjustment effects of quantity adjustment in the money market.

Another example is the labor market. If the government sees supply gap or demand shortfall in the labor market and adopts such quantity adjustment measures as adjusting the employment size or the ratio of permanent jobs to contract jobs, these measures, in spite of having no direct influence on wages, will undoubtedly influence the speed of labor migration and the direction of employment, which will sooner or later have an impact on wages as well as the demand and supply of labor.

The real estate market and the foreign exchange market are similar. As long as the government adopts some quantity adjustment measures, they will always have some price adjustment effects, and thus the demand and supply in these markets will be influenced by both quantity adjustment and price adjustment.

5.2.4 The Coordination of Quantity–Price Adjustment Measures in the Commodity Market

The mutually influential relation between quantity adjustment and price adjustment helps the government regulate the economy as it consciously coordinates quantity adjustment measures with price adjustment measures. Keep in mind that if the government cannot consciously enforce coordinated adjustment measures, the market itself will autonomously coordinate price adjustment and quantity adjustment so that they can work together. Under economic disequilibrium conditions, if sole market regulation (including price adjustment and quantity adjustment that the market perform autonomously) fails to mitigate losses from economic disequilibrium, the government can consciously coordinate quantity adjustment measures and price adjustment measures so that government regulation can work.

Next, we will separately discuss two situations, one in which only commodity supply gap exists and the other in which commodity supply gap and commodity demand shortfall coexist.

A. Coordinating Quantity–Price Adjustment Measures in Presence of Commodity Supply Gap

We have to first of all point out that the commodity market, the money market, the labor market, the real estate market, and the foreign exchange market are all closely interconnected, with changes in supply and demand in one market leading to changes in supply and demand in another market. We cannot think that we can alleviate or close the commodity supply gap by taking adjustment measures only in the commodity market. Although it seems necessary to adopt adjustment measures in the commodity market, as commodity supply gap is revealed by signs of supply shortages in the commodity market, the changes resulting from the adjustment measures in the commodity market with other markets unchanged will not improve or eliminate commodity shortages. Therefore, to coordinate quantity–price adjustment measures in the presence of commodity supply gap actually means to coordinate quantity–price adjustment measures both in the commodity market and in other relevant markets.

Per our earlier discussions, the priority for quantity adjustment measures and price adjustment measures when they are jointly performed in the presence of commodity supply gap should be determined by the degree of disequilibrium. That is, the higher the degree of disequilibrium, the heavier the quantity adjustment measures should weigh. When commodity supply gap and commodity demand shortfall exist simultaneously, the respective weights of quantity adjustment and price adjustment should also be determined by the degree of disequilibrium. Next, let me list the ways of coordinating quantity–price adjustment measures available in the presence of normal commodity supply gap[1]:

---

[1]I have discussed this issue in my book, *Management of National Economy* (Hebei People's Press, 1988), with reference to Tables 12–1 and 12–3. The analyses in this book are based on the discussions therein.

(i) In the commodity market, government regulatory measures targeting commodity supply gap that fall into the category of price adjustment include:

1. Increasing the selling prices of shortage commodities in order to reduce demand
2. Lowering the prices of the production materials used in producing shortage commodities in order to increase supply

   Government regulatory measures targeting commodity supply gap that fall into the category of quantity adjustment include:
3. Adjusting the range of the commodities sold at fixed price in order to reduce demand, for instance, selling certain commodities at fixed price instead of non-fixed price or vice versa.
4. Initiating quota controls over some commodities and removing or loosening quota controls over other commodities in order to reduce demand.
5. Adjusting the range of commodities sold at fixed price in order to increase supply, i.e., selling commodities at non-fixed price instead of fixed price or vice versa, which is the exact opposite of point (3).
6. Adjusting the range of commodities that are subject to sales quota in order to increase supply. The commodities that are subject to quota, freed from quota controls, or subject to lower controls are exactly opposite to point (4).

(ii) Some adjustment measures can be adopted in the money market to tackle commodity supply gap. They can be coordinated with the adjustment measures in the commodity market. Of these measures, those considered price adjustment are:

7. Increasing interest rate with the intention of suppressing the purchase of shortage commodities in order to reduce demand
8. Lowering interest rate with the intention of increasing the production of shortage commodities in order to increase supply

   Those measures applicable to the money market that are considered quantity adjustment are:
9. Shrinking the credit scale with the intention of suppressing the purchase of shortage commodities in order to reduce demand
10. Expanding the credit scale with the intention of increasing the production of shortage commodities in order to increase supply
11. In order to reduce demand, adjusting the respective weights of planned credit and market credit in total credit scale with the intention of reducing the demand for shortage commodities
12. In order to increase supply, adjusting the respective weights of planned credit and market credit in total credit scale with the intention of increasing the production of shortage commodities

(iii) Some adjustment measures can be adopted in the labor market to tackle commodity supply gap. They can be coordinated with the other adjustment measures in the commodity market. Of these measures, those considered price adjustment are:

13. In order to reduce demand, controlling the growth rate of wages until wages are lowered so that consumption funds in society and their growth rate can be reduced
14. In order to increase supply, increasing wages for the sectors that produce shortage commodities as well as for the sectors that supply production materials used in producing shortage commodities and allowing their wages to grow to a certain level

    Those measures applicable to the labor market that are considered quantity adjustment are:
15. In order to reduce demand, adjusting the credit scale, controlling the labor force and employment growth rate, and adjusting the respective weights of permanent jobs and contract jobs in total job openings so that the quantity and growth rate of consumption funds in society can be reduced
16. In order to increase supply, loosening restrictions on the number of people employed by the sectors that produce shortage commodities as well as those who supply production materials used in the production of shortage commodities and allowing the number of people employed by these sectors to grow to some extent

(iv) Some adjustment measures can be applied in the real estate market to tackle commodity supply gap. They can be coordinated with the other adjustment measures in the commodity market. Of these measures, those considered price adjustment are:

17. Adjusting rental rate so as to suppress aggregate demand in order to reduce demand
18. Adjusting real estate prices to ease the pressure from commodity shortages in order to reduce demand
19. Adjusting rental rate to increase the production of shortage commodities in order to increase supply
20. Adjusting real estate prices to increase the production of shortage commodities in order to increase supply

    Those measures applicable to the real estate market that are considered quantity adjustment are:
21. Increasing the supply of leasable and usable land and housing to ease the pressure from commodity shortages in order to reduce demand
22. Adjusting the size of leasable and usable land as well as that of housing supply to increase the production of shortage commodities in order to increase supply

(v) These price adjustment and quantity adjustment measures listed above are only applicable to the commodity market, the money market, the labor market, and the real estate market. However, there are other adjustment measures available to tackle commodity supply gap. Of these measures, those considered price adjustment are:

23. Using foreign exchange regulation to reduce domestic demand and increase domestic supply, for example, adjusting foreign exchange rates and using the changes of exchange rates to influence import, export, and money inflows and outflows
24. Using tax rate regulation (in which tax rate is basically treated as price adjustment) to suppress domestic demand and increase domestic supply, for example, adjusting tax rates and using the changes of tax rates to influence investment and consumption as well as the demand and supply of commodities and labor

    Those measures considered quantity adjustment are:
25. Imposing control on foreign exchange or loosening control on foreign exchange to influence import, export, and money inflows and outflows so as to suppress domestic demand and increase domestic supply
26. Adjusting fiscal expenditures to influence investment and consumption as well as the demand and supply of commodities and labor so as to suppress domestic demand and increase domestic supply

As a matter of fact, we can list a few other adjustment measures in addition to those listed above, and each one of them can be further broken down into several specific measures. Therefore, we will have various combinations of measures to choose from according to specific situations in each period to tackle commodity supply gap, taking advantage of both price adjustment effects and quantity adjustment effects and avoiding solely relying on one type of adjustment measures (i.e., price adjustment measures only or quantity adjustment measures only) or the negative effects from only adopting one type of adjustment measures in a market.

We also have to keep in mind that coordinating price adjustment and quantity adjustment in the presence of commodity supply gap that we are discussing has a third connotation, besides the first connotation (which refers to using both price adjustment measures and quantity adjustment measures) and the second connotation (which refers to using adjustment measures in the commodity market as well as some appropriate adjustment measures in other markets). The third connotation of coordinating quantity–price adjustment measures is that quantity–price adjustment can be carried out to suppress demand or increase supply. Only by understanding these three connotations of coordinating quantity–price adjustment measures can we truly recognize the role that quantity–price adjustment measures play in balancing national income.

The third connotation of coordinating quantity–price adjustment measures is undoubtedly an option available to manage the economy under the circumstance of commodity supply gap. But coordinating quantity–price adjustment measures is more important if commodity supply gap and commodity demand shortfall coexist. In this circumstance, it appears that it would be quite difficult to handle economic complexities if quantity–price adjustment measures had only the first and second connotations.

B. Coordinating Quantity–Price Adjustment Measures Under the Coexistence of Commodity Supply Gap and Commodity Demand Shortfall

When commodity supply gap and commodity demand shortfall coexist, adjustment measures are coordinated in the same way as when only commodity supply gap exists. In this circumstance, the government needs to not only coordinate quantity adjustment measures and price adjustment measures but also apply coordinated measures in many other markets that are correlated.

However, this situation is different from the one in which only commodity supply gap exists. When commodity supply gap and commodity demand shortfall coexist, it is more important to implement and coordinate adjustment measures with the purpose of both suppressing demand and increasing supply. The reason for this is that the coexistence of supply gap and demand shortfall makes it difficult to enforce government regulation. If the government tackles only one of the two issues, suppressing demand or increasing supply, demand may continue to grow while the government tries to suppress demand, or supply may continue to decrease while the government tries to increase supply. This is a phenomenon called economic "side effects." To alleviate the "side effects," we will have to adopt a combination of adjustment measures.[2]

There are five different ways of coordinating adjustment measures. They are as follows: coordinating the quantity adjustment intended to adjust demand with the price adjustment intended to adjust supply, coordinating the price adjustment intended to adjust demand with the quantity adjustment intended to adjust supply, coordinating the quantity adjustment intended to adjust demand with the quantity adjustment intended to adjust supply, coordinating the price adjustment intended to adjust demand with the price adjustment intended to adjust supply, and coordinating the quantity–price adjustment intended to adjust demand with the quantity–price adjustment intended to adjust supply. Next, we will discuss each of them separately.

1. Coordinating the quantity adjustment intended to adjust demand with the price adjustment intended to adjust supply. This way of coordination features its ability to adjust aggregate demand using relatively powerful measures so as to prevent significant price fluctuations and to narrow commodity supply gap. Meanwhile, to prevent the adjustments to demand from negatively impacting economic growth, e.g., to prevent the excessive suppression of aggregate demand from stunting the growth of supply, we can apply price adjustment measures targeting supply so as to gradually alleviate commodity supply gap, which will help ease both commodity supply gap and commodity demand shortfall.

   If the quantity adjustment intended to adjust demand and the price adjustment intended to adjust supply are well coordinated, the government's intention to adjust demand and supply can be realized simultaneously without any direct conflict. The main reason is that using quantity adjustment measures to adjust demand and using price adjustment measures to adjust supply to some extent allow microeconomic units to change their economic behavior in accordance

[2]I have discussed fairly thoroughly the economic "side effects" as well as the treatments in Chap. 8 of *Management of National Economy* (Hebei People's Press, 1988). This book examines the issue in greater detail on the basis of the discussions therein.

with different signals. For example, they can adjust investment and consumption according to the quantity signals so as to meet the government's requirement for demand adjustment, or they can adjust investment and consumption according to the price signals so as to meet the government's requirement for supply adjustment. This can reduce the frictions of economic behavior among microeconomic units and also help alleviate supply gap and demand shortfall in the economy.

2. Coordinating the price adjustment intended to adjust demand and the quantity adjustment intended to adjust supply. The coordination of these adjustment measures is basically the same as what we have just discussed. That is, both ways of coordinating adjustment measures can serve the government's purpose of gradually alleviating commodity supply gap and commodity demand shortfall while avoiding direct conflicts in the process of reaching the dual goals.

   However, this way of coordinating adjustment measures is different from the prior one in the following way: Since price adjustment measures are used to adjust demand, i.e., using changes in the price of some commodities or changes in interest rate or rent to influence investment and consumption, in addition to a possibility of relatively strong resistance from microeconomic units, the effects of the adjustment measures may also only be seen after a relatively long period of time. Therefore, this method of coordinating adjustment measures is primarily suitable for immature commodity supply gap. On the other hand, as supply is influenced by quantity adjustment measures, which have fairly quick adjustment effects, demand may experience relatively large swings as a result. Therefore, this method of coordinating adjustment measures is primarily suitable for immature commodity supply gap. In other words, if relatively severe commodity supply gap has already been in existence and demand adjustment has become a pressing task, the first method will probably be more appropriate in order to simultaneously alleviate commodity supply gap and commodity demand shortfall. If the situation is different, we can adopt price adjustment measures to suppress demand and quantity adjustment measures to increase supply.

3. Coordinating the quantity adjustment intended to adjust demand with the quantity adjustment intended to adjust supply. Under the circumstance where both commodity supply gap and commodity demand shortfall exist, adopting quantity adjustment measures with the purpose of adjusting both demand and supply is very likely to require the following preexisting conditions: The market has been in such a bad shape and the market mechanism has been so underdeveloped that price adjustment cannot function, and it is necessary to apply quantity adjustment to both demand and supply to alleviate commodity supply gap and commodity demand shortfall.

   At this point, there is one issue that is worthy of our attention: We need to prevent any conflict or offsetting effects between quantity adjustment measures intended to adjust demand and those intended to adjust supply. How can we do that? Generally speaking, we have to take the following three points into consideration:

   First, in terms of quantity adjustment, we need to apply different measures in different markets according to different situations. For example, in order to adjust demand, we can start with the money market and adjust the credit scale or turn to the real estate market and adjust the land available for transfer and the quantity of housing supplies. In order to adjust supply, we can start with the labor market and adjust the size of employment and the ratio of permanent jobs and contract jobs or target the commodity market and adjust the type and quantity of certain commodities that are sold at fixed price rather than non-fixed price.

Second, the quantity adjustment measures, though implemented in the same market or in the same area, can be treated appropriately based on the structural differences so that the offsetting effects between demand-targeted and supply-targeted measures can be avoided. For example, in terms of fiscal expenditures, we can appropriately adjust the structure of fiscal spending in the following way: We can adjust the fiscal spending amount of some projects in order to adjust demand while adjusting the fiscal spending amount of other projects in order to adjust supply. Another example is bank credit, which can also be appropriately adjusted through structural adjustment of credit expenditures: We can adjust credit availability to some industrial sectors or certain manufacturers in order to adjust demand while adjusting credit amount for other sectors or manufacturers in order to adjust supply.

Third, even if we can apply different quantity adjustment measures in different markets according to different situations in each market or adjust the structure of quantity adjustment according to specific measures adopted in each market and make proper arrangements, sometimes it is inevitable to see conflicts arising as long as quantity adjustment measures are adopted to adjust demand and supply simultaneously. Therefore, we need to consider the lagging effect, the direct and indirect effects of each adjustment measure, as well as the net effect resulting from positive effects being offset by negative effects. The timing of the lagging effect varies as quantity adjustment measures vary. As a result, we can prevent, to some extent, the adjustment measures intended to adjust demand from offsetting the adjustment measures intended to adjust supply during the same period of time. Since there are direct and indirect effects and various adjustment measures have different direct and indirect effects, the offsetting of the adjustment measures intended to adjust demand and those intended to adjust supply can be mitigated. The final effect of various adjustment measures adopted by the government is dependent upon the net effect as a result of positive effects being offset by negative effects. Commodity supply gap will not necessarily be exactly equal to commodity demand shortfall. As a matter of fact, either commodity supply gap is larger than commodity demand shortfall or vice versa. Therefore, the net effect of adjustment measures as a result of positive effects being offset by negative effects will help us detect which of the supply gap or demand shortfall has been largely alleviated.

4. Coordinating the price adjustment intended to adjust demand and the price adjustment intended to adjust supply. Generally speaking, the way of coordinating adjustment measures has a prerequisite that is slightly different from the former one (i.e., coordinating the quantity adjustment intended to adjust demand and the quantity adjustment intended to adjust supply). The prerequisite for

this way of coordination is largely applicable when the market is not in such a bad shape, and the market mechanism, although incomplete, is far from being severely underdeveloped. Thus, price adjustment measures, rather than quantity adjustment measures, can be adopted to alleviate commodity supply gap and demand shortfall.

Meanwhile, we will have to pay attention to the same issue as the one related to the former way of coordinating adjustment measures that we have discussed, i.e., we need to prevent potential conflicts between the price adjustment measures intended to adjust demand and the price adjustment measures intended to adjust supply as well as the effect of one measure offsetting another. Therefore, the arrangement under this way of coordinating adjustment measures is the same as under the former way, i.e., some price adjustment measures are applied in some markets while different price adjustment measures are applied in other markets. For example, to adjust demand, we can change interest rate or rent, while in order to adjust supply, we can change the prices of shortage commodities or lower the prices of production materials used to produce shortage commodities. In addition, we can take advantage of the structural adjustment of prices so that the price adjustment intended to adjust demand and the price adjustment intended to adjust supply will not conflict with each other. For example, in order to adjust demand, we can change the tax rate applicable to the production and sales of certain products, while we can change the tax rate applicable to the production and sales of the other products to adjust supply.

The lagging effect, the direct and indirect effect of the adjustment measures, as well as the net effect as a result of positive effects being offset by negative effects that we discussed in the former way of coordinating adjustment measures are also worthy of our attention when we apply the current way of coordinating adjustment measures. As long as different price adjustment measures are properly arranged, we will at least be able to significantly reduce, if not completely eliminate, any potential conflict between different price adjustment measures.

5. Coordinating the quantity–price adjustment intended to adjust demand with the quantity–price adjustment intended to adjust supply. Real economic activities can be complex. The four ways of coordinating adjustment measures discussed above may seem too simple when commodity supply gap and demand shortfall coexist and therefore are not necessarily applicable to complex economic activities. It is probably necessary to coordinate the quantity–price adjustment intended for both demand and supply, i.e., it is necessary to apply quantity–price adjustment intended to adjust demand while applying quantity–price adjustment intended to adjust supply.

   In this scenario, one of the main problems we will encounter is that these adjustment measures tend to be offsetting each other. All that has been discussed above is also applicable to this scenario.

   Yet we have to pay attention to the dual coordination. This means that in order to tackle commodity supply gap, it is necessary to coordinate quantity adjustment and price adjustment so that demand can be effectively controlled or that in order to tackle commodity demand shortfall, it is also necessary to coordinate quantity adjustment and price adjustment so that demand can be increased and supply can be decreased effectively. Therefore, the first tier of coordination lies in the coordinated quantity–price adjustment measures to tackle either commodity supply gap or commodity demand shortfall, and the second tier of coordination lies in the coordinated quantity–price adjustment measures to tackle the coexisting commodity supply gap and demand shortfall. These two tiers of coordination are important. If any tier of coordination is not well executed, adjustment measures may offset each other. Research on the socialist economic "side effects" as well as some treatments has revealed that the dual coordination of these two tiers is feasible and that the key point is to arrange measures properly and take the lagging effect of various adjustment measures into consideration.[3]

[3]This topic can be found in Chaps. 8 and 12 of my publication, *Management of National Economy*, Hebei People's Press, 1988.

Chapter 6
Easing Supply and Demand Mismatch Under Economic Disequilibrium Conditions

6.1 The Counter Effects of Government Price Adjustment

6.1.1 The Rigidity of Supply Gap Under Economic Disequilibrium Conditions

As we know, current economic disequilibrium in China is not only due to an underdeveloped market but also due to the fact that enterprises are not yet goods producers who make their own business decisions and take responsibility for their own profits and losses. Therefore, when commodity supply gap occurs, especially under the coexistence of commodity supply gap and commodity demand shortfall, even if quantity adjustment or price adjustment measures adopted by the government can be effective to some extent, government regulation will have limited results and the mismatch between supply and demand cannot be reduced to a large extent if the enterprise operation mechanism is not truly overhauled and enterprises are still affiliated with and controlled by government administrative institutions. This should be the starting point of our research on current Chinese economic issues.

To further illustrate these issues, let us start with the features of supply gap and demand shortfall under the conditions in which enterprises are not goods producers who can make their own business decisions or are responsible for their own profits and losses and the market has not been fully developed.

In the presence of supply gap, if the economy is in the midst of the abovementioned conditions, it will be unlikely for the market to deliver an accurate message about supply gap to enterprises because it has not been fully developed, nor will it be able to encourage enterprises to allocate resources available to produce commodities to fill the supply gap. As enterprises lack the operation mechanism of a normal goods producer who can make its own business decisions and is responsible for profits and losses, they are not only unable to receive an accurate message on supply gap but also unable to adjust their allocation of the means of production even after receiving those messages, or unable to obtain from the market all necessary

Y. Li, *Chinese Economy in Disequilibrium*, China Academic Library,
DOI 10.1007/978-3-642-39558-1_6, © Foreign Language Teaching and Research
Publishing Co., Ltd and Springer-Verlag Berlin Heidelberg 2014

resources needed to adjust production, or even unable to increase their own profits by providing the market with commodities in demand. Obviously, supply gap is rigid and cannot be alleviated via market self-adjustment.

In the presence of demand shortfall, the nature of demand shortfall and its characteristics are similar to that of supply gap in many ways. Supply gap drives prices higher, whereas in the case of demand shortfall, commodity overstock or sluggish sales do not necessarily lower the prices, which may even ride higher in tandem with the prices of shortage commodities. Why? It has something to do with economic disequilibrium. Because the market has not been fully developed, it is impossible for the market to deliver to enterprises accurate messages about demand shortfall, nor is it possible for the market to encourage enterprises to transfer the resources that experience inventory buildup or sluggish sales to other areas. Because enterprises lack the operation mechanism of a normal goods producer who makes its own business decisions and is responsible for profits and losses, they are not only unable to receive accurate information on demand shortfall but also unable to adjust the allocation of the means of production even after receiving the information, or unable to effectively transfer all excess resources after adjusting production, or may even incur some real losses due to providing the market with commodities that are not in demand. Obviously, demand shortfall is also rigid and cannot be alleviated via market self-adjustment.

Because the rigidity of supply gap and demand shortfall does exist under economic disequilibrium conditions, the market cannot fully develop and government adjustment measures, regardless of the implementation of quantity adjustment measures or price adjustment measures, cannot produce satisfactory results if the status of enterprises is not changed. Not only that, in some cases, some adjustment measures adopted by the government to reduce supply gap or demand shortfall may even bring about counter effects. That is, supply gap that is expected to shrink after the implementation of adjustment measures turns out to be wider after the adjustment, or demand shortfall that is expected to shrink after the implementation of adjustment measures turns out to be worse afterward. These counter effects are worthy of our attention.

6.1.2 *Commodity Supply Gap and the Counter Effects of Government Price Adjustment Under Economic Disequilibrium Conditions*

The potential counter effects from government regulation under economic disequilibrium conditions can be viewed from two different perspectives, supply gap and demand shortfall.

Let us assume commodity supply gap occurs and the government decides to apply price adjustment measures to increase supply and suppress demand. As long as enterprises lack a proper operation mechanism and the market is not fully developed, the following things may happen:

A. The government removes price control to stimulate supply and uses market price to support supply growth. However, as resources are constrained and limited resources are distributed by means of rationing, it is impossible for supply to grow proportionally after the price decontrol. In other words, the growth rate of supply will be lower than that of price. On the other hand, after price controls are lifted, because enterprises are not guided by the maximization of self-interest or budget constraints, rising prices may prompt them to harm consumers (i.e., passing higher costs along to consumers) or the nation (i.e., lowering fiscal income due to higher costs and lower income) in order to adapt to new economic conditions. As a result, removing price control as a method to stimulate supply growth will fail to reach its goals and only cause vicious price escalation.
B. After the government removes price control, as resources are limited and the market has not been fully developed, each enterprise will fare differently depending on whether it can obtain limited supply of resources via rationing. Some are neither able to secure the supply of production materials nor bear price increases or higher costs. As a result, they are forced to cut back or stop production, which directly reduces supply. Other enterprises are able to secure the supply of production materials via rationing. However, these enterprises, in anticipation of price increases due to limited supply of resources, are more likely to withhold production materials so that they can profit from reselling production materials instead of using them in production. This situation also leads to lower supply.
C. Assuming that the government chooses to lower interest rates to stimulate supply. This method may have another outcome. As banks and enterprises lack a proper operation mechanism, lowering interest rates stimulates the supply of some products, but the demand for these products increases by an even larger quantity. As a result, the growth of demand exceeds the growth of supply, driving commodity supply gap even wider. In other words, both aggregate imbalance and structural imbalance get even worse.
D. If the government removes price control or raises prices to suppress demand, there may be some unwanted consequences. One of the reasons for this is that enterprises lack budget constraints or the mechanism to maximize self-interest. The public sector is no different. These entities will not lower their purchasing power at all simply because prices are higher. As a result, price increases far outpace demand decreases, or demand basically stays put without any significant change. This is a very common occurrence. A commonly known phenomenon that is worthy of our attention—public purchasing power is not constrained by rising prices—can be explained by the lack of the profit maximization mechanism or budget constraints.
E. Another reason why the price decontrol or increase initiated by the government to suppress demand may usually give rise to unwanted consequences is that price

increases tend to bring about uncertainty or disturb people's expectations. When people realize that supply is not going to improve in the short term, they will accelerate consumption in order to avoid the depreciation of cash on hand or the deposits in their bank account, changing the situation of "withholding cash and waiting for purchase opportunities" to "using cash to expedite purchases," or the situation of "holding bank deposits and waiting for purchase opportunities" to "withdrawing bank deposits to expedite purchases." As a result, price rise will not curb demand. Instead, it will stimulate purchases. Using cash to expedite purchases or withdrawing bank deposits to expedite purchases will in turn aggravate commodity supply gap, drive prices higher, and further disturb people's expectations.

F. There is one more reason why the price decontrol and price increase initiated by the government to suppress demand may normally give rise to unwanted consequences. That is, when resources are scarce, commodities are in short supply and the market is not fully developed, and some microeconomic units (including not only small business owners, private enterprises, and enterprises but also residents) may add a special meaning to the purchase of consumer goods, which is called "extra investment," as people's economic behavior has been distorted. For example, people buy gifts, such as expensive cigarettes, luxury wine, high-end electronics, precious herbal materials, and luxury clothes. The purchase of these goods is not constrained by high prices. Since purchasers consider these commodities to be a sort of "extra investment," they believe the benefits exceed the costs. Because of high prices, these gifts are getting even more precious and their benefits are getting larger. In addition, rising prices are less likely to restrain consumers from spending as a way to show off wealth. Even though prices are high, spending of this nature will not necessarily decline.

G. If the government raises interest rates to suppress demand, it will be unlikely to see any good effect, at least not from the investment perspective. Because enterprises lack a proper operation mechanism and money supply is limited, enterprises will not necessarily lower their demand for capital because of higher funding cost. This demonstrates why relatively small increases in interest rates are unable to curb investment. Considerable increases in interest rates will likely have opposite consequences, i.e., normal business production and operation are impacted, and while demand is suppressed, supply is also subdued. Subdued supply is exactly contradictory to what the government has hoped for, i.e., closing the supply gap.

All the above has fully revealed that price adjustment implemented by the government to alleviate supply gap under economic disequilibrium conditions is likely to generate some counter effects. As long as we understand the current situations in China, we will not blindly trust price adjustment to alleviate supply gap.

6.1.3 Commodity Demand Shortfall and the Counter Effects from Government Price Adjustment Under Economic Disequilibrium Conditions

From the structural imbalance perspective, it is highly likely to have commodity demand shortfall concurrent with commodity supply gap. In the case of commodity demand shortfall, if the government decides to apply price adjustment measures to increase demand and suppress supply so as to reduce commodity inventories, it is likely to see counter effects resulting from government price adjustment, which prevents the government from achieving its goals. The reason remains the same. That is, enterprises lack a proper operation mechanism and the market has not been fully developed.

A. The government executes price adjustment by lowering the price of some commodities to stimulate demand and suppress supply. However, because the producers of these commodities are not responsible for their own profits and losses nor are the buyers of these commodities, price signals will not be effective in stimulating demand and suppressing supply as expected. Demand may increase slightly and supply may decrease slightly, but the changes are not compatible with the magnitude of price declines.
B. Assuming that some enterprises see the signal of declining prices and start to lower production. Because asset ownership is not clear, enterprises are not going to deal with excess production materials or labor. As a result, lowering production only causes higher losses that in turn reduce the proceeds that the state collects. The new macroeconomic situations may force the government to alter its original decision of lowering prices.
C. Assuming that some enterprises see the signal of lowering prices and start to increase the purchase of some commodities. Because enterprises operate under the circumstance of limited resources, they must adjust raw materials and production equipment to realign their product portfolios so as to increase the production of shortage commodities and reduce the production of the products that have poor sales. If they only increase the purchase of some commodities (attracted by lower prices) while unable to secure complementary products (due to resource supply constraints), they will have to stop buying the commodities of reduced prices, which makes it hard for the government to reach its goal of stimulating demand. Or they will have to store the commodities of reduced prices instead of using them to increase the supply of shortage commodities, hoping that they can resell at higher prices, which also makes it hard for the government to fulfill its plan of product restructuring.
D. If the government uses price adjustment measures to increase demand in the presence of commodity demand shortfall, it may impact the enterprises that do not make their own decisions and are not responsible for profits and losses in the following way: They not only increase purchases by taking advantage of reduced prices but also use the additional purchases to produce the commodities that have

already experienced inventory buildup or sluggish sales. As a result, although demand increases, unjustified supply also increases. Commodity demand shortfall, instead of shrinking, may end up wider, which is also inconsistent with the government goal.

E. If the government lowers interest rates to increase demand with the intention of reducing commodity demand shortfall, the increase of supply might not be lower than the increase of demand, because banks and enterprises lack a proper operation mechanism. On the contrary, if the government increases interest rates to control supply with the intention of reducing commodity demand shortfall, it may also end up with flat or slightly lower supply, for the same reason that banks and enterprises lack a proper operation mechanism. Therefore, if banks and enterprises lack a proper operation mechanism, interest rate adjustment with the intention of reducing commodity demand shortfall will barely fulfill government goals.

All the above has fully revealed that price adjustment implemented by the government to alleviate demand shortfall under economic disequilibrium conditions is likely to have some counter effects. As long as we understand the current situations in China, we will not blindly trust price adjustment to alleviate demand shortfall.

6.1.4 Behind the Dual-Track Price System: Potential Issues Related to Rationing Adjustment

Under economic disequilibrium conditions with a relatively large commodity supply gap, it is not possible for the government to remove price control. We have discussed this point earlier. During the transition from the traditional product economy to the new commodity economy, the dual-track price system will be maintained for a relatively long period of time. This is the second best choice. Under the dual-track price system, the economy has all kinds of frictions, causing all kinds of irrational economic behavior, as can be reasonably expected. We would like to discuss two points here. First, if the economy cannot remove price control immediately and transit to uniform market price, nor is it possible to return to the traditional product economy, i.e., uniform price under the mechanism of the planned economy, the only alternative currently available is the dual-track price system. Between two necessary evils, the lesser will be selected. It is harmful to either immediately adopt the uniform market price system at the current stage or return to the traditional sole price system of the planned economy. Either way will cause more damage than the dual-track price system does. Therefore, we would maintain rather than terminate the unreasonable dual-track price system at the current stage. Second, the dual-track price system will undoubtedly cause all kinds of issues. One of the most noticeable issues is the illegal trading carried out by someone who takes advantage of the gap between two prices and earns huge undue profits, which will harm not only consumers but also the nation. We should point out that the gap between two prices is inseparable from the dual-track price system. There would not be a dual-track price system if there were no gap between two prices. The issue is not the existence of price gap, but who illegally profits from the price gap and how he or she takes advantage of the price gap to earn undue profits. As a matter of fact, many of the issues related to the dual-track price system have precisely exposed the fundamental flaws inherent in the traditional economic system. Only after reaching behind the dual-track price system can we discover the core of the issues.

The first point mentioned above is almost indisputable. If we remove price control and terminate the dual-track price system, we will end up with nothing but social and economic turmoil. Currently, we cannot rush to this decision. Meanwhile, it is also impossible or unfeasible for us to return to the traditional sole price system of the planned economy. If we do that, the economy will shrink and dwindle.

As for the second point mentioned above, we need to discuss it in greater detail. The uniform price mechanism in the market can be realized only when demand is relatively close to supply. When supply gap is fairly large, even if we terminate the dual-track price system and revert to uniform market price, there will not be only one price in the economy, but two prices. At this time, these two prices are actually different from those under the dual-track price system. The two prices under the dual-track price system are fixed price, or planned price, and non-fixed price, or market price. After price control is lifted, two prices actually exist when supply gap is fairly large. One is open-market price and the other is non-open-market price. Why do we have these two prices at this time? In order to explain the reason why market price can be classified as open-market price and non-open-market price, we will have to analyze rationing adjustment at time of relatively large supply gap. We know that illegal trading arising from the gap of the two prices under the dual-track price system is associated with rationing adjustment. If we terminate the dual-track price system at time of relatively large supply gap, there are still two prices and a gap in between, which is also associated with rationing adjustment.

Rationing adjustment is a form of quantity adjustment. Rationing adjustment can be broken down into two types. The first type is the rationing adjustment that the market voluntarily performs, and the second one is the rationing adjustment that the government carries out according to some specific rules. Under the dual-track price system, there must be rationing adjustment performed by the government according to some specific rules to begin with. Then, on the basis of government rationing adjustment, the market autonomously performs rationing adjustment. Profiting from the gap between two prices exactly follows this pattern. For example, if a certain type of nonferrous metal is a scarce commodity, the government can allocate it among relevant enterprises according to the equalization principle, the target principle (or the priority principle), or the history principle. Regardless of which rationing principle the government uses for allocation, the price of the underlying commodity is always lower than its market price. There are always some enterprises who resell their share of allocated scarce commodities, and the principle that they follow is one for market rationing, including the priority principle (or the principle of first-come, first-buy), the monopoly principle (under which monopolistic enterprises determine to whom they sell), or other principles. Regardless of which principle is followed, the price of the underlying commodity is always higher than its fixed price, or planned price. As long as the supply gap of a specific commodity is relatively large, profiting from the price gap will be inevitable.

Let us assume that we terminated the dual-track price system for shortage commodities in this circumstance. What would happen then? It should be admitted that the relatively large supply gap would not disappear as a result. As we have pointed out earlier, aggregate supply will not see immediate significant increase because of various resource constraints. As long as shortage remains, the principle of market rationing will continue to work. Whether the market follows the priority principle (or the principle of first-come, first-buy) or the monopoly principle to allocate shortage commodities, buyers will have to pay some extra expenses on top of open-market price in order to secure those commodities, such as fees paid to retrieve relevant information and charges associated with the close of a transaction, which as a matter of fact becomes a part of non-open-market price of those commodities. Moreover, as long as a commodity is still short, buyers who purchase it at a certain price are still able to resell it, and its non-open-market price goes up every time it changes hands. Escalating non-open-market price will influence open-market price and drive it higher. It will end up with non-open-market price continuing to push open-market price upward and open-market price always trying to catch up with non-open-market price. As soon as open-market price appears to do so, non-open-market price will start to jump again. The catch-up game will undoubtedly lead to continuous escalation of both open-market price and non-open-market price and end up with prices way over its original level, but the gap between these two prices will persist.

Why will open- and non-open-market prices keep rising one after another after the dual-track price system is terminated? How can we stop these two prices from escalating? This is an issue that calls for further research. Obviously, this abnormal phenomenon is related to the scarcity of resources as well as the relatively small price elasticity in the circumstance of resource shortages. This is not the end of the story. If the potential buyers of these shortage commodities are subject to profit constraints and budget constraints, their demand for the commodities will be influenced by higher prices, as they will refrain from buying when prices reach a certain level. In other words, the fact that the demand curve slopes downward to the right demonstrates that buyers react against to higher prices by reducing their purchase volume. Their reactions will hinder and eventually stall the price rise. If buyers are not subject to profit constraints or budget constraints, the shape of the demand curve will change, i.e., it no longer slopes downward to the right, and the upward trend in price will no longer be influenced by buyers. In the current Chinese economy, enterprises are not buyers of shortage commodities who are subject to profit constraints and budget constraints. If enterprises stay the way they are, terminating the dual-track price system for shortage commodities will not only create two prices (open-market price and non-open-market price), but these two prices will also rise continuously (with open-market price chasing non-open-market price and non-open-market price continuing to rise in order to avoid being caught up by rising open-market price). Therefore, the behavior of profiting from the gap of two prices cannot be explained by the price itself.

6.2 Reforming the Enterprise Operation Mechanism

6.2.1 Reforming the Enterprise Operation Mechanism and Easing Supply and Demand Mismatch

The analyses above naturally lead us to the following conclusion: In order to resolve the current issue of large commodity supply gap in China, it is necessary to first and foremost turn enterprises into goods producers who are responsible for their own business decisions as well as profits and losses and establish a normal business operation mechanism under which entities pursue the maximization of self-interest and are subject to budget constraints. If the enterprise operation mechanism is not properly reformed, simply hoping to immediately terminate the dual-track price system will only bring about the outcomes that we have discussed above.

To resolve the issue of supply being unable to meet demand, we will undoubtedly have to increase supply. Supply increases need to be ultimately realized by increasing production capacity. Increasing supply means higher productivity. Increasing supply with the purpose of resolving the issue of supply being unable to meet demand is not only effective but also very important.[1]

To increase supply requires additional inputs. When supply is not able to meet demand, if we add inputs excessively or simply regard adding extra inputs as the way to increase supply, demand can increase, which is contradictory to the intention of suppressing demand in the first place. Therefore, we should not hope that supply will increase with additional inputs. Instead, we should do our utmost to increase supply by minimizing additional inputs.

How can we do that? The government can adopt several adjustment measures, such as quantity adjustment measures and price adjustment measures. Keep in mind that if the market has not been fully developed and enterprises are not motivated, not only price adjustment measures but also quantity adjustment measures will be less effective. The fundamental solution to the issue of insufficient supply is to recombine production factors and motivate enterprises and their employees. This is the issue of reforming the enterprise operation mechanism.

If enterprises have not become goods producers who take responsibility for their business decisions as well as operational profits and losses, or enterprise ownership has not been normalized, or the property right of enterprise fixed assets remains unspecified, it will be very difficult to recombine production factors. Reforming the

[1] See Li Yining [1].

enterprise operation mechanism refers to changing enterprises that are affiliated with and controlled by government administrative institutions to business entities that operate with clearly specified property rights under profit constraints and budget constraints. During the process of reforming the enterprise operation mechanism, we will see continuous improvement in the recombination of production factors because the reform will clarify enterprises' property rights, specifying who are the owners and the managers of enterprises' fixed assets, which will facilitate mergers and acquisitions, encourage enterprises to invest in other enterprises, accelerate the forming of enterprise conglomerates, and optimize the industrial structure and product structure. As a result, we can reach the goal of increasing the supply of products and services with as minimal additional inputs as possible.

Reforming the enterprise operation mechanism includes reforming how enterprises distribute corporate earnings. The mechanism that enterprises follow to distribute corporate earnings directly impacts the motivation of enterprises themselves as well as that of their employees. Reforming corporate earnings distribution mechanism can only be completed by normalizing enterprises' property rights and by truly transforming enterprises to goods producers who are responsible for their business decisions and operational profits and losses. If enterprises themselves as well as their employees are motivated, which is as important as recombining production factors, they will likely produce more products and services with as minimal additional inputs as possible.

The discussions have demonstrated that there are a series of alternative measures available to the government to increase supply and resolve the issue of supply falling short of demand. If the main hurdle to supply gap alleviation is enterprises' lack of a proper operation mechanism as well as a necessary interest-maximization mechanism and budget constraints, the main measure that the government adopts should not be price adjustment nor quantity adjustment, but the reform of the enterprise operation mechanism, i.e., transforming enterprises to goods producers who are responsible for their business decisions and profits and losses.

Let us further analyze the issue from the perspective of suppressing demand.

To increase supply is certainly the most important way to resolve the issue of supply being unable to meet demand. Yet to some extent, to suppress demand is also very meaningful, which can be done by applying price adjustment measures and quantity adjustment measures under government regulation. Although some of the adjustment measures to suppress demand may take effect in a relatively short period of time, they are after all temporary relief. These measures are nothing but forcing demand to adjust to the current level of productivity rather than increasing productivity to meet current demand. In addition, we also have to consider the side effects from suppressing demand. Demand needs to be suppressed appropriately. Excessively suppressing demand will bring difficulties to the economy in the future.

The issue that we have to discuss here is as follows: In order to suppress demand, should we start with reforming the enterprise operation mechanism, in addition to price adjustment measures and quantity adjustment measures implemented by the government? The answer is yes. We should point out that to suppress demand by first of all reforming the enterprise operation mechanism when enterprises lack a proper operation mechanism, the indispensable mechanism of pursuing the maximization of self-interest, and budget constraints, will not only be more effective than quantity–price adjustment measures but will also avoid some side effects, such as negatively influencing resource utilization efficiency, discouraging enterprises and their employees, and unfavorably impacting supply growth. We can look at this argument from two different perspectives, suppressing investment demand and suppressing consumption demand.

The primary method of suppressing investment demand should be to create a mechanism for the investment entity, i.e., enterprises, so that they can be self-restrained and make self-adjustments according to changing investment environment. If the investment principal lacks such a mechanism, any quantity–price adjustment measure that the government adopts will fail to produce satisfactory results. In order to create such a mechanism for enterprises as the investment principal, we will have to reform the enterprise operation mechanism so that they can be restrained by their self-interest and budget. As a result, enterprises will take their self-interest into consideration and stop making inefficient or ineffective investments. It is only on that basis that the price adjustment measures and quantity adjustment measures adopted by the government to suppress investment demand can gradually take effect as enterprises adjust their business behavior.

The primary method that the government adopts to suppress consumption demand is the same, that is, to create the mechanism for the consumption principal so that it can exercise self-restraint and make self-adjustments as the market changes. As for enterprises, controlling their consumption demand is closely related to the enterprise operation mechanism. On the one hand, enterprise is one of the consumption principals in society. If enterprises are not restrained by the maximization of self-interest nor subject to budget constraints, their consumption demand will unlikely be contained, which can be explained by the commonly discussed phenomenon that corporate purchasing power never appears to diminish. On the other hand, consumption demand from enterprise employees is related to their disposable income, which ultimately depends upon various types of income they receive from their employers. If the enterprise operation mechanism is not reformed, it will be impossible to have enterprise employees' income link up with labor productivity as well as the growth of labor productivity. This can also explain why enterprises constantly compare and show off their compensation such as salaries and bonuses, a topic that is commonly discussed.

Therefore, from the perspectives of increasing supply and suppressing demand, we can reach this conclusion: Under economic disequilibrium conditions, the basic approach to easing the mismatch between supply and demand is to reform the enterprise operation mechanism so that enterprises can be restrained by the maximization of self-interest and subject to budget constraints. If the issue of enterprise operation mechanism is resolved, we can increase the supply of products and services from the supply perspective with as minimal additional inputs as possible through recombining production factors and motivating enterprises and their employees. From the demand perspective, through establishing the mechanism under which enterprises exercise self-restraint in their investment decisions as well as their spending, we can not only control demand effectively but also reduce the side effects that come along with demand suppression.

6.2.2 *Reforming Enterprise Operation and Alleviating Structural Imbalance*

Alleviating the supply gap of some key commodities due to structural imbalance can be tackled by following the same basic method as we have discussed above, i.e., reforming the enterprise operation mechanism to increase supply and suppress demand. How do we alleviate the shortfall of demand for some key commodities due to structural imbalance? Should we go with reforming the enterprise operation mechanism as the basic approach to suppressing supply and increasing demand as well? The answer is also positive. If enterprises are not goods producers who take responsibility for their own business decisions and operational profits and losses, or they are not restrained by the maximization of self-interest nor subject to budget constraints, no matter what quantity adjustment measures and price adjustment measures the government adopts, supply will not necessarily decrease and demand will not necessarily increase, which will not necessarily lead to lower commodity demand shortfall. In our previous analysis of the commodity demand shortfall and the counter effects of government price adjustment under economic disequilibrium conditions, we actually explained the necessity of reforming the enterprise operation mechanism. Next, we will discuss in further detail from two different perspectives, suppressing supply and increasing demand.

When the supply of some key commodities exceeds their demand, it is necessary to suppress supply. How can we suppress the supply of these commodities without impacting the income of enterprises, enterprise employees, and the government? Simply relying on the government to adopt quantity–price adjustment measures can lead to lower supply, but these measures will not be able to maintain the income of enterprises, their employees, and the government. Moreover, these adjustment measures may not necessarily be effective when the reform of the enterprise operation mechanism is not complete. In this case, we can use such measures as accelerating resource circulation or transfers to suppress the supply of the commodities that have excess inventories or experience poor sales and to provide the production units that produce shortage commodities with resources via product restructuring or industrial restructuring, which will not only reduce the supply of the products from the units that are being targeted but also grow the units that we plan to grow. Meanwhile, the income of enterprises, enterprise employees, and the government will remain intact. In order to accelerate resource circulation or transfers, it is necessary to clarify the property rights of enterprise assets and allow enterprises to be goods producers who are responsible for their business decisions and operational profits and losses. All we have discussed so far has demonstrated that it is critical to reform the enterprise operation mechanism in order to suppress the excessive supply of some key commodities.

When the supply of some key commodities exceeds their demand, it is also necessary to increase the demand for these commodities. How can we increase the demand for these commodities without aggravating the demand that has already been somewhat inflated due to structural imbalance? What kind of methods can we use to direct enterprises to consume the commodities that have excessive inventories or poor sales? It appears that one viable solution is to utilize these commodities to produce other commodities that society needs through product restructuring, industrial restructuring, and technological restructuring. All of these are closely related to the reform of the enterprise operation mechanism. If the enterprise operation mechanism is overhauled, enterprises will be restrained by the maximization of self-interest and subject to budget constraints and will be able to choose investment opportunities as well as make independent operational decisions. Consequently, they will be driven by self-interest to pursue technological improvement, merge with other businesses, or set up business alliances to utilize the commodities that have poor sales and design new products. These enterprises are motivated due to the reform of the enterprise operation mechanism, which also makes it possible for enterprises to increase the purchase of commodities that have poor sales.

Of course, while emphasizing the impact of the reform of the enterprise operation mechanism on alleviating excessive supply or excessive demand under disequilibrium conditions, we are not denying the usefulness of quantity adjustment measures and price adjustment measures that the government adopts in a particular period of time according to some specific situations. What we are trying to explain here is nothing but the following: Reforming the enterprise operation mechanism is the premise of various quantity adjustment measures and price adjustment measures. If enterprises are still affiliated with and controlled by government administrative institutions and lack the interest-maximization mechanism and budget constraints, how can quantity–price adjustment measures adopted by the government be effective in tackling supply gap or demand shortfall?

6.2.3 *The Progressive Nature of Price Reform*

The dual-track price system is a price mechanism during the transition from the old economic system to the new economic system. The transition from the dual-track price system to the mechanism of pure market price is an important condition for the establishment of the new commodity economy. The mechanism of pure market price refers to a system in which price is completely open without direct interference from the government and it is totally determined by market demand and supply, with only indirect influences from government adjustment measures.

The above analyses have revealed that the existence of the dual-track price system is traced to the existence of commodity supply gap and commodity demand shortfall, especially the commodity supply gap. We have analyzed earlier that the reasons why commodity supply gap will last for a long time and why the trend of rising price level cannot be kept in check are not only because the market is not fully developed, but more importantly because enterprises are not responsible for their business decisions and operational profits and losses. Moreover, as we have pointed out earlier that to prevent the economy from sliding into recession and prices from rising continuously in the presence of commodity and resource shortages, the government will have to take adjustment measures to reach rationing equilibrium. From these discussions, we can clearly see that the transition from the dual-track price system to the mechanism of pure market price cannot be done by simply removing price controls. The transition is dependent on three basic conditions:

The first condition: Has commodity supply gap shrunk?

The second condition: Are enterprises responsible for their business decisions and operational profits and losses or be restrained by the maximization of self-interest and subject to budget constraints?

The third condition: Has the government adopted various adjustment measures during the period of dual prices and effectively reached ex post equilibrium, or rationing equilibrium, such that the trend of rising price level has been held in check or the inflation rate has declined slightly?

These three conditions must be met. If only two of them are met and one is unmet, then it is not yet the right time to transit from the dual-track price system to pure market price. Rushing into fully removing price controls before all conditions are met will certainly cause economic fluctuations. Should we do that, it would delay the removal of price controls, forcing the dual-track price system to maintain its status quo for an extended period of time.

Keep in mind that since dual prices turn out to be a measure to achieve rationing equilibrium under the condition of commodity supply gap, it is necessary to reduce commodity supply gap if we decide to terminate the dual-track price system that is incompatible with the market economy. If commodity supply and demand are balanced, commodity supply gap will disappear, and of course dual prices will no longer be needed. However, reaching the balance between supply and demand is not easy, regardless of aggregate balance or structural balance. It is impossible for us to imagine waiting for the day when the supply and demand of commodities are balanced to come before starting the transition from the dual-track price system to pure market price. That is unrealistic. What can we do then? Generally speaking, we should force commodity supply and demand to gradually approach a balance on the aggregate basis with commodity supply gap gradually shrinking. On the structural basis, we should treat different commodities in different ways. When the supply gap and demand shortfall of certain commodities have shrunk and approached an approximate balance, it demonstrates that the dual prices for these commodities can be terminated. If the supply gap of some commodities is still fairly large, it signals that it is not yet the time to terminate their dual prices and the dual prices should remain for a longer time. In summary, when the conditions for a specific commodity are met, its price can be opened up. When the commodities of the same category are ready, their price controls can be lifted. If conditions are not met, price decontrol should be postponed. In this way, we will gradually realize the transition from the dual-track price system to pure market price.

Regardless of how large commodity supply gap and commodity demand shortfall are or which commodities have or have not met the requirements of price decontrol, deepening the reform on enterprises is critical to the termination of the dual-track price system. As we have discussed many times before, if enterprises are responsible for their business decisions and operational profits and losses, they will be able to utilize market price signals to adjust production and operation, which helps them adapt to the new economic environment after price decontrol. However, this by no means indicates that we can terminate the dual-track price system in the presence of relatively large commodity supply gap, even though enterprises are responsible for their business decisions and operational profits and losses. This is because price rises are inevitable when commodity supply gap is relatively large. If enterprises were not responsible for their business decisions or operational profits and losses, it would be very difficult to control the rising price level. The reason why the rising price level can be controlled after enterprises take responsibility for their business decisions and operational profits and losses is that they will be induced to increase supply and decrease demand to alleviate supply gap. Whether or not the rising price level can be really controlled is still dependent on the magnitude of commodity supply gap and the severity of constraints on resource. This demonstrates that allowing enterprises to make independent decisions and take responsibility for profits and losses is a necessary condition, but not the only condition, of the termination of the dual-track price system.

Let us take another look at the third condition we discussed earlier, i.e., the government makes progress in controlling the rising price level by adopting adjustment measures. Let us assume that enterprises have become independent goods producers who are responsible for their business decisions and operational profits and losses after economic reforms and that commodity supply gap has shrunk to some extent. However, prices have not been stabilized due to structural reasons. Meanwhile, government adjustment measures have not been very effective in controlling rising prices. At this time, it is not yet the time to remove price controls. The reason is that society is not completely ready for the removal of price controls nor is the state as far as its financial position is concerned. Since prices have not stabilized, removing price controls may bring about the tremor of instability, which will induce people to increase the purchase of commodities or even withdraw their savings accounts to purchase commodities as inventories. As price has not been stabilized, it is unlikely that the austerity measures adopted by the government have reached its goal. Removing price controls at this time will render government measures self-contradictory and put the government in a difficult position. Price decontrol will not only create barriers to enforcing the austerity measures but may also end up in a new situation in which fiscal revenues are unable to catch up with higher government spending after prices are opened.

Therefore, these three basic conditions discussed above are all required for the transition from the dual-track price system to pure market price. If we understand this, we can naturally understand the following four issues:

A. The transition from the dual-track price system to pure market price in China can only happen by taking baby steps, i.e., gradually removing price controls step by step. The proposal of "reaching the goal by taking one giant and final step" or "reforming prices by taking giant steps" is both unrealistic and harmful.
B. The transition from the dual-track price system to pure market price in China can only happen in accordance with the progress of the enterprise reform. The progress of the enterprise reform determines that of the price reform. The proposal of using a "breakthrough" of the price reform in the first place to jump-start other reforms (including the enterprise reform) will only throw the economy into chaos and will be harmful to pushing reforms forward.
C. The transition from the dual-track price system to pure market price in China can only be realized when the upward trend in price is under control or the downward trend in price sets in. The proposal that ignores economic environment as well as the tolerance of society and the nation's fiscal situation will not only lead to price reform failure but also disrupt overall economic reforms.
D. In light of current situations in China, the government should continue to maintain the dual-track price system and apply rationing equilibrium to shortage commodities. Although the dual-track price system and the rationing equilibrium for commodities may somewhat harm the economy, it is undoubtedly less harmful than removing price controls right now.

Everyone who studies economic theories as well as the reality of economic reforms will know that the optimal solution in an economic reform does not really exist. Such an optimal solution only exists in the mind of theorists. In real economic reforms, what happens can only be the second best, and it is also a realistic and practical solution. "Price reform first" is perhaps doable in theory. If the Chinese economy were in type I disequilibrium conditions, I would have no doubt about that. My concern is that whether or not "price reform first" is doable under type II disequilibrium conditions. The question is, if the dual-track price system is changed to pure market price while enterprises have not become independent goods producers who make their own business decisions and are responsible for their own profits and losses, how can the enterprise reform proceed? Wouldn't the enterprise reform come to a halt? Therefore, we should follow the reality and go with the second best solution, which is to "first of all shrink supply gap and then proceed with the enterprise reform and lowering inflation." We should not be fascinated by the proposal of "price reform first," which may sound very appealing according to some "research."

Reference

1. Li, Yining. (1986). *Socialist political economics* (pp. 310–312). The Commercial Press, Beijing, China.

Chapter 7
Industrial Restructuring

7.1 Domestic Source of Funding for Industrial Restructuring

7.1.1 Funding Gap and Funding Potential Under Disequilibrium Conditions

Current economic disequilibria in China have revealed that domestic funding potential cannot be ignored despite an obvious funding gap. The concurrent existence of funding gap and funding potential is one of the features of the current funding problems in China.

A funding gap refers to insufficient supply of capital. During economic growth, the demand for capital has always been very large and the supply of capital has always been limited. Limited supply of capital in the economy is not able to keep up with the demand for capital, pushing the cost of capital higher. However, because the interest elasticity of capital supply is not large and neither is the interest elasticity of capital demand, purely relying on raising interest rates will not be able to increase capital supply and decrease capital demand. As a result, funding gap is inevitable. The situation forces the financial authority to focus on the credit scale to adjust capital supply and demand in its formulation of policies. In particular, quantity adjustment in the capital market is executed by using capital rationing to meet capital supply shortages, while the adjustment of interest rate is only considered a supplementary measure. The adjustment measures adopted by the Chinese financial authority in recent years turned out exactly the way we are discussing here, i.e., quantity adjustment measures are primary and price adjustment measures are secondary. We should consider that these policies have been largely consistent with current economic disequilibrium conditions in China.

However, we should note that while funding gap and funding potential coexist, the capacity of funding potential should not be underestimated. Funding potential

Y. Li, *Chinese Economy in Disequilibrium*, China Academic Library,
DOI 10.1007/978-3-642-39558-1_7, © Foreign Language Teaching and Research Publishing Co., Ltd and Springer-Verlag Berlin Heidelberg 2014

refers to the domestic capital embedded in the economy that can be discovered but has not yet been utilized. Potential capital is seen in the form of either idle cash or noncash resources. More specifically, it has the following five forms:

First of all, the most common form is personal cash on hand. A person's cash on hand is the person's disposable income after deducting his or her consumption and savings deposit at any financial institution. The amount of cash on hand far exceeds the amount of cash reserved by residents for their daily expenditures. Why is it so? It is because of unmet personal consumption needs and lack of domestic investment instruments, besides just a few available forms of assets such as cash, certificates of deposit, and bonds. In other words, insufficient supply of consumer goods and the lack of personal investment opportunities give rise to potential capital.

The second form of potential capital is petty cash on the hands of small business owners and private enterprises. Small business owners and private enterprises are business operators, and their petty cash on hand is different from personal cash on hand. They are reluctant to continue investing cash in production, as they are uncertain about whether they should expand production and operation or reinvest in their businesses. The amount of cash that is not invested in production is likely to be diverted into consumption and become exorbitant and extravagant spending or be reserved for new opportunities.

The third form of potential capital is cash or inventory that enterprises reserve above and beyond the needs of normal business operation. This refers to an excessive amount of petty cash, raw materials, fuel, or parts that are well above the normal quantity. In the presence of commodity supply gap and capital funding gap, enterprises tend to maintain above-normal cash and inventories out of precaution or for fear of supply interruption or sustained inflation. Regardless of whether it is petty cash or inventory materials that enterprises maintain, capital is unreasonably tied in that form of asset as long as it is above the normal level, which will worsen the capital supply shortages in the economy. If we can persuade enterprises to maintain cash and inventory materials below the normal level, it will be equivalent to decreasing the demand for capital and increasing the supply of capital. Besides enterprises, small business owners and private enterprises sometimes also keep inventory supplies above the normal level. By the same token, that residents store excessive consumer goods (with the purpose of protecting against supply interruption or rising prices) signals that capital is utilized unreasonably.

The fourth form of potential capital is represented by relatively low capital utilization efficiency. Given a fixed amount of total capital supply in the economy, the more inefficiently capital is utilized, the tighter the capital supply will be. In addition, if capital turnover slows down, capital supply will become tight. This demonstrates that given the total amount of capital supply, relatively low capital utilization efficiency and slow capital turnover have both revealed some funding potential. This conclusion tells us that as long as we can increase capital utilization efficiency by diverting capital from where utilization efficiency is relatively low to areas with relatively high utilization efficiency and accelerate capital turnover, we will be able to alleviate the capital supply gap and the imbalance between capital supply and demand.

The fifth form of potential capital is noncash resources. For example, idle labor or production facilities indicate that potential capital exists in the form of noncash resources. If idle labor and production facilities are put into use, we can generate additional income, part of which will become savings that will in turn be diverted into investment. In this way, noncash potential capital can be turned into real capital in the form of cash. The addition of capital is conducive to alleviating the imbalance between capital supply and demand.

The five points discussed above have led to this conclusion: While we need to pay attention to the funding gap under current economic disequilibrium conditions in China, we cannot ignore domestic funding potential. Both economic growth and industrial restructuring require a relatively large amount of capital. If we see only funding gap but fail to see funding potential, we will likely come up with an overly pessimistic assessment of the situation of domestic capital supply and demand.

7.1.2 Main Approaches to Discovering Domestic Funding Potential

Recognizing the coexistence of funding gap and funding potential will help us formulate the right policies for industrial restructuring.

How to discover domestic funding potential? We can come up with some detailed measures according to the five different situations discussed earlier. The measures available to us are discussed in detail as follows:

First of all, in order to increase the personal savings rate and reduce as much personal cash on hand as possible, we should create more personal investment opportunities, particularly using the equity market as an investment vehicle to reduce cash on hand.

Secondly, in order to encourage small business owners and private enterprises to reinvest, and so as to reduce their cash on hand or to turn the portion of cash on hand that has been designated for exorbitant and extravagant consumption into production funds, we should introduce appropriate policies to strengthen their confidence in investment as well as property ownership rights.

Thirdly, we should try to eliminate enterprises' concerns over supply interruption or sustained inflation so that they no longer have to maintain above-normal cash and inventory and can instead utilize their capital appropriately. Therefore, we should apply measures to increase the supply of raw materials, fuel, and parts, develop the trading of commodity futures, and reduce the impact of rising prices on normal business activities. These measures will in turn reduce capital demand from enterprises.

Fourthly, in order to increase capital utilization efficiency in society, accelerate capital turnover, and minimize capital deployment by society, we should appropriately adjust the direction and structure of capital deployment by diverting the capital that is utilized less efficiently to the production areas where capital is utilized more efficiently. Meanwhile, we should adopt various measures to accelerate capital turnover, such as improving technologies, shortening manufacturing cycles, organizing balanced production, accelerating the transportation and distribution of finished products, and collecting accounts receivables in a timely manner.

Fifthly, in order to fully utilize idle labor and production facilities to create additional income and increase savings, we should adopt various measures to promote the circulation and recombination of production factors. These measures will help turn potential noncash capital into real cash capital.

From the above discussions, we can understand that as long as appropriate measures are adopted, potential capital can be discovered. The five measures we discussed above can be summarized into the following two points: On the one hand, we should continue pushing economic reforms forward to discover funding potential; on the other hand, we should rely on various measures that aim to adjust product structure, industrial structure, regional economic structure, consumption structure, and technological structure so that we can increase capital utilization efficiency and reduce unreasonable capital utilization.

The economic reforms hereby referred to cover many areas. In terms of financial reforms, the focus should be placed on allowing the establishment of various financial institutions and the commercialization of state-owned commercial banks. Establishing various financial institutions will help absorb idle capital from society and facilitate the transformation of savings into investment. The commercialization of state-owned commercial banks will not only significantly improve capital utilization efficiency and reduce inappropriate capital deployment but also mobilize and encourage banks to absorb and utilize idle capital in society. Moreover, financial reforms will accelerate the development of the capital market and contribute to the formation of a perfect capital market. Based on how the capital market is developed and perfected, we can gradually remove the controls over interest rate so that it can adjust to changing supply and demand in the capital market.

In terms of the reform of the enterprise operation mechanism, the most important measure applicable to discovering funding potential is to turn enterprises into goods producers who make their own business decisions and are responsible for operational profits and losses and to set up a shareholding system for appropriate enterprises. Recognizing enterprises as independent decision-makers who take responsibility for their own profits and losses will help enterprises save capital and avoid unnecessary capital deployment, hence increasing capital utilization efficiency. To set up the shareholding system by way of stock offering can not only absorb idle capital from society and divert the capital raised to production but also encourage corporate mergers and acquisitions or the formation of business alliances, helping recombine production factors and direct the capital in society to the development of production capacity for the benefit of the economy. These measures are essential to discovering funding potential.

Reforming the social security system will also help discover funding potential. One of the main purposes of the reform is to change the old way of purely relying on the state to provide social security and to establish a social security system that mainly relies on individuals themselves, i.e., a social security system that consists of personal savings, corporate contributions, and state subsidies. Through the reform, pension funds and various social security and welfare funds will have significant amount of capital under management. These funds can be allocated to where they are needed to alleviate the shortages of capital supplies in society.

We cannot underestimate the importance of investment system reform to the mobilization of idle capital in society and the efficient utilization of capital. We should do the following: Establish and perfect the system of fixed asset investment funds, arranging investment according to capital position and leverage funds provided by the state to pay the interest of the capital collected from society and so as to attract more capital; at the same time, the government should no longer concern itself with the details of operational investment projects, but delegate them to commercial investment companies, who are both investors and future operators of these projects. These commercial investment companies will sell or lease the projects once they are completed, contract with other companies to perform project management, or structure them into a subsidiary by issuing stocks to the public. These measures will effectively contribute to the efficient utilization and payback of investment capital.

The series of economic reforms discussed above are the basic approaches to resolving the capital supply and demand imbalance under the current condition of insufficient capital supply.

Next, we will discuss how to discover funding potential in terms of adjustment measures targeting product structure, industrial structure, regional economic structure, consumption structure, and technological structure.

7.1.3 Restructuring Versus Increasing Capital Utilization Efficiency

We still have to start this topic by discussing type II disequilibrium.

If the market is not fully developed and enterprises are not motivated, it will be very difficult to execute restructuring plans (including the adjustments to not only product structure and industrial structure but also regional economic structure, consumption structure, and technological structure), and the attempt to discover funding potential via restructuring will also be fruitless. It is from this perspective that we consider pushing economic reforms forward and encouraging restructuring by means of economic reform the basic approach to discovering funding potential in China. We have discussed this point previously.

Undoubtedly, if economic reforms proceed smoothly, the financial system, the enterprise system, the social security system, and the investment system will all be changed fundamentally and the market will gradually become perfect. Under such circumstances, restructuring will accelerate and capital utilization efficiency will improve. The question we have is: If economic reforms are still in progress without making any fundamental changes in the underdeveloped market, will it be impossible to proceed with restructuring, which is relatively important to us, or is it absolutely impossible to increase capital utilization efficiency via restructuring? The answer is: Not necessarily. We cannot wait until after the completion of economic reforms before carrying out restructuring. If we did that, we would lose time. By the same token, we cannot wait until everything is ready before proceeding with increasing capital utilization efficiency via restructuring, or we would be struggling with tight capital supply. The right thing to do is to coordinate economic reforms and restructuring so that both can move forward and work together to discover domestic funding potential, increase capital utilization efficiency, and alleviate capital supply and demand imbalance.

In this circumstance, an applicable restructuring measure is quantity adjustment by the government, which mainly includes the adjustment of credit quantity and the adjustment to the rationing of scarce production materials that are intended to increase capital supply and decrease inefficient capital utilization. This does not mean that quantity adjustment performed by the government is the best alternative that supports restructuring. At least it is a practical choice in these circumstances.

The adjustment of credit quantity mainly refers to the changes to the quantitative credit structure initiated by the government in accordance with its goals, provided that the total credit scale is under control, with the purpose of changing product structure, industrial structure, regional economic structure, consumption structure, and technological structure. Restructuring credit quantity is to terminate credit support for those enterprises or units who generate low economic returns or those who demonstrate low capital utilization efficiency and to redirect capital to those enterprises or units that have high economic returns or capital utilization efficiency. Meanwhile, restructuring credit quantity is to adjust economic development across different regions, initiate changes to the structure of personal consumption, and facilitate the coordination of the technological structure with the economy. All these measures will be conducive to gradually realizing the government's restructuring plan. Although the adjustment of credit quantity will not tackle the fundamental issues of the enterprise operation mechanism or the banking system, it will still be very effective during economic reforms when the interest rate elasticity of investment is relatively low and the supply gap in the capital market is relatively large, which prevents interest rates from floating freely in a short period of time.

Ration adjustment of scarce production materials can be determined by the target principle, which is used by the government to allocate the quota for scarce production materials (such as electricity, nonferrous metal, and certain chemicals) in order to support the sectors that can help alleviate the supply gap, utilize idle labor and production materials more efficiently, and restrict the growth of those enterprises that have low capital utilization efficiency. Ration adjustment of scarce production materials will not only impact product structure and industrial structure but also directly or indirectly accelerate the adjustment of regional economic structure, consumption structure, and technological structure. Although ration adjustment of scarce production materials does not tackle the fundamental issues of the economic system and to some extent even prevents the market from working, which may hinder competition among enterprises, we cannot ignore its importance to the economy in alleviating the insufficiency of capital supply in the current economic situations. We have to keep in mind that quantity adjustment measures (including quota adjustment of scarce production materials) are more powerful than price adjustment measures when supply and demand mismatch is relatively severe, which happens to be one of the features of the disequilibrium economy. Moreover, our main task at the moment is to discover funding potential and increase the supply of domestic capital. To this end, we must cut investment in those enterprises or sectors that have low capital utilization efficiency and increase investment in those that have relatively high capital utilization efficiency. While we are trying to reach this goal via restructuring, quantity adjustment can also play a more significant role than price adjustment. Some of the side effects of quantity adjustment (e.g., dampening the motivation of some enterprises, thus putting certain enterprises and sectors in a difficult position) can only be regarded as the inevitable costs of restructuring and the alleviation of capital supply insufficiency. They are acceptable as long as benefits exceed costs.

From the government's perspective, there will always be potential side effects that come along with the adjustment, whether it is credit quantity adjustment or the ration adjustment of scarce production materials. Therefore, it is necessary to try our best to reduce these side effects. The government can do the following:

A. Determining the restructuring goals and action plans in a more scientific way by trying to avoid making blind decisions as much as possible and collecting sufficient information to support credit quantity adjustment and the ration adjustment of scarce production materials.
B. Upon determining the restructuring goals and action plans, having the government departments responsible for the execution of credit quantity adjustment and the ration adjustment of scarce production materials strictly stick to the rules set by the government and banning any action in pursuit of illegal personal benefits in the name of quantity adjustment.
C. Introducing a dual-track credit system or a dual-track distribution system for certain production materials. To some extent, this can mitigate the disadvantages of quantity adjustment. The dual-track credit system refers to a system in which the market provides credit in addition to the government adjustment of credit quantity. Credit provided by the market allows interest rates of deposits and loans to be set by the market, and the government only sets the upper limit on floating interest rates. Under the dual-track credit system, the government should strictly prohibit any fund loaned to enterprises via the adjustment of credit quantity from entering into the market. Otherwise, there will be new problems. The dual-track distribution system for certain production materials refers to a system in which the production materials with various degrees of scarcity can be distributed partly by ration adjustment and partly by open-market transactions executed in the production material market, except for some extremely rare and vital production materials that are completely controlled by the government via ration adjustment. The price for open-market transactions is determined by the market, and the government can choose whether or not to set a price ceiling. The ratio of distribution by ration adjustment to distribution via open-market transactions depends on the scarcity of a particular production material.

7.1.4 The Relationship Between Industrial Restructuring and Economic Growth During the Mobilization of Domestic Capital

Economic growth requires additional input of capital, and so does industrial restructuring. With limited supply of domestic capital, if more additional capital is committed to economic growth, capital allocated to industrial restructuring will have to be lessened. The conflict that arises during the distribution of additional capital is real. Of course, if more domestic funding potential is discovered at time of capital supply shortages, tight capital supply can be somewhat alleviated. However, newly mobilized capital will face the same issue, i.e., how should it be allocated between economic growth and industrial restructuring. Thus, we still need to decide on who gets more capital and who gets less.

Between economic growth and industrial restructuring, we can neither prefer one to another nor emphasize only one of them. The reason is that if we only emphasize economic growth and ignore industrial restructuring, economic growth under the current industrial structure will encounter more and more difficulties and we will face the coexistence of supply gap and demand shortfall of some production factors during economic growth, which will lower economic growth rate and cause subsequent structural imbalances. On the contrary, if we only emphasize industrial restructuring and ignore economic growth, industrial restructuring will falter. One of the reasons why industrial restructuring will falter is that lowering economic growth will mothball some production factors, thus lowering enterprises income, personal income, and fiscal income and hindering industrial restructuring from following the goals set by the government.

Therefore, the choice that we have is to balance economic growth and industrial restructuring and to carry out industrial restructuring during economic growth and maintain continuous economic growth by means of industrial restructuring. Specifically, to execute industrial restructuring during economic growth refers to the following: While maintaining an economic growth rate similar to the past, we will increase the percentage of the output from new industrial sectors in aggregate output and decrease the percentage of the output from traditional industrial sectors in aggregate output (as the absolute value of the output from traditional industrial sectors may remain unchanged or change slightly). To maintain economic growth by means of industrial restructuring refers to the following: While the percentage of output from traditional industrial sectors in aggregate output keeps declining, the economic growth engine will mainly rely on higher absolute value of the output from new industrial sectors as well as its rising share in aggregate output. Obviously, to balance economic growth and industrial restructuring requires production factors to circulate and recombine. It is also related to the redistribution of capital among various sectors as well as the guidance on societal consumption, savings, and investment.

The key point that we need to focus on here is how economic growth and industrial restructuring are related to mobilizing domestic capital. If the government mobilizes domestic capital by means of voluntary savings, e.g., adjusting interest rates and giving favorable tax treatment to investment to encourage people to increase the share of income allocated to savings and investment, the way that newly discovered domestic capital is actually distributed between new and traditional industrial sectors will depend to a large extent on the differential interest rates and preferential investment tax treatment. The government can determine the differential interest rates and preferential investment tax treatment at a high level according to the current situation and the target model of the industrial structure as well as the probability of economic growth and historical economic growth rates. In summary, mobilizing domestic capital by means of voluntary savings and distributing capital among various sectors appropriately will lead to fewer hurdles, if any, than other ways. If any hurdle does arise, it may originate from the traditional values behind consumption and savings (i.e., people may or may not react to the changes in interest rates or preferential investment tax treatment and correspondingly change their consumption and savings behavior by raising savings rate and increasing the propensity to invest) or from the financing capability of financial institutions (i.e., they may or may not be capable of effectively and efficiently discovering idle capital in society and using the capital to support the development of new industrial sectors).

If the government tries to discover domestic funding potential by means of compulsory savings in an attempt to mobilize domestic capital, for instance, forcing people to buy government bonds, raising direct and indirect tax rates and increasing the prices of some consumer goods, or lowering the level of cash amount that enterprises are required to hold with the purpose of raising additional capital to be invested in new industrial sectors, we will have the following two outcomes. Firstly, the government will be able to raise a certain amount of cash fairly quickly and allocate the capital to various areas and sectors according to its predetermined goals. On the other hand, as this way of raising funds is to mandatorily change personal consumption behavior and directly interfere with how enterprises conduct businesses and distribute income, personal and business motivation may be hurt, economic growth may be influenced, and business growth may be interrupted, which may hurt economic growth. Therefore, even if the government is not absolutely prohibited from using compulsory savings to raise capital during the process of mobilizing domestic capital, it must act appropriately. Otherwise, it will be difficult to balance economic growth and industrial restructuring.

However, we should realize that both voluntary savings and compulsory savings are acceptable as long as they help support industrial restructuring during the process of pursuing economic growth and maintaining sustained economic growth through industrial restructuring. As the economic regulator, the government has to manage voluntary savings and compulsory savings according to the specific situations at different times. Voluntary savings play a more powerful role in motivating individuals and businesses, while compulsory savings, if used appropriately and accounting for appropriate ratio, can raise capital fairly quickly to help promote economic growth and restructure industries. Given the current situations in China, how to manage voluntary savings and compulsory savings in such a way that balances economic growth and industrial restructuring is an important topic on which we need to do further research.

7.2 Industrial Restructuring and Long-Term Orientation of Corporate Behavior

7.2.1 *Main Reasons for Corporate Shortsightedness and Impediments to Industrial Restructuring*

We know that corporate behavior consists of the decisions related to input, output, and income distribution. Whether an enterprise is focused on only its short-term interests is related to the economic benefits it receives from its input, output, and income distribution decisions. If an enterprise is uncertain about its self-interest, it does not care about any long-term benefit from its decisions on input, output, and income distribution. Instead, it will focus on its short-term interests, thus giving rise to corporate shortsightedness. Under the traditional economic system, an enterprise was nothing but a subordinate of its administrative institution, and the interests of its superior administrative department superseded its own interests. The senior management of an enterprise included officials dispatched by its superior administrative department. They followed every instruction from its superior administrative department that managed every specific area. Decisions on input, output, and income distribution were not made by the enterprise itself, and its self-interest related to input, output, and income distribution had no direct impact on the enterprise itself. It is hard to judge whether the behavior of enterprises under the traditional economic system was long-term oriented or shortsighted. We can even objectively say that this issue is not relevant. The reason is this: If a superior administrative department had long-term considerations and arrangements, an enterprise would exhibit long-term-oriented behavior when making decisions on input, output, and income distribution; if a superior administrative department had short-term considerations and arrangements, an enterprise's decisions on input, output, and income distribution would certainly focus on short-term interests. An enterprise as of that time is not yet a real corporation.

After the subcontracting system was implemented during economic reforms, enterprises were given rights to make their own decisions on input, output, and income distribution during the subcontracting period. But these decisions obviously reflected the shortsightedness of corporate behavior. For example, subcontractors were unwilling to make an investment that would generate long-term returns, especially an investment that brought no returns but only inputs in the short term. Rather than caring about the fixed assets of an enterprise and keeping them well maintained, a subcontractor would try to utilize the assets to the fullest to get every penny out of them. In terms of earnings distribution, they tend to ignore reinvestment and instead try as hard as possible to satisfy their employees' request for higher compensation. All of these are symptoms of corporate shortsightedness. The nature of the subcontracting system demonstrates that corporate shortsightedness is unavoidable. Of course, there are measures to improve the subcontracting system. These measures, for example, include using a comprehensive index of net income and total taxes paid, not just a single index, to evaluate business performance, appropriately extending the term of a subcontracting period or favoring current contractor at contract renewal according to specific business operational situations, and compensating incumbent subcontractors during the subcontracting period for any investment that produced long-term returns and allowing incumbent subcontractors to receive a portion of future benefits. These measures can overcome some of the shortcomings related to the corporate shortsightedness arising from the subcontracting system, but they are still unable to totally eliminate corporate shortsightedness. This is exactly the defect that the subcontracting system fails to overcome.

It is not difficult to understand why corporate shortsightedness is detrimental to economic growth, as has been revealed by the fact that economic efficiency fails to grow sustainably or may even continue to decline and that the size of corporate investment is subject to constraints. In other words, business investment rate is hardly maintained at the existing level due to the shortsightedness of decisions on distributing corporate income and also exhibits a downward trend. We know that economic growth depends on two basic factors, investment rate and investment result. Maintaining a certain economic growth rate requires not only a stable investment rate but also relatively good results from the investment. Given the corporate shortsightedness, low economic efficiency and the downward trend in investment rate will surely reduce the potentiality of economic growth, which is worrisome.

In that case, it is easy to imagine the difficulty in performing industrial restructuring. From the enterprise perspective, they do not care about developing new industrial sectors because they, as subcontractors, only care about their short-term interests. And they do not have sufficient capital to develop new industrial sectors either. In addition, production factors were not allowed to flow freely under the subcontracting system, and there were also many economic constraints on the optimization and recombination of production factors. This shows that the subcontracting system is incapable of aligning enterprise decisions on input, output, and income distribution with the needs of industrial restructuring, even though subcontractors understand the importance of industrial restructuring and know that more investment in new industrial sectors will benefit enterprises themselves as well as the national economy. From a macroeconomic perspective, because macroeconomy is based on microeconomy, the shortsightedness of microeconomic units makes it difficult for the economy to achieve higher efficiency and may even lead to lower efficiency. Therefore, the amount of capital allocated to industrial restructuring by the government is obviously insufficient. Industrial restructuring needs fiscal support. When enterprises themselves are incapable of changing current industrial structure, fiscal support becomes particularly important. However, the insufficient funds that the government can tap into limit its capability of realizing the predetermined industrial restructuring goals.

Of course, the difficulties in carrying out industrial restructuring in the current economic environment in China are not only due to corporate shortsightedness. The market is not fully developed, there are obstacles to the free flow of production factors and shortage of some key production materials, goods are not priced reasonably, and new industrial sectors lack technological capabilities. These situations make it even more difficult to carry out industrial restructuring. In spite of many other reasons, corporate shortsightedness is an important one that we cannot ignore. In addition, some of the abovementioned reasons that hinder industrial restructuring are also related to corporate shortsightedness. For example, an underdeveloped market and unreasonable prices for comparable commodities surely forced enterprises under the subcontracting system to focus only on their short-term interests, which in turn made it very difficult for the market to fully develop and impossible for unreasonable commodity prices to turn around to bring on additional supplies. As another example, the free flow of production factors encountered obstacles, some key production materials experienced shortages, and new industrial sectors lacked sufficient technological capabilities. All these factors were not only influenced by the shortsightedness of enterprises that adopted the subcontracting system but also responsible for causing corporate shortsightedness. It is hard to imagine enterprises that adopt the subcontracting system and care only about its short-term interests would invest a large amount of capital in a major investment project that brings long-term benefits and develops future technological capabilities. They simply would not do that.

7.2.2 Investors' Interests Functioning as Internal Constraint on Corporate Shortsightedness

Now, we have to clarify a theoretical issue: Wouldn't corporate shortsightedness be constrained by the corporate operation mechanism? Why does the subcontracting system fail to eliminate corporate shortsightedness, while the shareholding system is capable of balancing short-term interests with long-term interests? We should clearly point out that any enterprise that adopts the subcontracting system is not really constrained by its investors' interests. If the interests of the subcontractee were supposed to be aligned with that of the investor, it would only manifest during the competitive bidding process, during which the subcontractee can select a subcontractor from multiple bidders that best fits his or her interests. After the completion of the bidding process, it would be difficult to leverage the investors' interests to constrain the shortsightedness of the subcontractor. In addition, when property rights are not normalized and the government is not separated from enterprise, a subcontractor per se may still be affiliated with and controlled by a government institution and is not yet an entity that makes its own business decisions and is responsible for its profits and losses. Therefore, investors' interests do not really function as a constraint even during the process of soliciting bidders to bid for a contract.

The shareholding system is drastically different. An enterprise under the shareholding system that we are discussing here refers to a normal corporation that has shareholders and is established on the basis of public ownership. The interests of various investors, including the central government, local governments, and state-owned enterprises, are fully manifested. This is because every investor expects two types of income from an investment in a shareholding enterprise, dividend and capital appreciation. Between these two types of income, the latter is likely to be more important and attractive than the former. If an investor has a few alternative investment opportunities to choose from, he or she will compare both the first and second type of income from different shareholding enterprises. If one enterprise has a higher dividend rate but lower expected capital appreciation, as compared with another enterprise that comes with a lower dividend rate but higher expected capital appreciation, an investor will more than likely choose to purchase the stock of the latter enterprise. The investor would think in the following way: If the purpose of the investment is purely to receive dividend rather than equity appreciation, why do I only invest in a stock? Wouldn't it be more reliable to invest in bonds or certificates of deposit that pay interest without equity investment risks? It is these investment considerations and the ensuing investment decisions that urge a shareholding enterprise to carefully formulate its long-term growth strategy and operating policy.

In this circumstance, a shareholding enterprise must pay attention to how to accumulate capital and reinvest, unlike those operating under the subcontracting system that try to pay out as many dividends as possible. By the same token, shareholding enterprises, unlike their peers under the subcontracting system that try to deplete all resources and skip equipment maintenance, must focus on technological innovation, try to develop new products, and tap into new markets so that business can grow. Only by doing so can they achieve share appreciation and attract more investors. Otherwise, investors who own the stock would sell off their holdings and instead purchase the stock of other enterprises that have higher growth potential and expected share appreciation. This is how investors' interests function as the constraint on corporate shortsightedness.

Hence, the decision-maker of a shareholding enterprise must consider both long-term and short-term interests. A shareholding enterprise cannot afford ignoring the importance of capital accumulation and retained earnings reinvestment to its survival. If it does not have enough growth potential, it may appear unattractive to investors, even though it still pays relatively large dividends or maintains a relatively high dividend payout ratio. What an enterprise operating under the subcontracting system lacks the most is exactly the constraint on the shortsightedness imposed by the self-interest of its investors. If such an enterprise is not transformed into a shareholding enterprise, corporate shortsightedness cannot be eliminated.

7.2.3 *Investors' Interests Functioning as External Constraint on Corporate Shortsightedness*

The constraint that investors' interests impose on corporate shortsightedness as we discussed in the above section can be called internal constraint, because it arises from the selection of investment opportunities by equity investors. Next, we will discuss a different constraint, i.e., corporate mergers and acquisitions, one that exists in reality and can control corporate shortsightedness. This can be called the external constraint that investors' interests impose on corporate shortsightedness.

We have to know that in a competitive market, every enterprise falls into its competitors' radar screen. Let us assume that a shareholding enterprise realizes a 10 % rate of return, which its management may be happy about. However, its competitor may reach a different conclusion after analyzing the enterprise's current status and business prospect. For instance, the competitor may come to the viewpoint that "it is totally possible to reach a 30 % rate of return based on its current technology and equipment, employee quality, business reputation, business contacts, and product sales." The enterprise that is capable of achieving a 30 % rate of return only achieves 10 %. This reveals that it has earning potential, but its current management is incompetent and lacks sufficient operational and managerial skills. Accordingly, the competitor can start purchasing the stock in the market or even launch a hostile takeover campaign. After the competitor has gathered enough shares, a takeover will take place. It will reshuffle the board of directors of the acquiree and reelect its chief executive officer. The enterprise will be managed in a different way to increase profitability and reach the expected rate of return of 30 %.

This demonstrates that as long as the market is competitive, any shareholding enterprise operates in an environment in which it is not only a potential takeover target but also a possible acquiring enterprise. Listing shares on a stock exchange makes mergers and acquisitions possible. Those enterprises that are poorly managed or even those who have earning potential but fail to fully discover it are likely to be taken over by their competitors. Those that are well managed can grow their business by pursuing mergers and acquisitions. This also reveals that a shareholding enterprise, if it wishes to survive in a competitive market, will have to balance its short-term and long-term interests, try its best to improve management and optimize business operations, and maintain a decent earnings retention rate, reinvestment amount, and dividend payout rate. Only after it captures all potential profits as well as reaches the goals of profitability, earnings retention, and the reinvestment for future growth can it retain current investors and avoid being taken over. On the contrary, if a shareholding enterprise only pays attention to its short-term interests and develops severe shortsightedness, its competitors will notice that its operation and development are on a wrong track. They will work on a plan to take it over, reenergize its growth, and redevelop an operational plan. As a result, they will benefit from the long-term growth and profit from share appreciation.

Here, we can clearly see that the internal and external constraints on shareholding enterprises due to investors' interests are closely connected and work at the same time. From an internal perspective, investors will sell off the shares of any enterprise that fails to support share appreciation or maximize potential profits and invest in other enterprises instead. From an external perspective, the competitors of such enterprise will consider purchasing its shares and launching a takeover. The internal and external constraints arising from investors' interests exert influence at the same time. Every shareholding enterprise will face the following choice: either continuing to focus on short-term interests while ignoring long-term interests and bearing the risk of being acquired or changing its growth strategy and operational plan to balance its long-term and short-term interests while improving business operations and management, increasing reinvestment, and continuing to pursue business growth.

7.2.4 Long-Term-Oriented Corporate Behavior and Rationalization of Industrial Restructuring

The growth of macroeconomic productivity is directly linked to the emphases that enterprises place on capital accumulation, technological innovations, and the discovery of manufacturing and operational potential. All of these will certainly contribute to the rationalization of industrial restructuring.

We will analyze the relationship between long-term-oriented corporate behavior and the rationalization of industrial restructuring from the following three aspects:

First of all, when enterprises place emphasis on long-term development strategy and operational plan, they will certainly adjust earnings distribution, determine reasonable dividend payout, and increase the retention of internal capital. In this way, the tight capital supply, a major issue troubling the economy, can be alleviated. Regardless of how an enterprise invests in a new industry, using retained earnings or fiscal or financial support, the result is conducive to industrial restructuring.

Secondly, advancing technology, improving labor quality, regularly maintaining equipment, as well as increasing capital accumulation, all of which result from long-term-oriented corporate behavior, will enhance the potential of economic growth. Enhanced potential of business growth indicates enhanced potential of economic growth, thus ensuring sustainable economic growth. As we know, the industrial restructuring during sustained economic growth will be much easier than that during economic slowdown or recession. In other words, the industrial restructuring in an environment that promotes long-term-oriented corporate behavior will be much easier than that in an environment dominated by corporate shortsightedness.

Thirdly, industrial restructuring assumes that production factors can be circulated and recombined. If enterprises adopt the shareholding system, corporate shortsightedness will be constrained by investors' interests. Meanwhile, the shareholding system will support the circulation and recombination of production factors. It is in this sense that we conclude that long-term-oriented corporate behavior and the rationalization of industrial restructuring are closely related.

Based on the discussions above, we can reach the following conclusion: Long-term-oriented corporate behavior or corporate shortsightedness is not an issue that is only related to long-term corporate growth or the fate of a corporation but more of a strategic issue that concerns economic growth and industrial restructuring.

If we dive a little deeper into the issue, it will not be difficult for us to find out that long-term-oriented corporate behavior and the rationalization of industrial restructuring are linked to efficiency.

Efficiency refers to the degree of effectiveness of resource allocation and utilization. When we say a nation, region, sector, or enterprise has relatively high efficiency, we refer to a nation, region, sector, or enterprise where resources are reasonably allocated and effectively utilized, with every kind of resource put to use. If we say someone has relatively high efficiency, we mean that the person tries his or her best or does what he or she is capable of and coordinates seamlessly with other resources, such as production materials and labor (including his or her coworkers). This is also related to the efficiency of resource allocation and utilization. Now, we have to think about this question: Where does efficiency come from?

In terms of resource allocation and utilization, efficiency comes from three aspects: motivation, quality, and environment. Human resources are the most important resource among all and are represented by the labor force. To achieve relatively high efficiency, the labor force must be motivated. If an enterprise is regarded as an entity consisting of a group of individuals, its production and operation must be driven by motivation, and every member of the entity must also have motivation in order to achieve relatively high efficiency. Motivation varies. They can be economic or noneconomic, such as social responsibility, personal career ambitions, and personal interest or hobbies. In any case, motivation is critical to efficiency.

Efficiency also comes from quality. By quality, we mainly refer to the quality of people. People of high quality can enhance the quality of materials, even when the materials are of relatively low quality. People of high quality can gradually replace the materials of low quality with ones of high quality. The quality of people, including knowledge and technology skills, operational skills, innovation skills, mentality, and moral integrity, also varies. It is less likely for people of low quality to achieve relatively high efficiency.

Efficiency also comes from the environment. People live and work in a certain environment. An enterprise that consists of a group of people also operates in a certain environment. If the environment restricts the motivation of people and enterprise or influences the quality of people or the environment prohibits people from renovating low-quality materials, such environment will not support but limit or kill high efficiency.

We can learn from our discussions that the relatively low efficiency of resource allocation and combination in China is due to relatively poor motivation, quality, and environment. Regarding corporate shortsightedness, a hot topic nowadays, we should ask why enterprises tend to act only out of their short-term interests. If we look at it from the motivation perspective, isn't it because enterprises themselves lack the motivation to operate and grow for the long run and enterprise employees also lack the motivation to work hard for the long run? If we look at it from the quality perspective, isn't it because enterprises themselves lack the quality to organize and achieve major technological innovations and enterprise employees also lack the quality to achieve major technological and managerial breakthrough? If we look at it from the environment perspective, isn't it because the current environment in which enterprise employees live and work stifles people's motivation and prevents the enhancement of personal quality? Since all three conditions, motivation, quality, and environment, are the way they are, how can enterprises avoid shortsightedness?

Let us look at the industrial structural imbalance that is often discussed and ask why the industrial structure is out of balance and whether it is hard to turn it around in a short time. If we look at the structural imbalance from the motivation perspective, isn't it related to the lack of motivation to recombine production factors as well as the lack of motivation to develop new products and new industries? From the quality perspective, even though we try to turn industrial structural imbalance around in a relatively short period of time, the quality of enterprise employees as well as enterprises themselves are not up to the standard, nor are macroeconomic management institutions staffed with quality personnel who are capable of developing and managing new industries. If we look at it from the environment perspective, a series of issues regarding industrial restructuring are traced back to the environment, including the issues concerning the supply of capital, labor, technology and information, infrastructure, tax and price, and especially property rights. If these issues concerning the environment are not resolved properly, it will still be difficult to proceed with industrial restructuring despite the high quality of enterprises themselves or of their employees.

Therefore, based on the research on corporate behavior and industrial restructuring, we are very clear about the solution to the issue of efficiency. We must systematically resolve the issues concerning motivation, quality, and environment that are related to the creation and increase of efficiency. Only after we resolve these issues can corporate shortsightedness be transformed into long-term-oriented behavior and the industrial structure be gradually rationalized, thus bringing along high efficiency.

7.2.5 Resource Allocation and Long-Term-Oriented Societal Behavior

After we redirect the focus of our research from corporate behavior to societal behavior, and from analyzing the industrial structure to analyzing the economic structure, we will find out that the low efficiency currently in China is not only due to corporate and societal shortsightedness but also due to industrial and economic structural imbalance. This is exactly the issue at which we need to take another look.

Societal shortsightedness means that the behavior of all walks of life in society, in addition to the behavior of enterprises and their employees, focuses on short-term interests, and even the behavior of some government institutions follows the same pattern. For example, peasants are not willing to grow crops to produce food, students are not willing to study hard in school, and private business owners are not willing to reinvest, all of which demonstrate behavioral shortsightedness. Moreover, the leaders of some government institutions are satisfied with the current situation and fail to have long-term consideration. Some families constantly feel that they are living in uncertainties and are unclear about their future. These examples are all reflective of behavioral shortsightedness. With regard to this issue, I will analyze in further detail in the section on institutional innovation. For now, I will withhold more detailed discussions but only talk about the relationship among economic structure, resource allocation, and societal behavior.

The fundamental cause of societal shortsightedness is the lack of certainty of people's expectations for society. To most enterprises, enterprise employees, peasants, students, private business owners, and government officers, the future is full of uncertainties and very difficult to predict. All sorts of social and economic uncertainties lead people to focus on their short-term interests and to take action without long-term consideration. A society that mainly focuses on short-term interests is one without efficiency and one with ineffective resource allocation and utilization. If we base our analysis on the three aspects we discussed earlier, motivation, quality, and environment, we can reach the same conclusion: Societal shortsightedness is traced to the uncertainty of expectations, which is due to environmental constraints and lack of motivation and required quality. Among various environmental constraints, the most important one is abnormal property rights, which negatively impact economic activities and restrict the motivation of every entity in society. If property rights are normalized, business expectations will stabilize to some extent and businesses will feel motivated at least during the process of business transactions, which may facilitate the transformation from societal shortsightedness to long-term orientation. Of course, it is not enough to merely normalize property rights. Nonetheless, we cannot deny that it is after all the basic solution to societal shortsightedness and it is especially important to China at this time.

When we redirect our discussions on the industrial structure to those on the economic structure, we will see that relatively ineffective resource allocation and utilization is related to not only industrial structural imbalance but also economic structural imbalance. The economic structural imbalance manifests in the following ways: In terms of ownership structure, cooperative businesses that are more conducive to mobilizing workers and real collective businesses account for a relatively small percentage in the aggregate economy. In terms of regional economic structure, regional advantages are constrained, economic cooperation and specialization among different regions are hindered, and more developed regions that should play a larger role in the economy are restricted in various ways and are forced to go with the flow, while less developed regions are increasingly reliant on state assistance due to their lack of an economic mechanism to grow and improve the regional economy on their own. In terms of technological structure, we see obvious structural imbalance: We have mastered a few top-notch technologies of the world and established some advanced industries, but raw and primitive labor technologies still account for a large share of the economy, especially in rural and remote areas, where those raw and primitive labor technologies are still dominant. The analysis of economic structure is not limited to that of ownership structure, regional economic structure, and technological structure that we have just discussed. As a matter of fact, in a broader sense, some other structures related to those we have just talked about, such as structure of enterprise size, employment structure, energy structure, and foreign trade structure, all exhibit various degrees of imbalance. Therefore, the opinion that the overall Chinese economic structure is out of balance is not blemishing the Chinese economy at all. We can fully understand why resource allocation and utilization is relatively ineffective in this circumstance. When we set the rationalization of resource allocation as one of the targets of economic reforms, we have to reach the following verdict: If economic reforms failed to rationalize the economic structure after the establishment of the new economic operational mechanism, then we had not reached the target of rationalizing resource allocation, just as low efficiency would be inevitable if economic reforms had not transformed societal shortsightedness (not limited to corporate shortsightedness) into long-term-oriented societal behavior through a series of measures to normalize property rights.

Obviously, economic structural imbalance, resource misallocation, and societal shortsightedness influence one another. It is difficult to resolve one issue if there is no significant improvement to the other. In order to achieve a balanced economic structure, effective resource allocation, and long-term-oriented societal behavior, the key is to deepen economic reforms. Only during the process of deepening economic reforms can we gradually resolve the issues of motivation, quality, and environment that are critical to increasing efficiency; gradually balance the economic structure, including the industrial structure; raise resource allocation and utilization efficiency; and, correspondingly, develop long-term-oriented behavior and prevent society, including enterprises, from behaving only out of their short-term interests.

In our discussions on resource allocation and long-term-oriented societal behavior, we naturally come up with a question that is often perplexing to many economists. When economic downturn sets in, economists are often asked this question: "When will the economy come out of recession?" A common answer to this question will be like this: By analyzing the cyclical economic trend and using the change of output (or economic growth rate) as the primary indicator, we consider the economy as having come out of recession as long as output bounces back after declining for a few consecutive periods, or economic growth rate starts to increase after declining for a few consecutive periods. Economic growth rate is a primary indicator that is widely used in the world to analyze cyclical economic trend. However, for China's economy, which is currently in type II disequilibrium, using economic growth rate to indicate whether the economy has or has not emerged from a recession is obviously questionable.

The change of output can shed some light on current economic situations, but it cannot reveal the true picture. Given the current economic situations in China, especially with enterprise and societal shortsightedness in presence, increasing output does not necessarily indicate that the economy has turned around. As long as enterprises still lack the constraints imposed by self-interest and budget, they will even likely increase production and ignore real losses or real product sales. Under the influences of societal shortsightedness, it is very likely for the public to focus only on short-term interests while ignoring long-term interests during the process of purchasing goods, which may lead to higher production that is not reflective of the real economic condition. The government is also constrained by shortsightedness, as seen in its attempt to artificially recover output for various reasons. For example, if a superior government institution decides to use output increase as the indicator to evaluate the performance of the subordinate government institution, the latter will try its best to increase output while totally ignoring everything else. Let us assume that output keeps declining for a few consecutive months. If output increase is used as the main metric to evaluate performances, a subordinate government institution will try every way to increase output, e.g., encouraging manufacturing facilities to commence operations by providing various fiscal and credit support, urging various commercial departments to purchase manufactured goods, and encouraging residents to purchase more goods. In other words, when the change of output is used as the main indicator to judge whether or not the economy has emerged from a recession, it is relatively easy for the economy to come out of it since the government can use fiscal and credit measures to artificially increase output. Emerging from a recession in this way is not necessarily indicative of an improving economy, but only glosses over the real economic situation. Since problems are still unresolved, we can surely conclude that the economy will turn south again after some time or run into another recession. To a shortsighted government or enterprise, there is nothing to worry about. The reason is simple. At least we have come out of the previous recession. Even though another recession comes, can't we just do the same and come out of it in the same way? Under disequilibrium conditions, corporate and societal shortsightedness will only lead us to this result.

The main indictor that is truly reflective of whether the economy has emerged from a recession should not be based on the change of output, but the change of enterprise productivity as well as the change of actual fiscal revenues from enterprises. Only from the changes of these indicators can we tell whether the economy has improved or not. Enterprise productivity is reflected in the profitability per hundred-*yuan* capital, or the profitability per hundred-*yuan* output, or the profitability per hundred-*yuan* sales. These profitability ratios can measure the performance of business operations more accurately. If enterprise productivity keeps declining for a few consecutive periods, we can say that the economy has encountered some difficulties. Although output during that time keeps rising, the economy may not be really improving. Enterprise productivity reflects not only the operational results of those enterprises themselves but also the situation of resource allocation and industrial structure. If resources are misallocated and the industrial structure is out of balance, business production cost will surely rise, sales will slow down, and profitability will decline. At the same time, as enterprise productivity is closely tied to state fiscal revenues, actual fiscal revenues can also be used as the main indicator to evaluate whether or not the economy has come out of recession. In particular, actual fiscal revenues are calculated net of inflation and various debt proceeds. If actual fiscal revenues keep declining for a few consecutive periods, we can also say that the economy has met with difficulties. Even though output during these periods keeps rising, it does not mean the economy has really improved.

From the analyses of whether or not the economy has come out of recession, we can learn that the key to avert declining enterprise productivity and actual fiscal revenues under the current economic conditions in China still lies in the deepening of economic reforms so as to overcome the negative impact of enterprise and societal shortsightedness on resource allocation, industrial structure, and economic structure and to build a solid foundation for economic stability and growth.

7.3 Industrial Restructuring and Unbalanced Economic Growth

7.3.1 A Theoretical Dilemma

One of the unconcluded research topics on the Chinese economy is to find out how to establish a balanced relationship among economic reforms, economic growth, and industrial restructuring so that they can help one another move forward, which will not only lead to effective economic growth during economic reforms but also establish a new resource allocation mechanism by means of economic growth and industrial restructuring and transform the traditional economic system into the new economic system.

This is a challenging task. Keep in mind that the current Chinese economy is in disequilibrium. The market has not been fully developed, resources are in short supply, and enterprises are not real goods producers who act out of self-interest. In this circumstance, if we mainly rely on the market and let it set prices, lack of the constraint by enterprises' self-interest and the restrictions on the circulation of production factors due to abnormal property rights will drive prices higher and cause market signals to malfunction. As a result, industrial structure will not move toward rationalization, and the industrial structural imbalance that has developed over the long time in history may get even worse, stalling potential economic growth in the future. On the other hand, if we mainly rely on government regulation, i.e., allowing the government to use price limits and commodity quotas, we may to some extent support the relatively fast growth of some industrial sectors while controlling production increases from other sectors, maintaining overall economic growth. However, because enterprises' motivation is contained, they are not motivated to increase efficiency. This will surely delay or block the establishment of a new resource allocation mechanism. The growth of the economy is achieved by sacrificing efficiency. The industrial structure cannot get out of imbalance due to the lack of guidance by accurate market signals. This is the dilemma that Chinese economists are facing. To resolve this issue, we need to start with analyzing the investment principal.

7.3.2 Determining the Investment Principal of Industrial Restructuring

The principal of economic growth is enterprise. The principal of industrial restructuring is also enterprise. The principal hereby discussed refers to an investment principal. If we want enterprise to be a real investment principal, we must first and foremost allow enterprise to become a real entity with its own interests. In other words, enterprise must have its own independent interests, enterprise must care about its own interests, and enterprise must invest to realize its own interests. Also, enterprise must act under self-control during the investing process with the purpose of realizing its own interests. When we devise economic development plans and industrial restructuring policies, we can probably find a new way if we regard enterprise as an investment principal that has its own independent interests and is constrained by self-interest. If we start with this perception, the primary issue is the enterprise system reform, which is to grant enterprise the status of an entity with self-interest as well as an investment principal and to allow the process of enterprise selecting investment opportunities to constrain and support economic growth and industrial restructuring so that economic reforms, economic growth, and industrial restructuring can coordinate and move forward at the same time.

We know that, in reality, industrial restructuring is to reduce investment in some industrial sectors and increase investment in some other industrial sectors. The industrial structure is reflected not only by the ratio of the outputs from various sectors but also by the ratio of the inputs into various sectors. Inputs constrain outputs and the ratio of input to output also constrains output. The comment of "letting enterprise be the investment principal of industrial restructuring" has two connotations. First, an enterprise chooses its investment direction and decides on whether to increase or decrease inputs in a certain sector according to its self-interest, which influences the ratio of output from various industrial sectors. Second, an enterprise adjusts its own ratio of input to output. To put it in another way, an enterprise increases or decreases output by means of increasing efficiency. In these two connotations, the second one is probably more important. It is because only after an enterprise has become an entity of self-interest will it be relatively better motivated to increase output by means of increasing efficiency. This is a more reasonable way to resolve commodity shortages, especially when resources are in short supply and various inputs are subject to physical constraints.

If we look at this point from a different perspective, allowing enterprise to be an investment principal also means that enterprise becomes a buyer of production factors. When enterprises adjust their investment directions and the combination of production factors in accordance with their self-interest, they change the demand for production factors, which in turn influences the sales of products produced by others. This will also practically influence the production and capacity of some other industrial sectors and meanwhile point out a direction for industrial restructuring. Therefore, after enterprises become entities with self-interest, they will be able to influence industrial restructuring from the perspective of input (including the quantity of resource inputs and the ratio of input to output) and from the perspective of buyers of products made by other enterprises. Economic growth is ultimately dependent upon the growth of output from each and every enterprise. Since the growth of enterprise output is achieved during the process of industrial restructuring, economic growth and industrial restructuring share the same processes. When enterprise with independent self-interest becomes the principal of economic growth, it also becomes the principal of industrial restructuring.

7.3.3 *The Role of Rationing Equilibrium in Industrial Restructuring Under Disequilibrium Conditions*

When we treat enterprise as an investment principal and place emphasis on the role of enterprise's investment and purchase decisions in industrial restructuring, we should keep in mind that it operates under disequilibrium conditions, in which underdeveloped market and resource shortages will inevitably significantly influence its decisions in selecting investment and purchases. With this in mind, we cannot ignore the importance of the roles that the government plays in industrial restructuring. The greater the degree of economic disequilibrium, the more important the role the government plays in industrial restructuring.

The government must be responsible for nonprofit investment projects. This is directly related to the responsibility of a government, from which no government should try to escape. We hardly need any further proof on this point. What we need to discuss now is as follows: Under the circumstances where the market is not fully developed and resources are in short supply, what should the government do as the economic regulator to influence enterprises' decisions on investment opportunities and commodity purchases so that the industrial structure can be adjusted and become more reasonable? The government can meet this goal mainly by rationing equilibrium.

Rationing equilibrium by government can be realized according to the target principle, the average principle, or the historical ratio principle. Every principle is applicable in certain areas and has potential shortcomings. Therefore, the principle that the government uses in certain circumstances should be reviewed according to the specifics of the situation before a decision is made.

The target principle means that the government decides on the pecking order according to the level of importance of each industrial sector and allocates limited resources accordingly. The way of allocating resources helps ensure that the target of economic growth and the goal of industrial restructuring set by the government can be reached. It can also fairly quickly support the growth of some industrial sectors while limiting the growth of others. But the questions are as follows: Is the pecking order of the industrial sectors reasonable? Can we make sure that the ratio of limited resources allocated by the government rationing and by open-market transactions contributes to realizing the goals of economic growth and industrial restructuring at the same time? Is such resource rationing consistent with the efficiency criteria of resource utilization? Lastly, can we make sure that the resources allocated to an industrial sector either by government rationing or by open-market transactions will not be utilized for other purposes or resold for undue profits? The side effects of the target principle are as follows: Some sectors and enterprises receive special attention, but they are not necessarily highly efficient, while others are practically excluded from the list of the recipients of resources. Despite being highly efficient, they are forced to lower their efficiency due to insufficient supply of resources. Therefore, in the case where the target principle is applied to rationing (even though the principle is appropriate), yet without corresponding measures to support the flow of resources between sectors and to facilitate product modifications and upgrades, rationing equilibrium under the target principle will have to sacrifice resource utilization efficiency of society.

The average principle means that the government divvies up resources evenly according to the demand and availability of resources. From the perspective of industrial restructuring, the average principle may prevent the government from realizing its predetermined goal of industrial restructuring, because applying the average principle means the industrial structure will maintain its status quo. From the perspective of maintaining economic growth, rationing equilibrium achieved by using the average principle at least stays away from relatively significant economic fluctuations. In addition, from the perspective of supply and demand of consumer necessities, utilizing the average principle to allocate limited resources also helps maintain social stability. Under the average principle, however, the resource utilization efficiency of society will be lower, but the lowered efficiency is attributed more to the insufficient aggregate resource supply than to the structural changes of the industrial sector, as the industrial structure basically maintains its status quo.

The historical ratio principle means that the government allocates resources among sectors and enterprises according to the historical ratio or the ratio that was being used in the past. This way of allocating limited resources has effects similar to that of the average principle, i.e., basically maintaining the status quo of the industrial structure while staying away from relatively significant economic fluctuations. But the question is: Since the historical resource allocation ratio is used as the basis to allocate current resources, how reasonable is the allocation ratio? In this circumstance, can we at the same time make sure that the resources allocated to certain sectors and enterprises are not used for different purposes or resold to other sectors and enterprises for undue profits? Moreover, the historical ratio is not automatically adjusted according to the ongoing real situations. If we want to make adjustments to the historical ratio, how should we adjust new rations for limited resources?

The analyses have revealed that balancing the goals of economic growth and industrial restructuring without harming the motivation of enterprises or lowering resource utilization efficiency is indeed a very difficult task. Regardless of which principle is used by the government in rationing, the way that target rations, average rations, or historical rations are determined must first of all be reasonable. Only by reasonably determining these ratios can the government reduce as many errors and conflicts as possible during the rationing process. Secondly, regardless of which principle is used, we should try to avoid the leakage of shortage resources, i.e., to prevent the shortage resources that have been allocated to certain sectors or enterprises from being resold to other sectors and enterprises.

A compromise is to apply a portion of all three principles to reach rationing equilibrium under government regulation. Among these three principles, the target principle is a method that can relatively better facilitate the government's efforts to reach its predetermined goals for industrial restructuring. The historical ratio principle is a method that can relatively better support economic growth and will less likely cause relatively violent economic fluctuations. The average principle is a method that is relatively less likely to cause frictions among buyers or harm enterprises' motivation. If the government intends to utilize rationing equilibrium to perform industrial restructuring under disequilibrium conditions, it can mainly use the target principle while taking the features of the historical ratio principle and the average principle into consideration to come up with a systematic ratio for the allocation of shortage resources.

7.3.4 Applying the Policy on Leading Industries and Unbalanced Economic Growth

Economic growth under the circumstance of resource shortages is linked to resource rations among various sectors. If the allocation of shortage resources mainly relies on the target principle, we can surely achieve economic growth during the process of industrial restructuring, and economic growth realized in this way will be tilted. In other words, economic grow this unbalanced.

Now we have an issue of how to evaluate unbalanced economic growth. Keep in mind that the growth of an economy always takes place against a particular economic backdrop, which we call the initial state of economic growth. After certain periods of time, the economy will grow and end up in an expected situation, which we call the final stage of economic growth. In evaluating balanced and unbalanced economic growth, we must not disregard either the initial state or the final stage of economic growth. If the industrial structure of the initial status of economic growth is balanced and that of the final stage of economic growth is also balanced, it is obvious that balanced economic growth is the ideal way to grow the economy. During this period, unbalanced economic growth may be unnecessary or even detrimental to realizing the goal of a balanced industrial structure. However, since the Chinese economy is currently in disequilibrium and the Chinese industrial structure during the initial state of economic growth has been severely unbalanced, it is not only impossible to achieve balanced economic growth but also inconsistent with the requirements to grow the economy under the rationing equilibrium of shortage resources. Therefore, whether unbalanced economic growth is right or wrong cannot be judged without taking the reality into consideration.

In terms of whether unbalanced economic growth under rationing equilibrium executed by the government allows it to reach its predetermined goals of economic growth and industrial restructuring, it depends not only upon whether the policy on leading industries adopted by the government is reasonable or not but also upon how well the policy on leading industries is executed. If the government does not propose any policy on leading industries and leaves everything to the market and expects it to establish leading industries on its own, both economic growth and industrial restructuring can be realized. However, this normally occurs in a relatively developed market in which enterprises are constrained by self-interest. Despite that, industrial restructuring may still progress very slowly, because when commodity supply or demand is limited, the rationing adjustment done by the market itself (which allows shortage resources or limited market to be allocated autonomously) can only reach its anticipated results through numerous transactions and resource transfers. Current situations in China have demonstrated that because the market has not been fully developed, enterprises have not been constrained by self-interest, and there have been some difficulties transferring resources autonomously among various sectors, the results of the rationing adjustment by the market itself will not necessarily be consistent with the economic growth and industrial restructuring goals set by the government. Therefore, obviously, it is quite necessary for the government to determine the policy on leading industries and apply it to achieve unbalanced economic growth through rationing equilibrium.

The policy on leading industries is one that favors certain industries. We should, however, note that any leading industry must coordinate with several other industries to which the leading industry is directly related. These industries are further connected to several other industries. Hence, even though the government applies a policy that favors some industries, it cannot only care about one single industry or a few industries while totally ignoring the other related industries. This type of policy can only ration shortage resources according to how closely an industry is tied to the leading industries. This means that when, under disequilibrium conditions, rationing equilibrium is the only way for the government to realize unbalanced economic growth and to consolidate resources in support of leading industries to realize industrial restructuring, the degree of preference (for the leading industries) of the industrial policy will have to be appropriate rather than excessive. Otherwise, this preference will not only fail to accelerate the growth of the leading industries, but even likely prolong or exacerbate industrial structural imbalance.

From these analyses, we have clearly learned that the struggle between balanced and unbalanced economic growth is not what people have thought it would be, nor is it about whether balanced economic growth is better or worse than unbalanced economic growth. If the initial state of growth is accompanied by unbalanced industrial structure, this hotly debated topic will inevitably fall on the magnitude of the imbalance of economic growth, or the degree of preference of the industrial policy. Excessive preference for some industries is more harmful than no preference. Excessively unbalanced economic growth is likely to exacerbate industrial structural imbalance. If the initial state of economic growth is accompanied by unbalanced industrial structure, balanced economic growth obviously will not help resolve industrial structural imbalance, but more than likely maintain the existing industrial structure rather than worsen structural imbalance. This is exactly what the government should pay attention to when formulating the policy on leading industries.

Now we have come to the question of how to apply the policy on leading industries and how to come up with an appropriate degree of preference of the industrial policy set out by the government. To analyze this issue, we will have to study the roles of enterprise operation mechanism and price signal in the execution of the policy on leading industries.

7.3.5 *Enterprise Self-Control and the Constraining Effect on Excessive Preference of the Industrial Policy*

The policy on leading industries is initiated and executed by the government. Nonidealized government behavior causes the policy on leading industries to somewhat deviate from the predetermined goals on economic growth and industrial restructuring. It is very difficult for the government to come up with the perfect degree of preference of the industrial policy. In this circumstance, another force is needed to counter the effect of excessive preference of the industrial policy. Now, where does the countering force originate? It is not from the government itself, but from enterprises that are investment principals and entities of self-interest.

If enterprises are unable to sever their subordination to administrative institutions, they will not be constrained by self-interest nor choose investment opportunities according to their current and expected interests. Undoubtedly, when the government ostensibly favors some industries (by granting excessively preferential status to some industries), which will change the supply and demand in the market as a result, it is unlikely for enterprises to respond to these changes brought about by the government policy. The policy that excessively favors some industries will exacerbate industrial structural imbalance and cause a large supply gap for some commodities and at the same time a large demand shortfall for some other commodities. These problems will remain unsolved until they get worse. Usually, a long time has passed before the government takes action to address those issues. The time lag is usually very long and the consequential damage to the economy is severe. In addition, because the preference for some industries under the industrial policy is tied to the rationing of shortage commodities and enterprises lack the constraint of self-interest, they may take advantage of such industrial policy to earn undue profits. For example, some enterprises may take advantage of shortage resources to develop products that are not urgently needed or to earn profits from activities that are unrelated to manufacturing. These activities not only fail to correct the preference of the industrial policy but may instead cause the industrial policy to be even more unreasonable and heighten the scarcity of shortage resources.

If the abovementioned issues do occur, which is contradictory to the anticipation of the government who initiates the industrial policy that favors certain industries, and in the meantime the government does not believe that the root cause of those issues is that enterprises lack the constraint of self-interest, it may lead the government to a wrong conclusion, i.e., blaming unreasonable prices or the dual-track price system. As a result, the government may try to terminate the dual-track price system and remove price controls to correct severe industrial structural imbalance and resolve commodity supply gap and commodity demand shortfall. These actions seem reasonable theoretically, because the right price signals will guide resources to where they are most needed and the quick reactions of enterprises to price signals will direct them to produce shortage commodities and increase investment in the vulnerable segments of the economy, which can streamline the industrial structure. However, the reality is completely different under disequilibrium conditions. If the government did that, the results would be nothing but further imbalance and more severe economic trouble. The key issue here is still that it is impossible for an enterprise that is not responsible for its business decisions or operational profits and losses to become an entity with self-interest that can truly function in adjusting the industrial structure.

As we have discussed earlier, it is a known fact that resources are in short supply and the industrial structure is out of balance in its initial state and that the market is not fully developed and that enterprises lack the constraint of self-interest. In the circumstance that resources are short, rationing equilibrium will be inevitable. This has to be completed either by the government or by the market. The dual-track price system indicates that government rationing exists concurrently with market rationing. Government rationing will be carried out on the basis of the target principle (or the average principle, or the historical ratio principle). In this circumstance, if the government decides to replace the dual-track price system with pure market pricing, this in fact indicates that government rationing will be terminated and it is the market that will take full control of the allocation of shortage resources. The market will do so by following the principle of "first-come, first-served" or the monopoly principle. However, as long as the market has not been fully developed, property rights have not been normalized, and enterprises lack the constraint of self-interest, relatively low price elasticity of supply as well as relatively low price elasticity of demand will certainly generate two new prices, i.e., open market price and hidden market price (or black market price), regardless of which principle that the market applies to allocate resources. Open market price and hidden market price will chase each other but always keep a distance from each other, causing prices to escalate time after time. This is the current Chinese economic reality under disequilibrium conditions. Therefore, replacing the dual-track price system with pure market pricing will not help alleviate industrial structural imbalance, but will only make it worse.

If the government recognizes the economic disequilibrium conditions and considers the fact that enterprises have not become independent goods producers, it surely should not open up prices and terminate the dual-track price system prematurely when it works toward to the goal of completing industry restructuring effectively. Instead, it should maintain government rationing while reforming the enterprise operation mechanism and leverage the enterprise self-control mechanism to balance the excessively preferential arrangements of the industrial policy. The analysis presented in Chap. 6 of this book is also applicable to this issue.

As an investment principal and an entity of self-interest, an enterprise, in making decisions on investment and business operations, will exercise self-control if the enterprise operation mechanism functions. That can serve as the offsetting force to balance the excessively preferential arrangements of the industrial policy. The reason is that enterprises adjust the direction and amount of investment on the basis of their own economic interests. If the official industrial policy excessively favors certain industries, an enterprise under the dual-track price system will have the following two alternatives:

The first alternative for an enterprise is to accept market rationing. That is, it adopts the market price that is higher than the fixed price to produce the shortage commodities that meet the market needs as well as its own economic interests. This can relieve the shortages of these commodities due to excessive preference of the industrial policy. Of course, when an enterprise chooses to do so, it will be exposed to some investment and operational risks. However, as an entity with self-interest, the enterprise is not only empowered to do so but also willing to take these risks. When there are investment and operational risks, there are returns. Motivated by profits, an enterprise will likely pursue this alternative.

The second alternative for an enterprise is to reject market rationing. This is primarily because the excessive preference of the industrial policy can lead to highly concentrated government rations and the enterprise, taking its own economic interests into consideration, feels that the price tag for market rations is too high, which may significantly increase its investment and operational risks. Insufficient government rations will surely cause some enterprises to change production capacity and product lines, including producing different products, shutting down product lines, reducing production volume, and merging with or establishing alliance with other enterprises. The flow of production factors and the recombination of resources are guided by the self-interest of enterprises, which are in turn guided by the demand of the market. This helps alleviate the shortages of some commodities arising from the excessively preferential arrangement of the industrial policy. Motivated by profits, enterprises may go with this alternative.

Regardless of which of the two alternatives an enterprise goes with, its choice will first of all help make up some of the shortages arising from the excessively preferential arrangement of the industrial policy. We can regard the self-control of enterprises as the constraint on the excessively preferential arrangement of the industrial policy. In addition, the self-control of enterprises can serve as a different constraint on the excessively preferential arrangement of the industrial policy. Such constraint is manifested in the changes in the marketplace after enterprises choose one of the two abovementioned alternatives, which prompts the government to alter its original industrial policy that excessively favors some industries or its rationing plan that is excessively concentrated on certain industries.

For example, an enterprise chooses the first alternative to produce a shortage commodity by using production materials purchased from the market at a price higher than its fixed price. As a result, the supply of the production materials will increase, and the price of the shortage commodity made of those production materials produced by the enterprise will fall, which can provide the government who rations such production materials and shortage commodities with a signal indicating that its original rationing plan (which excessively favors certain industries and results in overly concentrated rations) has been out of sync with market changes. Therefore, it is possible for the government to adjust rationing according to the development in the market.

If an enterprise chooses the second alternative, i.e., it reacts to excessively concentrated government rations by reallocating production factors and recombining resources, the result from the enterprise reactions will lead to increased supply of some shortage commodities in the market, hence changing the market. When the government sees the changes, it will also reconsider its original rationing plan and make necessary adjustments according to the development in the market.

Therefore, only when enterprises are no longer controlled by government institutions and have become independent goods producers who are responsible for their business decisions and their own profits and losses can the equilibrium of the government rationing help improve the industrial structure and prevent industrial structural imbalance from remaining unresolved for a prolonged period of time due to unreasonable government rationing. On the contrary, if the government hopes to perform industrial restructuring by terminating the dual-track price system before reforming the enterprise operation mechanism, the ultimate results can deviate from the goals predetermined by the government.

These discussions have fully illustrated the relationship of economic reforms, economic growth, and industrial restructuring under disequilibrium conditions. In short, if we do not first and foremost effectively reform the enterprise operation mechanism, it will be very difficult to realize the goals of economic growth and industrial restructuring and to achieve economic growth and industrial structuring in the future.

Chapter 8
Government Regulation of Agriculture

8.1 Demand and Supply of Agricultural Products Under Disequilibrium Conditions

8.1.1 Agricultural Disequilibrium

In our analysis on industrial restructuring, we should treat agriculture and the demand and supply of agricultural products in a special way by specifically studying the demand and supply of agricultural products as well as the development of agriculture in a separate section.

If we regard an underdeveloped market and limited supply of resources as the main features of economic disequilibrium, it will be obvious that the Chinese agriculture has exhibited the features of disequilibrium, which are first of all reflected by the limited supply of land and secondly by the substantial constraints on the free transfers of resources in the agricultural industry. Western economists usually regard agriculture as a perfectly competitive sector and the agricultural produce market a perfectly competitive market. If the agricultural industry and the market of agricultural products they refer to are in a developed capitalist country, the viewpoint is more or less applicable. However, to a developing country, especially China in its current situation, this viewpoint is far from the truth. The current agricultural disequilibrium in China is mainly reflected in the following three aspects:

First, in the circumstance of limited supply of resources, resources are substantially constrained from being freely transferred due to the system. Free transfer is constrained not only inside the agricultural sector but also between agricultural and nonagricultural sectors and between rural and urban areas.

Second, main agricultural products are in short supply, and hence, there are gaps between the supply and demand of these products. There are also constraints on the market of main agricultural products. Government rationing is applied and so is market rationing. The existence of the dual-track price system reflects that the market of main agricultural products is under imperfect competition.

Y. Li, *Chinese Economy in Disequilibrium*, China Academic Library,
DOI 10.1007/978-3-642-39558-1_8, © Foreign Language Teaching and Research
Publishing Co., Ltd and Springer-Verlag Berlin Heidelberg 2014

Third, in terms of the agricultural products that are not subject to government rationing, they are traded in the marketplace with high transaction costs, and the competition of these products is imperfect for several reasons, such as incomplete information, various tangible and intangible constraints on product transfers between different geographical areas, underdeveloped intermediary organizations, and the absence of some necessary institutions.

All these demonstrate that we should not rely on the measures that only focus on price and market, but need to take measures that apply to areas beyond price and market according to specific disequilibrium conditions to resolve agricultural problems in China. Moreover, the reality nowadays has indicated that the primary measures are those other than price and market.

8.1.2 Demand and Supply of Agricultural Products Versus Government Regulation

Based on the features of disequilibria in the agricultural sector discussed above, the government should place its regulatory emphasis on motivating producers of agricultural products, supporting circulation of resources, and ensuring the availability of necessary supplies for agricultural product producers to increase production so that the supply of agricultural products can be increased. Of course, emphasizing on these measures does not mean that there is no need for other measures such as raising the fixed price of agricultural products and expanding the scope of the agricultural products that are free to trade without restriction. We only mean that in the case of disequilibrium conditions, regulatory measures beyond price and market are relatively more important.

Measures beyond price and market available to the government to increase the supply of agricultural products include the following:

1. Establishing the agricultural production stabilization fund. The government will determine the main categories of agricultural products that are in need of price support from the government in order to maintain production volume and producers' income. When the price of a listed agricultural product falls below its support price, the agricultural production stabilization fund will purchase the product at its support price. The agricultural production stabilization fund is mainly funded by the fiscal budget. Profits from using the fund to manage the purchases and sales of these agricultural products can also be a supplementary source of capital for the fund. The support price of each agricultural product is publicized in advance and kept relatively stable during a certain period of time, which can stabilize producers and avoid violent fluctuations in the production volume of the core agricultural products. In the current circumstance, the support price can be set a little bit higher. Even with the increase of supply of agricultural products and the decline of supply gap in the future, the agricultural production stabilization fund, once established, should be maintained in the long run, and the support price for each product should be adjusted in a timely manner according to demand and supply in the market.

2. Developing farm servicing companies and supporting the relative concentration of land via financial intermediaries. When agricultural producers are not highly motivated to plant and grow crops, together with the constrained circulation of agricultural resources, it is necessary to maintain the stability of the labor force engaging in agricultural production. Therefore, the government should encourage and support the establishment of farm servicing companies and allow them to grow relatively quickly. These companies can be formed by funds in the market to sign contracts with those households who do not have sufficient labor to grow crops or the required experience or skills to manage their farmland on their own. Farm servicing companies are staffed by relatively stable farm workers, have high productivity, and make profit by charging service fees or by obtaining a percentage of the actual harvest. They can significantly increase production output given the same area of arable land and hence raise land utilization efficiency.

   Supporting relative concentration of land via financial intermediaries means that we establish some financial institutions, such as a land savings bank (or a land savings credit union or a farmers' land savings fund) to accept land as deposit from those households who are neither willing to grow crops nor willing to give up their contracted land by paying certain amount of interest. These financial institutions can in turn gather the land received from each depositor and lend it to skilled farmers or farm servicing companies, or they can enter into farm servicing contracts with farm servicing companies, who get paid service fees or a percentage of harvest from the land. These financial intermediaries can be established using funds from society and earn profits from the spread between the deposits of land and the loans of land or from managing the land on their own. The combination of financial institutions, skilled farmers, or farm servicing companies will be the way to economies of scale.
3. Establishing a network of specialized distributors of agricultural production materials and cooperative suppliers of agricultural production materials. In light of the shortages of agricultural production materials and market underdevelopment, we should not terminate but rather enhance government rationing of some key agricultural production materials (such as fertilizer, pesticides, farming equipment and fuel, and agricultural film). The exclusive distributor system is a viable way at the moment. Government rations should mainly follow the target principle and meanwhile take into account the average principle and the historical ratio principle. When determining the rationing target for key agricultural production materials, the government should first and foremost focus on grain. However, it is not enough to rely on government rations and exclusive distributors only. We should also establish a network of cooperative suppliers of agricultural production materials as early as possible. The network of cooperative suppliers of agricultural production materials mainly refers to a network that primarily handles and supplies agricultural production materials organized and funded by agricultural producers. The network is not only monitored and managed by agricultural producers but also capable of serving them at the same time.

The above describes the measures that the government can adopt to increase the supply of agricultural products. They can also be coordinated with other measures such as raising the price of agricultural products.

8.1.3 Demand for Agricultural Products Versus Government Regulation

In order to regulate demand for agricultural products, the government can also adopt appropriate regulatory measures. The focus of government regulation applicable to this area should also be placed on measures beyond price and market. However, this does not mean that government regulation of the price of agricultural products is useless in reducing the supply gap of agricultural products. Rather, it means that government regulation of the price of agricultural products cannot be the primary measure to effectively alleviate the mismatch between the demand and supply of agricultural products under disequilibrium conditions. The government can still perform rationing on some key agricultural products when faced with extreme shortages. However, this is not a fundamental measure that attempts from the demand side to alleviate the mismatch of the demand and supply of agricultural products.

Among measures beyond price or market that aim to adjust the demand, there are mainly three measures available to the government:

1. Applying differential tax rates, differential interest rates and differential credit quota to the users who use agricultural products as raw materials so as to adjust the demand for agricultural products. The users of agricultural products can be categorized into three main groups. The first group is enterprises or other production units. They need agricultural products as raw materials. When certain agricultural products are in relatively severe shortage, the government should try its best to reduce the demand for agricultural products from the users who use agricultural products as raw materials and adjust the structure of their demand for raw materials. Although the government may get the same result by adjusting the price of agricultural raw materials or by rationing agricultural raw materials, the former measure may have a relatively large impact, whereas the latter measure may hurt the motivation of enterprises or other production units who use agricultural products as raw materials, nor will it necessarily guarantee more efficient utilization of agricultural products as raw materials. Therefore, one of the alternatives available to the government is to adopt such measures as differential tax rates, differential interest rates, and differential credit amount to guide enterprises or other production units to adjust the structure of raw materials and reduce the usage of shortage agricultural products. Adjusting the structure of raw materials requires additional inputs. However, if the government adopts differential tax rates, differential interest rates, and differential credit amount to benefit the enterprises or other production units that make adjustments to the

structure of raw materials and cut the usage of agricultural products as raw materials, these enterprises or production units may feel the benefits of following the government. As a result, such government initiatives will benefit the whole of society, including users who use agricultural products as raw materials.

2. Using differential tax rates, differential interest rates, and differential credit amount, as well as differential foreign exchange retention ratios to adjust the structure of export commodities and reduce the export of agricultural products. Among those three main groups of agricultural product buyers, the second group is agricultural product exporter. They handle the export of agricultural products. When some agricultural products suffer from relatively significant shortages, the government can try to reduce the export of agricultural products by those enterprises. Of course, if necessary, the government will not rule out the possibility of using harsh measures such as applying export quota to reach its goal. However, doing so may negatively influence the motivation of exporters. A better way is to use differential tax rates, interest rates, and credit amount, as well as differential foreign exchange retention ratios so that exporters can adjust the structure of export commodities according to the demand and supply of agricultural products and reduce the export of shortage commodities. In doing so, the government can motivate exporters relatively easily. Meanwhile, the flexibility of these measures also enables exporters to be more empowered when adjusting their export structure.
3. Applying various methods to change the ratio of personal savings to consumption as well as the consumption structure and guiding consumers to reducing the demand for shortage agricultural products. Among the three main groups of agricultural product buyers, the third one is consumer, who is the direct or indirect buyer of agricultural products. For example, food is the main product that consumers purchase directly, while the main buyers of cotton, linen, silk, and wool are enterprises. Since cloth or clothing that consumers purchase is made from agricultural products such as cotton, linen, silk, and wool, these agricultural products can be considered commodities that consumers purchase indirectly (the same is with manufactured food, which is considered agricultural products that consumers purchase indirectly). In order to reduce the direct and indirect purchases of agricultural products, the government can try to change the ratio of personal savings to consumption so as to change consumer consumption structure, including the structure of food, clothing, and housing, besides using price adjustment measures and applying rationing. There are a series of measures available to the government in this regard. Here are some examples:

   (a) The government can adjust tax rate or interest rate to adjust the ratio of savings to consumption.
   (b) The government can levy new taxes to change the ratio of personal savings to consumption (including the structure of food consumption by consumers).
   (c) The government can sell houses or gold and silver jewelries to change the structure of personal consumption and sell stocks or issue government bonds to change the ratio of personal savings to consumption as well as the consumer consumption structure.

(d) The government can adopt some measures to encourage consumers to increase spending on services (such as tourism, cultural, and educational services) and so as to reduce their direct or indirect purchases of agricultural products.
(e) The government can adopt fiscal and credit measures to reduce the demand for agricultural products when aggregate demand exceeds aggregate supply.

These adjustment measures can be used together with price adjustment or government rationing of agricultural products.

8.2 Trend of Balanced Demand and Supply of Agricultural Products

8.2.1 Long-Term-Oriented Behavior of Agricultural Product Buyers and Sellers

It is not painless to adjust the demand and supply of agricultural products. The difficulty is that these adjustment measures that we have discussed earlier are not directly related to price or market. Those measures change the demand and supply of agricultural products either via fiscal or credit policies or via certain adjustments to the system (such as establishing land savings banks or farm servicing companies). If farmers lack the willingness and motivation to increase scale of production, or they are not interested in changing the structure of raw materials or consumption, or they believe such changes are too costly and bring in low returns, any measure that the government undertakes to change the supply and demand of agricultural products will not be effective at all. In other words, if the buyers and sellers of agricultural products are all only focused on their short-term interests and have no idea of how their short-term interests are related to the government measures devised to adjust the demand and supply of agricultural products, it will be impossible for them to operate their businesses following the adjustment goals that the government sets for demand and supply. They probably care less about their long-term interests. In this way, we can easily understand why government regulatory measures are not so effective.

Now we have a question: What kind of regulatory measures should the government apply to guide the buyers and sellers of agricultural products so that they can turn their attention to their long-term interests instead of focusing only on their short-term interests? Basically, whether a microeconomic unit (an enterprise or a person) acts in its long-term interests or not is dependent upon three conditions: Does it have a clear development goal when it engages in economic activities? Is it motivated internally to realize the predetermined development goal? And is it likely to realize the predetermined development goal with its own efforts? On the contrary, if a microeconomic unit does not have a business development goal and only cares about its short-term interests, or if it is not motivated and believes that its development goal has nothing to do with itself, or if it loses confidence in the long-term prospect or has inconsistent expectations, believing that it will be impossible to realize the development goals regardless of how hard it tries, it will inevitably focus on its short-term interests or ultra-short-term interests. In our discussions on current Chinese agriculture and its development, we will first of all analyze the real situations of agricultural product suppliers from the perspective of the three conditions discussed above that are critical to microeconomic units' long-term-oriented behavior.

(a) The Development Goal of Economic Activities

Here, the most important issue is the determination of the development goal for agricultural product suppliers. Producing agricultural products is just a way to realize their development goal. We cannot regard the development goal of agricultural product suppliers simply as farming, feeding poultry, and providing the market with agricultural products. If they understand that producing agricultural products is making contribution to society, we can regard their development goal as making larger contribution to society. If they believe that producing more agricultural products will bring more income, improve their standard of living, and create more wealth, we can regard increasing material wealth as their development goal. If these two beliefs (social responsibility and material wealth) are combined, the development goal will be more meaningful. Anyway, if the development goal is determined, agricultural product producers will clearly know what they need to do. However, currently, such a goal has become quite vague. Social responsibility is thought to be too general to be a development goal, and material wealth is thought to be unrealistic because, in real life, producers of many other products may create more material wealth than those of agricultural products do. Therefore, many agricultural product producers are more and more unclear about their development goals.

(b) The Motivation to Achieve a Predetermined Goal

Without a development goal, there is no point in discussing motivation. In the circumstance where many agricultural product producers are more and more unclear about their development goals, it is difficult to believe that agricultural product producers are fully motivated, especially in terms of committing additional investment to increase the supply of agricultural products. Of course, this does not mean that they are not motivated at all to do any business. That they do not care about increasing the supply of agricultural products only indicates that they lack the motivation in this regard. Although pursuing short-term interests can also be considered a "goal," it is not the same as the development goal of economic activities. Because of lack of motivation, any government adjustment measure, be it fiscal, credit, or others, will fail to induce agricultural product producers to adapt their business activities to the intention of the government.

(c) The Confidence in Realizing the Development Goal Through Hard Work

This issue is similar to the motivation problem that we have just discussed. If the development goal is unclear and motivation is insufficient, what is the point of discussing the confidence in realizing the development goal? It is not difficult to find an explanation for behavioral shortsightedness among agricultural product producers. What we need to discuss is as follows: Even though some agricultural product producers may have their own development goals and prepare to increase the supply of agricultural products to realize their goals, can they really do so by working hard on their own? Admittedly, their confidence is low. In the circumstance where the market is underdeveloped and resources are in short supply, agricultural product producers may not necessarily reach their goals by working hard on their own. As their confidence wanes, so do their efforts to increase the supply of agricultural products. Therefore, it will be difficult for the government to fulfill its plan of increasing the supply of agricultural products by means of various adjustment measures.

The above analyses are based on behavioral shortsightedness from the perspective of agricultural product producers. Next, let us look at agricultural product buyers. Let us simplify the categories of agricultural product buyers and classify them into two groups, enterprises and individuals. When the market is not fully developed and enterprises lack the constraint of self-interest and business budget, it is impossible for any enterprise to come up with a development goal, let alone the motivation and confidence to realize that goal. Therefore, it is not easy for an enterprise to cut its purchases of agricultural products as raw materials by adjusting the structure of its raw materials and lowering its production costs. With enterprise shortsightedness, agricultural product buyers will surely care about their short-term interests only. As for individual agricultural product consumers, we cannot deny that they are not free to change their consumption structure, especially food structure, when their income is relatively low. On the other hand, they will not likely change the way they directly or indirectly purchase agricultural products in response to government measures, because the market is not fully developed, resources are in short supply, and personal expectations are not stable. In other words, unstable personal expectations determine that individual agricultural product consumers only care about their short-term interests.

These situations can be described as the irregularity of the relationship between government regulation and the demand and supply of agricultural products.

8.2.2 The Optimal Scale of Agricultural Production

One important issue in our research on agricultural disequilibria in China is to find out how to resolve the behavioral shortsightedness of the buyers and sellers of agricultural products. Although the behavioral shortsightedness of agricultural product buyers is closely related to the alleviation of the mismatch between the demand and supply of agricultural products, it is not the primary task we need to deal with in agriculture. The real difficulty we are facing is how to overcome the shortsightedness of agricultural product producers and to increase the supply of agricultural products. It is necessary to provide the producers with a clear development goal and necessary motivation to realize the development goal and to build their confidence in realizing the predetermined development goal through their hard work. Apparently, these are the points that we need to focus on to resolve agricultural issues.

To agricultural product producers, the issue of land ownership and right of use is directly linked to the goal, motivation, and confidence we have discussed. If we can come up with an appropriate proposal for land ownership and right of use according to the actual situations in China, it will not only help motivate agricultural product producers to produce goods but also change the behavior of agricultural product producers and direct them to be more long-term oriented. Now, can we establish private land ownership? Some foreign scholars who propose privatization of land ownership believe that private land ownership can enhance the motivation of agricultural product producers to increase inputs into the land and motivate them to care about their personal properties, harvests, and land, thus leading to higher production. I disagree with this proposal. Public land ownership has been in place for years in China, and people from all walks of life have accepted the concept of public land ownership. If China were to abolish public land ownership and adopt private land ownership, social disorder would arise with detrimental consequences, especially in rural areas. In addition, private land ownership certainly brings forth the issue of land owners selling their land at will, which would damage agricultural productivity and intensify social conflicts. Moreover, should land ownership be privatized, land owners would care about and preserve their land and cultivate their land with meticulous care, but we cannot rule out the possibility that some land owners profit from land purchases and sell or use their land to engage in some nonagricultural activities. Isn't this behavior also shortsighted? Therefore, we must discuss how to overcome the shortsightedness of agricultural product producers under public land ownership. At the current stage, we can maintain status quo in rural areas, i.e., collective land ownership, and maintain the household responsibility system based on collective land ownership. As for land ownership system in the future, we can imagine the following scenario: First of all, all land inside the People's Republic of China shall be declared as owned by the state at a certain point of time in the future, and a state land commission shall be established to monitor and manage all land in the country, disallowing any encroachment of the land that belongs to the whole nation. Meanwhile, a regulation on land occupancy and utilization under public land ownership shall be promulgated, which would specify that the state is the owner of all land and designate a particular occupier and user to every piece of arable land in the agricultural sector. These specific land occupiers and users are microeconomic units engaging in agricultural production (farmers or agricultural enterprises). The state has the ownership of all arable land in the agricultural sector. A microeconomic unit that specifically occupies and uses a piece of arable land can use, transfer, or leave the land to its successor. As for land transfer or lease, any microeconomic unit (a farmer or agricultural enterprise) that occupies and uses land has no right to determine on its own the transfer or lease of land to another user who intends to use the land for nonagricultural purposes, nor does it have the right to transfer or lease the land to a foreigner because the owner of land is the state and the "transfer" that we are discussing hereby is applicable to the right of use, so is "lease" or "successor." In addition, when a microeconomic unit transfers the land to another land user who intends to use the land for agricultural purposes, it must register with relevant land management agency—the State Land Commission—who represents the owner of land, records the transfer, and pays certain charges (such as land transfer fees).

Due to the clarification of public land ownership, the property right of land is clearly defined as far as ownership is concerned. Any microeconomic unit that uses land for agricultural purposes can use it for a long term and transfer the right of use to its successor, as long as state ownership of land is not encroached and rule of law on land management is not violated. As a result, microeconomic units will care about land more than before, and land utilization efficiency will increase significantly. Most importantly, it will direct agricultural product producers to be more long-term oriented.

With the long-standing public land ownership and the long-term use of land by microeconomic units, economies of scale in agriculture will make noticeable headway. Keep in mind that it is very difficult to achieve economies of scale with the collective land ownership and the household responsibility system currently in place, not only because land is dispersed and farmers do not have a clear understanding of economies of scale but also because farmers behave in a shortsighted manner without much care about the land or even lack personal interest in economies of scale. Therefore, only a few pilot programs with voluntary participation requirement are currently carried out in a few regions to test agricultural production on an optimal scale. If we could adopt the occupier and user system under public land ownership in the future, arable land would be relatively centralized via leasing or transferring land, and farmers, as they care more about land, would be more interested in agriculture and motivated to engage in optimal agricultural production in various forms (including various degrees of cooperative production). As a result, the trend of balanced demand and supply of agricultural products would become more and more obvious.

Chapter 9
Establishing the Order of the Socialist Commodity Economy

9.1 Establishing the Order of the Socialist Commodity Economy: Necessity and Difficulty

9.1.1 The Connotation of the Order of the Socialist Commodity Economy

As we discussed in Chap. 1 of this book, the socialist economic system can be classified into three types, the traditional economic system, the dual-track economic system, and the new economic system. Among these three types of economic system, the traditional economic system is the product economy. The economic order under the traditional economic system is classified as the order of the product economy. The dual-track economic system is the transitional stage when the traditional economic system and the new economic system overlap and coexist. At this time, the order of the product economy is still largely in place, and the order of the commodity economy that is compatible with the new economic system has not been fully established. To put it differently, the order of the commodity economy is still in its infancy. The new economic system established after economic reforms will be the socialist commodity economy, and the compatible economic order is the order of the socialist commodity economy.

The economic order is a set of rules that people must follow in economic activities. Once the economic order is established, people can act accordingly and avoid economic disorder. All kinds of conflicts may emerge in the economy, but they can be reconciled and resolved in accordance with these agreed-upon rules. On the contrary, if the economy were out of order and economic activities were not following certain rules, people from all walks of life would lose confidence in the future of the economy, feeling that they would do business in an extremely uncertain environment without any protection of expected profits or even of their personal properties, which would surely lead to shortsightedness. The shortsightedness is

Y. Li, *Chinese Economy in Disequilibrium*, China Academic Library,
DOI 10.1007/978-3-642-39558-1_9, © Foreign Language Teaching and Research
Publishing Co., Ltd and Springer-Verlag Berlin Heidelberg 2014

applicable to not only enterprises but also individuals, the government, and society. In the absence of an economic order, economic chaos or even social turmoil would be inevitable.

In this sense, any society or era calls for an economic order to regulate personal behavior so that people can carry out economic activities in an orderly way. Even having the order of the product economy, which was not conducive to economic growth, is better than having no economic order at all. In other words, what troubles people most in economic activities is the absence of rules. Without rules, expectations of business activities cannot be stabilized. In that case, people may even think that any type of economic order will do, even one that is not ideal, because having something is better than having nothing.

China is currently under the dual-track economic system. Although the economy is not totally out of order, the real situation is that the order of the product economy still reigns partially, and the order of the commodity economy is still in its infancy. The existence of the dual-track economic system and the dual-track economic order (with one outdated but not totally retired and the other compatible with the commodity economy yet in its infancy) is not only very abnormal but also detrimental to the economy. This can be partially blamed for stagnation, inflation, and stagflation as well as resource misallocation. Therefore, it is an important task for us to establish a set of rules as soon as possible to regulate economic behavior, ones that are conducive to the development of the commodity economy and consistent with the coming new economic system, i.e., the order of the socialist commodity economy.

9.1.2 The Order of the Socialist Commodity Economy and the Furthering of Economic Reforms

It is necessary to establish the order of the socialist commodity economy, not only because it provides people with a set of rules to follow during business transactions and prevents people from developing behavioral shortsightedness in business activities due to lack of stable expectations, but also because it is critical to the furthering of economic reforms and to the transformation from the dual-track economic system to the new economic system.

The new economic system that we are about to establish is one in which an enterprise as a microeconomic unit makes its own business decisions and is responsible for its profits and losses. Apparently, the order of the commodity economy is compatible with the new economic system. After the new economic system is established, the order of the commodity economy will control all economic activities. This should not be questionable. Here, we should point out that the reason why we emphasize the establishment of the order of the commodity economy is not only to prepare for the new economic system in the future, but more importantly, to accelerate the transformation from the dual-track economic system to the new economic system through establishing the order of the commodity economy so as to terminate the order of the product economy as well as the product economy itself in a relatively short period of time. In other words, establishing the order of the commodity economy represents a step forward to some degree, and establishing a series of rules can accelerate the development of markets and the formation of a mechanism under which enterprises pursue self-growth and exercise self-control.

As we know, the economy was in a state of disequilibrium under the traditional economic system and so is the economy under the dual-track economic system. Even after the new economic system is established, there will be signs of resource supply constraints, indicating that economic disequilibrium has not disappeared despite somewhat declining intensity of disequilibrium. In support of a relatively smooth transition from the dual-track economic system to the new economic system under disequilibrium conditions, economic reforms need to go further in at least the following three aspects: (1) furthering the enterprise reform and transforming the enterprises that have not severed from their affiliation with government institutions into goods producers who make their own business decisions and are responsible for their own profits and losses; (2) furthering the reform of the planning mechanism so as to reach rationing equilibrium in the commodity market; and (3) transforming government functions, including separating the function of the government as asset owner and regulator of the economy and having the government gradually use economic regulatory measures to regulate the economy.

Furthering economic reforms in these aspects facilitates the establishment of the order of the commodity economy and the transformation from the dual-track economic system to the new economic system. In terms of the first aspect we discussed above, asset ownership will be standardized so that the economic and legal status of enterprise can be changed and they can be directed to serve the market. In terms of the second aspect, the relationship between planning and market will be specified, and some rules on the relationship among government, market, and enterprise will be set up so that government and market can fully function during resource allocation. As for the third aspect, the most important task is to clarify government functions and set up certain rules for the government to adhere to as the asset owner and the regulator of the economy. In summary, if we start establishing the order of the commodity economy while under the dual-track economic system, it is unlikely for us to complete the task during the same period, but it is conducive to accelerating the transition from the dual-track economic system to the new economic system.

9.1.3 The Relationship Between Order Establishment in the Socialist Commodity Economy and Institutional Innovation

The establishment of any economic order calls for the consolidation of a set of principles via institutions. The form of institutions reflects economic order. The institutions hereby mentioned are discussed in a broad sense. They include not only the mechanisms that are established by the legislature but also certain norms that were established by culture and tradition. The establishment of a new economic order means the termination of an old economic order. A new economic order is represented by new institutions. Therefore, the replacement of the old economic order by a new one is the replacement of old institutions by new ones. We have every reason to believe that the establishment of the order of the socialist commodity economy can be called a series of institutional innovations.

Institutional innovation is the transition from the old institutions to the new institutions. The order of the product economy, which is compatible with the product economy, is represented by a series of traditional institutions. We can use the relationship between government, market, and enterprises to illustrate the features of the traditional institutions under the order of the product economy.

(a) The Relationship Between Government and Enterprises

To meet the needs of the product economy, the government supervised enterprises. Enterprises were controlled by the government in terms of staff, capital, and assets and became the affiliated entities of various government institutions. Enterprises had no rights to make business decisions, let alone take responsibility for profits and losses. All of these have been consolidated by relevant institutions.

(b) The Relationship Between Enterprises and Market

In the product economy, the market was not only limited in terms of coverage but also unauthentic in terms of nature. Business transactions between enterprises were conducted outside the market. Even though some business transactions were conducted inside the market, the real market did not exist as transaction counterparties lacked other alternatives. All of these are also reflected by the various institutions established during the time of the product economy.

(c) The Relationship Between Government and Market

This relationship has also clearly demonstrated that the market was controlled by the government, as has been confirmed by various institutions applied in the product economy. The government dominated the market. Not only that, but the government also directly controlled and manipulated the market as a complete monopoly. The government obtained all the resources it needed not only from various sources outside the market but also from the market that is under its control.

This is the order of the product economy validated by its institutions. Although the institutions that established the order of the product economy came into being on a gradual basis, some introduced as laws and some not as laws, they had guaranteed that the economy could run in a proper manner in the product economy. Currently, if we wish to establish the order of the socialist commodity economy, the very action we need to take is to replace the traditional institutions with new ones. Whether it is about the relationship between government and enterprises, or between enterprises and market, or between government and market, we need new institutions to reflect the order of the commodity economy compatible with the system of the commodity economy. Without these institutional innovations, the establishment of the order of the commodity economy would be no more than empty talk. Therefore, it could be said that the establishment of the order of the commodity economy is no other than institutional innovation that reflects the establishment of such a new economic order.

9.1.4 *Difficulties in Establishing the Order of the Socialist Commodity Economy*

The transition from old institutions to new ones has always been difficult. This is because institutions represent the special interest of a group, a class, or a stratum. The transition of institutions is the transition and reallocation of interests. Even though old institutions may have been outdated for a long time, they will not disappear; new institutions may be able to raise productivity, but the birth of new institutions will encounter many difficulties. All of these are linked to adjusting and reallocating interests. Of course, people may ask this question: Taking China as an example, why was it relatively easy to establish the product economy and the economic order compatible with the system in the 1950s, while it was fairly difficult to establish the commodity economy and the corresponding economic order in the 1980s? Since the establishment of a new economic order is in fact a series of institutional innovations, why was the institutional innovation in the 1950s easier than in the 1980s? This is a very interesting question. We have to admit that there are some other reasons, besides the important roles of the adjustment and reallocation of interests that we just discussed.

Next, we will compare the transition of the economic order and the change of institutions during the 1950s and 1980s from five different perspectives:

First of all, China completed the transition from an extremely underdeveloped commodity economy to the product economy during the 1950s.

Because the commodity economy was extremely underdeveloped, it was much easier to transform from the commodity economy to the product economy and establish the corresponding economic order. On the contrary, the Chinese economy transformed from a highly developed product economy to the commodity economy in the 1980s. Because the product economy had been well developed, it was more difficult for the economy to complete its transition into the commodity economy and establish the economic order.

Secondly, the transition from the commodity economy to the product economy during the 1950s had mainly relied upon administrative orders.

History has demonstrated that a series of policies initiated from the top and executed by each level of government institutions in the 1950s, including centralized purchases and sales of goods in rural areas and centralized rationing of goods in urban areas, managed to establish the order of the product economy within a fairly short period of time. When the product economy started its transition to the commodity economy in the 1980s, the central government was no longer able to enforce from top-down similar policies that distorted the balance among production, distribution, and sales. In addition, it must allow enterprises and rural producers to develop a self-control mechanism and pursue self-growth in the marketplace and straighten out various economic relations during the natural evolvement of markets. As a result, it was a slow and natural process going from the dissolution of the order of the product economy to the establishment of the order of the commodity economy.

Thirdly, the product economy has an obvious feature compared with the commodity economy, i.e., the existence of various rigidities.

Keep in mind that because the market under the commodity economy is fully developed or almost fully developed, not only price is elastic, so are wage, interest, rent, and employment. Meanwhile, the status of enterprises as well as their management positions are also flexible and can be changed if necessary. The elasticity or flexibility energizes economic activities in the commodity economy. The product economy, however, was drastically different. In the product economy, price was rigid, so were wage, interest, rent, and employment. Moreover, the status of enterprises and their management positions were not flexible. Once an enterprise was established, it would go on almost forever. Even though it was unprofitable and unable to cover operating expenses, it could still go on unless its administrative institution decided to shut it down. Despite being shut down, enterprise management and permanent employees would not lose their jobs, and their salaries would not be cut either. The management would likely be assigned to similar positions elsewhere, and workers would likely be relocated to another place. This particular type of rigidity, compared to all other types of rigidities, is the one that is most unlikely to energize the economy, which can be termed "enterprise rigidity." It is because of the various rigidities in the product economy, especially "enterprise rigidity," that have caused many problems during the transition from the product economy to the commodity economy. The institutional innovation in this regard was much more difficult than that during the transition from the commodity economy to the product economy.

Fourthly, if we compare the net interest before and after institutional innovations, we can see that they are very different when the commodity economy transitioned to the product economy versus when the product economy transitioned to the commodity economy.

The net interest we are talking about refers to the total benefit net of related costs. Keep in mind that in initiating any institutional innovation, the initiator and undertaker (who can be an individual, a group, or government) of such institutional innovation will always expect the net interest to be greater than zero. Otherwise, it will not be necessary to perform the institutional innovation. But the question is: What are the criteria for the measurement of net interest from an institutional innovation, how can it be calculated, and most importantly, who is the recipient of net interest? When the commodity economy was transformed into the product economy during the 1950s, it was the government who initiated and undertook the institutional innovation. No one else was able to do that. The government must have believed that net interest was obviously larger than zero and that it would receive all net interest. The government could utilize all resources available to do whatever it wanted to do. When the product economy was transformed into the commodity economy during the 1980s, the government was still the primary entity that initiated and undertook the institutional innovation. In other words, it assumed the leadership role, among all entities, to initiate and undertake the institutional innovation. However, how large was the net interest of the institutional innovation? Who received the net interest? Could the government obtain resources from the net interest and use them to develop various projects? The answers to all these questions are not clear. We can draw a conclusion only by taking a look at the process of the institutional innovation as well as the actual situations during the establishment of the order of the commodity economy. Thus, the government who initiated and undertook the institutional innovation was not as decisive and resolute in developing policies during the transformation of the product economy to the commodity economy as in deciding to break away from the commodity economy and establish the product economy. We can expect the government to have hesitant moments during a certain period of time.

Fifthly, for all other entities who initiated and undertook institutional innovation (except the government), their roles in and attitudes toward an institutional innovation were quite different when the commodity economy was transformed into the product economy compared with when the product economy was transformed into the commodity economy.

When the commodity economy was transformed into the product economy, the government was the true sponsoring entity of the institutional innovation, and the other entities did not actually exist, or the other entities (such as enterprises and individuals) simply listed their names as initiators and undertakers of the institutional innovation while as a matter of fact they did not act as initiators or undertakers at all. Therefore, when the commodity economy was transformed into the product economy, the relationship among all these entities that participated in the institutional innovation was simple—the government called the shots. All the other entities, except the government, did not act as sponsors and thus had no say in institutional innovation decision-making or implementation. However, when the product economy was transformed into the commodity economy, the government, despite being the primary entity of the institutional innovation, was no longer the only sponsoring entity. All these entities worked with the government to initiate and implement the institutional innovation. Hence, the relationship between the government and all other entities was much more complicated. This is because some of a series of rules that constituted the order of the commodity economy were proposed and implemented by enterprises and individuals who participated in market activities, and in the meantime, normal market activities also relied upon various agreements or contracts between these enterprises and individuals. In other words, every enterprise or individual who participated in market activities is a proactive factor that contributed to the establishment of the commodity economy, contrary to the product economy in which they were simply passive entities. Since the establishment of the commodity economy and its economic order was the result of voluntary actions taken by all entities participating in the institutional innovation, including government, enterprise, and individual, it was impossible for these entities to have no conflicts or differences at all. Therefore, to some degree, this sheds some light on why the process of establishing the commodity economy was not as smooth as that of establishing the product economy.

These analyses fully demonstrate that the task of establishing the commodity economy and the economic order compatible with the commodity economy in a highly developed product economy will be difficult and requires a relatively long time to accomplish the goal. However, as long as the economy is on its way of transition from the product economy into the commodity economy, the trend will be irreversible and the institutional innovation cannot be stopped. The current challenge for our economists is not to study the necessity of institutional innovation, but mainly to analyze how to minimize the difficulties involved in institutional innovation so that a new economic system and economic order can be established relatively smoothly.

9.2 Interest Adjustment During the Process of Establishing the Order of the Commodity Economy

9.2.1 The Expected Net Interest of Various Institutional Innovation Sponsors

In the previous section, we discussed that when the order of the commodity economy was established, different institutional innovation sponsors assessed their own net interest and came up with their own estimate of net interest they could receive from the institutional innovation so that they could decide on how to participate in the institutional innovation. Now we will be looking at institutional innovation from a different perspective—that of three types of entities: government, enterprise, and individual.

1. The Government Acting as an Institutional Innovation Sponsor During the Process of Establishing the Order of the Commodity Economy

During the transition from the product economy to the commodity economy, we need to establish the order of the commodity economy, which includes specifying property rights, setting out transaction rules and regulations for various markets, clarifying the roles of various economic departments of the government, and institutionalizing and standardizing government behavior. After the new economic order is established, the government will be highly capable and efficient. It will no longer directly manage enterprises. Instead, it will regulate the market via economic adjustment measures and use laws, regulations, and policies to maintain normal operations in the marketplace. This is drastically different from the roles of the government in the product economy and the net interest that the government received from the order of the product economy.

In the product economy, the government could obtain as many resources as possible by all means and control the maximum amount of resources provided by society during each period in history. The net interest that the government receives after the commodity economy is established is certainly lower. With property rights clarified and enterprises retaining a portion of their income, the government can only impose taxes as the regulator and receive its own share of income as an investor. The government cannot obtain all the resources it wants by fiscal means or by printing money. Establishing the order of the commodity economy, in a sense, serves as a sort of restriction over the approaches that the government can use to obtain resources as well as over its share of resources. As discussed above, the government, as an institutional innovation sponsor, was sometimes hesitant and indecisive, due to lower expected net interest from the institutional innovation.

But there is another side of the story. If the government had ever been hesitant, such hesitation would have been unnecessary. From the dynamic perspective, the government's expected net interest would not decrease, but instead increase if the commodity economy were established. This is because the development of the commodity economy and the new economic order will energize the market and generate significant growth in enterprise and personal income. As a result, we expect the government to gain higher tax revenues as the regulator and higher investment income as an investor. The comment that expected net interest of the government would decrease is merely based on a static interpretation of the decrease in the government's share of total revenues. The upward trend in total revenues is neglected.

We should not consider the restrictions over the approaches that the government adopts to obtain resources and the share of resources obtained after the order of the commodity economy is established a bad thing detrimental to the government. Unrestricted utilization of resources by the government may allow resources to be allocated to inappropriate areas and lead to low efficiency, zero efficiency, or even negative efficiency. On the other hand, it may impede market activities and discourage enterprises and individuals from participating in market activities. In addition, if government behavior (including obtaining resources) were not restricted, the government itself and its officials might be corrupted.

2. Enterprise Acting as an Institutional Innovation Sponsor During the Process of Establishing the Order of the Commodity Economy

What does the order of the commodity economy really mean to enterprises? Basically, it means two things: One, property rights will be normalized; two, transactional activities will be market-oriented and contract-based. As one of the institutional innovation sponsors that establish the order of the commodity economy, enterprise expects its net interest to be greater than zero. The expected positive net interest derives from the abovementioned two aspects.

After property rights are normalized, investors of an enterprise (including a state-owned enterprise) will become the owner of its assets. The portion of investment made by the state shall be owned by various asset supervisory institutions of the state, whereas the portion of investment made by the enterprise itself shall be owned by such institutions as enterprise foundation. The management of an enterprise has the right to manage its assets. As a result, all enterprises will become goods producers who make their own business decisions and are responsible for their profits and losses. An enterprise is a legal entity and all enterprises are legally equal. The relationship between an enterprise and the government that invested in the enterprise is one between an investee and an investor. The relationship between an enterprise and the government as the regulator is that the enterprise must abide by the law and pay taxes in accordance with relevant rules and regulations. Enterprises' expected net interest will increase in three ways: First, enterprises only pay taxes pursuant to relevant rules and regulations. They are no longer liable for other obligations such as fees, contributions or allocated charges, nor do they accept any assignment from their administrative institutions. Second, enterprises can take advantage of its capital accumulation and allow assets to appreciate and income to grow. Third, enterprises can take advantage of their accumulated capital to set up business alliance with other enterprises, participate in equity ownership in other enterprises, and establish conglomerates. In summary, normalizing property rights will definitely increase enterprises' net interest.

For every enterprise, market-oriented and contract-based transactional activities are critical to ensuring the steady growth of revenues. In terms of production and sales activities, enterprises will always react to expected prices, expected profitability, and expected interest rate. Without market transactions, contractual protection, and equitable solutions to transactional disputes, enterprises will not maintain stable expectations, which may cause corporate shortsightedness, and in the meantime transaction cost will also increase, lowering enterprises' real income. It is for this reason that enterprises, as institutional innovation sponsors that establish the order of the commodity economy, will proactively participate in institutional innovation activities to execute market-oriented and contract-based transactions, as they are closely related to raising their expected net interest.

Therefore, we can reach this conclusion: If enterprises were neither able to make their own business decisions nor to take responsibility for their profits and losses in the product economy, no institutional innovation at that time could bring higher expected net interest to enterprises, and enterprises were destined to be passive in an institutional innovation. On the contrary, after the product economy is transformed into the commodity economy, enterprises, in anticipation of higher net interest, will propose and endorse any institutional innovation that normalizes property rights and supports market-oriented and contract-based transactions. The reason is obvious and self-explanatory.

3. Individual Acting as an Institutional Innovation Sponsor During the Process of Establishing the Order of the Commodity Economy

As one of the institutional innovation sponsors during the process of establishing the order of the commodity economy, individual functions in the following three ways:

First of all, as workers, individuals are obviously directly related to establishing the order in the labor market, and the development of market-oriented and contract-based activities in the labor market also influences the expected net interest of every member of the labor force. Therefore, individuals or any group that represents workers will not only actively support the establishment of the order of the labor market and the institutional innovation in this regard, but also make significant contributions to substantiating the new economic order.

Secondly, individuals are suppliers of capital, or savers, who are directly related to establishing the order of the capital market. What concerns people most is the absence of the protection of interest income or even principal after funds are transferred. Individuals are also afraid of fraudulence or breach of contracts in the capital market. Should these incidents happen, people would no longer be willing to offer their money as capital. Therefore, the progress of market-oriented and contract-based activities in the capital market influences everyone's expected net interest. Individuals request that certain institutional innovations in the capital market and the new economic order be established. They function as the originator and supporter of the institutional innovation.

Thirdly, individuals buy goods. As consumers, they are also directly related to the order of the commodity market. Because of the varying degrees of resource supply and demand constraints under disequilibrium conditions, we can often see either shortages or excess of commodities. Especially in the circumstance of commodity shortages, individual consumers may worry about declining product quality and higher prices, and meanwhile, they are also concerned about monopolies in the market, all of which will hurt consumers. Therefore, as commodity buyers, individuals require that the institutional innovation and the new order in the commodity market be established to minimize losses and bring about higher expected net interest. Individuals actively call for and support the institutional innovation in the commodity market and become an important force that drives market-oriented and contract-based activities in the commodity market.

We can imagine that people's economic requests were suppressed or at least not taken seriously in the product economy. If there were any institutional change in the product economy, which served to consolidate the order of the product economy, individuals would be completely passive. Even though they clearly knew that an institutional change would infringe upon their real net interest or expected net interest, they could do nothing. Only when the product economy started to transform to the commodity economy will it be possible for individuals to actively participate in the institutional innovation to increase their expected net interest.

9.2.2 Conflict of Expected Net Interest Among Different Institutional Innovation Sponsors

Government, enterprise, and individual are institutional innovation entities during the process of establishing the order of the commodity economy. Each of these entities can use institutional innovation to increase their expected net interest.

Generally speaking, the interests of government, enterprise, and individual are aligned. This statement has two implications: First, as long as the commodity economy grows and productivity increases, gross domestic product will increase. Even though government, enterprise, and individual keep their respective shares of total national income flat, their total interests will be higher. On the other hand, the interests of government, enterprise, and individual are coexistent and codependent. Should the interests of any one of them be hurt, the other two entities would not benefit in the long run. Many real cases in economic activities have demonstrated that the interests of these entities are aligned as stated. It is the alignment of the interests that drives government, enterprise, and individual to actively pursue the order of the commodity economy and to proactively propose, support, and execute institutional innovation during the process of establishing the order of the commodity economy.

However, we have to admit that government, enterprise, and individual are different entities in the institutional innovation during the establishment of the order of the commodity economy. Hence, their expected net interest will conflict with each other. For example, as the fiscal relationship and government functions are clearly defined, a series of rules applicable to industrial and commercial administration, price, wage, tax, and auditing will be introduced, which will impose certain constraints on the behavior of each of them. Government, enterprise, and individual must follow the order of the commodity economy to estimate their expected net interest. They cannot fall back on the old order of the product economy. The expected net interest under the old economic order will differ from the one under the new economic order in amount, which brings about changes to expected net interest and results in interest reallocation among various groups of society. Here is another example: When the economic order is established in the capital, labor, and commodity market, enterprise can be the supplier, and individual can be the buyer in a certain market, or it can be exactly the opposite, with enterprise being the buyer and individual being the supplier. If it were under equilibrium conditions where every market had equilibrium prices, the market price were the equilibrium price, transactions were concluded only at the equilibrium price, and demand equaled supply, both suppliers and buyers would be able to realize their expected net interest, and the conflict of interest would not be very obvious or could even disappear. However, this is not the case in real life. Despite the establishment of the order of the commodity economy after the transition to the commodity economy is completed, the economy may still be in the state of disequilibrium, and the equilibrium price may actually be nonexistent in the market as long as there are resource supply or demand constraints. As a result, it is inevitable to see conflicts of expected net interest between enterprise and individual that function as the supplier and buyer in the marketplace. The establishment of the order of the commodity economy can only prevent any conflict of interest between suppliers and buyers from escalating, some nonmarket factors from excessively interfering with the interests of suppliers and buyers, and non-market-based transactions from causing excessive damage to the interests of suppliers or sellers, but it will not completely eliminate the conflict of interest between them. Under disequilibrium conditions, even if property rights are clearly specified, all transactions are market-oriented and contract-based, and every market participant (an enterprise or an individual) is able to make its own business decisions and is constrained by its self-interest, there will be occasional commodity shortages or surpluses causing conflict of expected net interest between enterprise and individual. This will happen regardless of whether institutional innovation sponsors like it or not.

9.2.3 Conflict of Interest Between Various Types of Rigidity in the Economy and Institutional Innovation Sponsors

In our discussions on the difficulties of the transition from the product economy to the commodity economy, we have mentioned that "enterprise rigidity," together with some other types of rigidity under the product economy, such as wage rigidity, employment rigidity, and benefit rigidity, had made it very difficult for the economy to make the transition. To some extent, this is related to the conflict of interest between institutional innovation sponsors during the process of establishing the order of the commodity economy.

From the perspective of an individual who is a member of the labor force, a market-oriented and contract-based labor market meets the need of developing the commodity economy as well as his or her personal interest. On the other hand, because of the establishment of some new economic systems, e.g., enterprise employment system has been reformed and permanent employment has been abolished. Thus, enterprises are granted the rights to lay off or terminate their employees, and some workers' income will be lower compared to the past, thus widening income gaps among workers. Those workers who see their income rising at a lowered rate will be disappointed, and they may become a new obstacle to the institutional innovation in the labor market.

The problems do not end here. When the enterprise employment system is reformed, permanent employment is abolished, and layoff or termination is allowed, some workers will become unemployed in some circumstances, and conflict of interest between enterprises and workers will arise. Enterprises hope to eliminate unreasonable wage rigidity and employment rigidity by means of a series of institutional innovations. But workers (at least permanently employed workers) will normally try to maintain some wage rigidity and employment rigidity, which is reflected by a commonly known phrase: "Old rules apply to old people and new rules apply to new people." This is another obstacle to the institutional innovation in the labor market. It is reflective of the conflict of interest not only between enterprises and workers but also among different groups of workers.

Let us take another look at the conflict of interest among enterprise, government, and individual during the innovation of tax institutions. This will also help illustrate the conflict among these different institutional innovation sponsors. To establish the order of the commodity economy, it is necessary to normalize taxation so that taxes are both reasonable and standardized, clearly specified in laws and regulations, and can be checked and monitored more easily. In this sense, the interests of government, enterprise, and individual are aligned. However, the attitudes toward the types of taxes, the level of tax rates, and penalties for tax evasion, tax omission, or late tax payment vary among government, enterprise, and individual. If we say that there are disagreements among these institutional innovation sponsors, these disagreements can be considered conflict of interest. We can take the analysis one step further by dividing the government into the central government and local governments; the separation of taxes collected by the central government and local governments as well as the allocation of some taxes between them reflect conflict of interest, as the central government and local governments are different institutional innovation sponsors, despite the fact that both of them support the reform of the tax system and the establishment of a new tax system to promote economic development and ensure growth in fiscal revenues.

As a matter of fact, conflict of interest during the innovation of tax institutions is related to the abovementioned "enterprise rigidity" as well as other relevant types of rigidity. Generally speaking, enterprises wish to do business under the commodity economy, and that they can make their own business decisions and take responsibility for their profits and losses gives them hope for a bright future. However, many enterprises are still unable to forget the product economy in which they are not held responsible for any loss, especially when they are under pressures from market competition. They feel that the old way in which the government took care of everything and eliminated the danger of bankruptcy may not be too bad after all. In the old way, enterprises did not care about what types of taxes the government levied or how high tax rates were. The conflict of interest in terms of taxes had been minimized. If enterprises are responsible for their own profits and losses and are subject to shutdown or bankruptcy risks in a new economic environment, they will surely try to minimize taxes and fight for tax benefits in order to make up for any loss arising from the termination of the "enterprise rigidity." This is a clear conflict of interest between enterprise and government during the tax reform. In addition, as taxpayers, individuals will also consider their benefits from the "enterprise rigidity" and some of the other relevant types of rigidity. In the product economy with different types of rigidity, individuals paid almost zero taxes. Hence, there were no conflict of interest between government and individual in terms of direct taxes. When the economy completes the transition from the product economy to the commodity economy and the "enterprise rigidity" and some other relevant types of rigidity start to disappear, it is easy for people to understand that individuals begin to be sensitive about taxes, especially direct taxes. They start to feel uncertain about living necessities, for enterprises are susceptible to shutdown or bankruptcy; salaries can be suspended, discounted, or changed; employment is no longer stable; and benefits can be impacted. In such an environment, if direct taxes or some relevant measures are adopted, such as the requirement to file personal income tax and register personal properties, people may feel highly uncertain about the security of daily living, despite a relatively high minimum income required to file taxes. As a result, conflict of interest between government and individuals during the tax reform will be exposed.

In addition, we can also see conflict of interest between institutional innovation sponsors due to the "enterprise rigidity" and some other relevant types of rigidity in different areas, such as innovating financial or foreign trade institutions. Take credit as an example: Should we lend to selected enterprises, or should we lend to enterprises with the purpose of saving them from bankruptcy, even when they are unprofitable? This represents the conflict of interest among government, banks, enterprises, and workers. Unprofitable enterprises definitely wish to keep the unreasonable "enterprise rigidity" and some other relevant types of rigidity, such as wage rigidity and employment rigidity, and so do the workers of unprofitable enterprises. Therefore, they all believe that banks should lend to unprofitable enterprises. As one of the entities undertaking the innovation of the financial system, banks will undoubtedly oppose that. As for the government, its attitude is rather complicated. From the perspective of the economy, the government believes that it is necessary for banks to issue loans on the basis of the profitability principle. From the perspective of society, however, it believes that it is not inappropriate for banks to take care of unprofitable enterprises as well as their employees. Conflict of interest among the entities involved in the innovation of financial institutions certainly makes it more difficult to perform institutional innovation. It is the same with the innovation of foreign trade institutions. As the "enterprise rigidity" and some other relevant types of rigidity had been existent for a long time, we have encountered obstacles during the innovation of foreign trade institutions, which requires that specialized foreign trade enterprises be held responsible for their profits and losses and that export goods manufacturers freely participate in the competition in the international market, due to differences in profitability across various enterprises and different attitudes among their employees, despite the acknowledgment of the necessity to pursue institutional innovation by the government.

What we have discussed has once again revealed the difficulties in establishing the order of the commodity economy.

9.2.4 The Roles of the Government in Alleviating Conflict of Interest in Institutional Innovation

As the most important entity of institutional innovation during the process of establishing the order of the commodity economy, the government not only should play a role in alleviating conflict of interest during the process of the institutional innovation, but also has the capacity to do so. This is determined by the position of the government in the economy.

As discussed earlier, in the commodity economy, the government acts as the regulator to monitor and regulate the economy. The government also acts as an owner and investor to protect, own, and operate state assets. Besides, the government represents the interests of the entire nation. In other words, it is the representative of the country's interests and is responsible for reconciling the interests of the nation, collective groups, and individual persons. When the interests of these three parties are not aligned, the government should act out of national interest as well as out of long-term interests and reconcile any inconsistency that may arise. Of course, this does not mean that national interest can replace collective interest and personal interest, nor does it mean that the government can augment national interest by sacrificing collective interest and personal interest. To alleviate conflict of interest during the institutional innovation, the government must consider and reconcile the interests of these three parties.

How much can government do in this regard? We need to analyze this question in a realistic way. Generally speaking, government behavior cannot be idealized. After all, the government has limited information, its assessment of real situations may not be entirely consistent with the reality, and it is difficult for the government to prevent unexpected economic events from happening. What's more, the effectiveness of government policies lags and microeconomic units take precautionary measures. All of these issues may influence the government's efforts to alleviate conflict of interest during the institutional innovation. Therefore, the government cannot completely reconcile and simultaneously satisfy national interest, collective interest, and personal interest on its own. Nevertheless, the government should not feel relaxed. It is still able to work to alleviate conflict of interest to some extent during institutional innovation, which is demonstrated by the following ways:

1. A series of institutional innovations with regard to the establishment of the order of the commodity economy should be validated by laws and regulations. Although some of the innovations may not be complete or perfect enough at a certain time, having some institutions will be better than having no institution at all, and having some laws and regulations will be better than having no laws and regulations. During the process of formulating laws and regulations, the government should listen to all parties and select the best option. These laws and regulations should be reflective of national interest, collective interest, and personal interest at the same time.
2. After laws and regulations concerning the order of the commodity economy are established, even though such laws and regulations reflect national interest, collective interest, and personal interest, it is likely that one party may be neglected during the enforcement of these laws and regulations, causing conflict of interest among the institutional innovation sponsors. Therefore, the government should reinforce the monitoring and supervision of law enforcement so that national interest, collective interest, and personal interest can be effectively protected and that the order of the commodity economy can be established by gradually aligning the interests of the three parties.
3. The economic adjustment measures that the government takes can not only stabilize the economy and support economic growth but also ensure coordinated economic and social development. Simultaneously satisfying national interest, collective interest, and personal interest and alleviating conflict of interest during the process of developing the commodity economy and the institutional innovation is one of the tasks that ensure coordinated economic and social development.

Therefore, the government can consider actual economic situations and use appropriate economic adjustment measures pursuant to laws and regulations to avoid harming the interests of any of the three parties. This also demonstrates the role of the government.

4. During the process of the institutional innovation, conflict of interest among institutional innovation sponsors not only refers to the battling of real interests but also includes the psychological discomfort arising from increasingly widening gap among these three entities. This means that if any one of the three interest groups (especially enterprise or individual) feels that its secured interest is not as much as that of the other groups or that its interest is not growing as fast as that of the other groups, it may come to the belief that it has incurred losses. It is hard to avoid the psychological discomfort during the process of establishing the order of the commodity economy. During any institutional innovation, it is impossible to guarantee that every interest group receive equal share of benefits, and hence it is difficult to prevent people from developing resentment or contradictory attitudes. In an attempt to resolve this issue, the government, as the superior economic regulator and the representative of national interest, should use ideological education and propaganda to help people gain a relatively correct understanding of different entities' interests as well as the interest gap among different entities so as to minimize the psychological discomfort. We should admit that these education and propaganda efforts by the government are better than nothing.
5. Adjustment of the Relationship of Various Institutional Innovation Sponsors' Interests

As lawmaker, law enforcement body, economic regulator, and economic administrator, the government can probably alleviate the conflict of interest among the institutional innovation sponsors during the process of establishing the order of the commodity economy. Nonetheless, we will have to mainly rely on market-oriented and contract-based transactions to adjust the interests of the institutional innovation sponsors. Even if the economy could be in disequilibrium after the traditional economic system and the dual-track economic system were terminated, i.e., the market could still be underdeveloped and the supply and demand of resources could be faced with multiple constraints during a certain period of time, the interests of the institutional innovation sponsors could be naturally adjusted by business transactions as long as these transactions are market-oriented and contract-based. In addition, the results of the adjustment will also be accepted by both parties of a transaction. Therefore, to understand the meaning and function of market-oriented and contract-based transactions is critical to understanding the institutional innovation during the process of establishing the order of the socialist commodity economy.

Why can market-oriented and contract-based transactions play such a critical role in the adjustment of the interests of various entities? Why can't this role be assumed by the government? These questions can be answered from the following four aspects:

First of all, we have clearly learned from the functions of the market in allocating resources that the reason why various interests can be adjusted by market-oriented and contract-based transactions is the establishment of the market mechanism with fair competition.

Fair competition hereby discussed is in relative terms, for completely fair competition is impossible under disequilibrium conditions and equilibrium is only a theoretical assumption. For most Chinese enterprises and individuals, being able to set up a market mechanism with fair competition through the establishment of the order of the commodity economy is already quite impressive. With a market of relatively fair competition, every region, sector, and enterprise, except for extremely few that need special attention, is generally placed on a level field. They are standing on the same starting line. The situation in which some regions can receive favorable treatment or some sectors can obtain cheap supplies of raw materials and fuel or some enterprises are granted favorable prices will no longer exist. There is only one policy that is applicable to all market participants when they do business in the market. As a result, even if competition leads to income gap among market participants, the result will be acceptable to all.

Secondly, all market participants share a common benefit from market-oriented and contract-based transactions, i.e., they can have stable expectations for one another.

Keep in mind that the behavioral shortsightedness of enterprise, individual, and government as well as government officials can be traced back to the uncertainty of business prospects. Since the economic prospect is unpredictable, it is hard to prevent people from focusing on their near-term interests. From the perspective of enterprises and individuals who conduct market transactions, the biggest loss incurred by transactions under volatile expectations will be their inability to effectively estimate costs and benefits, which may lead to missed opportunities for investment or profit or losses that could have been avoided. As a result, they may lose confidence in operating their businesses. If the order of the commodity economy were established, business transactions would be market-oriented and contract-based, and the losses would decrease significantly as transaction participants could develop relatively stable expectations. In the circumstance where expectations are relatively stable, the adjustment of various entities' interests is based on how each entity endeavors to minimize its avoidable losses. In other words, the way that various entities' interests are adjusted is traced to their investment decisions and strategic business plans after they effectively weigh costs and benefits.

Thirdly, market-oriented and contract-based transactions will lower transaction costs significantly, which means a higher expected net interest for every market participant (including enterprises and individuals).

Transaction costs refer to the costs of the services provided by service providers in market transactions. In addition to transportation cost, transaction costs also include information cost (or cost related to obtaining market information), contract negotiation cost (or negotiation cost associated with signing a contract), and contract execution cost (or cost associated with executing a contract). Transaction costs always vary with the size of the market. The more developed and complete the market is, the lower the marginal costs of information, negotiation, and execution will be. In other words, the average transaction cost for every unit tends to decrease as the size of the market increases and the market becomes more developed and complete. If a transaction is not conducted inside the market but done outside the market or a transaction is not conducted in the form of a contract and is not binding on both parties of the transaction, either an enterprise or an individual will be subject to higher transaction costs. Higher transaction costs are not only the direct losses of the enterprises or individuals involved in the transaction but also detrimental to the national economy. This is because the continuous decline in transaction cost is one of the factors that can contribute to economic growth and higher gross domestic product, and also, the adjustment of various entities' interests will be much easier during economic growth and growing gross domestic product than during stagnant gross domestic product in a sluggish economy. This is the common benefit brought to the various institutional innovation sponsors by the lowered transaction costs through market-oriented and contract-based transactions.

Fourthly, in the circumstance where transactions are done in the market and based on contracts, the average rate of return from different investments tends to converge gradually as long as production factors are allowed to flow freely and property rights are clearly specified. This is another way to adjust the interests of various institutional innovation sponsors.

From a static perspective, conflicts may arise during the distribution of interests among various institutional innovation sponsors during the process of establishing the order of the commodity economy due to certain institutional or historical reasons. It is even likely that every entity believes it has not received enough interest and other entities have obtained too much interest. The conflict is hard to avoid. In a static economic environment, it is very difficult to transfer interest from one entity to another, unless the government uses some administrative adjustment measures. However, if the government were to use some administrative adjustment measures to do so, new conflicts would arise and another entity might be dissatisfied. From a dynamic viewpoint, any conflict of interest may tend to diminish as the average rate of return of investments for each entity converges. Market-oriented and contract-based transactions will allow production factors to flow freely and facilitate the convergence of average rate of return, which to some extent is fair to all institutional innovation sponsors. Of course, market-oriented and contract-based transactions will not eliminate any difference in the rate of return among different investors. The gap in average investment return may get even larger. In this case, can we ask whether this is contradictory to the convergence of average rate of return that we discussed earlier? Why can we believe the average rate of investment return is converging while the gap in investment return may widen on the other hand? As a matter of fact, they are not contradictory.

When we say that the average rate of investment return for each investor will tend to converge when transaction activities are market-oriented and contract-based, we refer to the general trend of cost integration, price integration, and revenue integration due to free circulation of production factors, including capital.

When we say that the gap in investment return for different investors will widen when transaction activities are market-oriented and contract-based, we have considered the outcomes from the rise and utilization of new investment opportunities, the development of new industrial sectors, the application of new technologies, the establishment of new markets, and the adoption of new managerial styles, which are not contradictory to the convergence of the average rate of investment return for each investor. In many cases, these two scenarios represent two different stages of the same process. That is, after the gap in investment return widens among different investors, there is a certain period of time before the average investment return of different investors gets more or less the same. While the average rate of return for each investor is converging, new investment opportunities, new industrial sectors, new technologies, new markets, and new managerial styles will emerge, pushing the rate of return of various investors to widen once again.

The process of economic activities basically follows this pattern. Therefore, the conflict of interest among different institutional innovation sponsors will likely improve if transaction activities are market-oriented and contract-based. On the other hand, different investors will see their returns vary for various reasons, such as capturing new investment opportunities. Because widening returns among investors are related to the emerging and capturing of new investment opportunities, it is reflective of the existence and consequence of competition in the marketplace. It demonstrates a certain degree of fairness. Normally, market participants recognize and accept the consequences. In addition, as long as the economic order is established and competition is fair, any investor can take advantage of a new investment opportunity and pursue higher returns. The possibility of achieving higher returns is conducive to offsetting the psychological discomfort arising from the widening gap in investment return.

These four aspects have illustrated the roles that market-oriented and contract-based transactions play in adjusting the interests of different institutional innovation sponsors. These four aspects are actually correlated. They reveal one important issue: Since the conflict of interest among different institutional innovation sponsors is inevitable under disequilibrium conditions and the government is subject to certain constraints when adjusting the interests of different institutional innovation sponsors, it is necessary, both in theory and in practice, to mainly rely on the market to adjust the interests of these entities so that the conflict of interest among them can be somewhat alleviated.

Chapter 10
The Standardization of Institutional Innovation

10.1 The Role of the Government in Standardizing Institutional Innovation

10.1.1 Contractual Violations During the Process of Establishing the Order of the Commodity Economy

During the process of establishing the commodity economy, economic growth may face multiple setbacks if business transactions are neither market-oriented nor contract-based. We have analyzed this issue in our discussions about establishing the order of the commodity economy and the institutional innovation. Now, what we have to study is this: Even though business transactions are done in the market and based on contract, how is the commodity economy impacted by breach of contract that may often occur? How can we resolve contractual violations?

The consequences of contractual violations are very obvious. They will not only harm the real interests of stakeholders, but also, and more importantly, lead to uncertainties in the expectation of growth and hinder future transactions as well as the expansion of business connections. More specifically, when violations of contracts increase, people may lose confidence in contract-based transactions, which tends to increase the proportion of cash-based spot transactions. The increasing proportion of cash-based spot transactions is incompatible with the trend of developing the commodity economy.

Many factors can lead to a contractual violation. Under the dual-track economic system, the potential causes of a contractual violation include the interference by government administrative institutions in enterprise and individual business activities, relatively significant price fluctuations, unfavorable influences of resource supply constraints on the supply of products, the existence of special interest tied to non-market-oriented and non-contract-based transactions, and the lack of legal restrictions on contractual violations. Some of the phenomena under the dual-track economic system, such as breaching a subcontract, a lease contract, or a supply

Y. Li, *Chinese Economy in Disequilibrium*, China Academic Library,
DOI 10.1007/978-3-642-39558-1_10, © Foreign Language Teaching and Research
Publishing Co., Ltd and Springer-Verlag Berlin Heidelberg 2014

order and nonpayment or delayed payment of payables or loans, are caused by the abovementioned factors. Of course, when we analyze violations of contracts, we will need to distinguish intentional violation and unintentional violation. The existence of either intentional violation or unintentional violation demonstrates, once again, the necessity and importance of establishing the order of the commodity economy and pushing forward the institutional innovation for business transactions.

After the transition of the dual-track economic system to the new economic system, both intentional and unintentional contractual violations may still persist as long as the economy is in disequilibrium, i.e., there are constraints on resource supply or constraints on demand for resources. To a large degree, intentional violation is related to the existence of special interest tied to non-market-oriented and non-contract-based transactions. The special interest from non-market-oriented and non-contract-based transactions originates from constraints on resource supply or constraints on demand for resources. An unintentional violation of a contract is closely related to constraints on resource supply or constraints on demand for resources, even if the violator does not really intend to secure special economic interests. Therefore, if we wish to eliminate violations of contracts, we should rely not only on establishing the order of the commodity economy and institutional innovation but also on reducing the degree of disequilibrium in the economy.

10.1.2 The Government as Institutional Innovation Sponsor

In our earlier discussions on the necessity of establishing the order of the commodity economy and adjusting the interests of various entities during the establishment of the order of the commodity economy, we have talked about the roles of the government as an institutional innovation sponsor. The roles of the government can be summarized as follows: In order to establish the order of the commodity economy, the government must establish a series of laws and regulations that are followed and enforced. For example, market-oriented and contract-based transactions must follow certain laws and regulations. Hence, the government as an institutional innovation sponsor must play their part in stipulating and enforcing the laws and regulations. Now, what exactly should the government do as an institutional innovation sponsor with regard to the violations of contracts that hinder the growth of the commodity economy?

First of all, as a party of a contract in a transaction, the government must abide by the rules and respect the sanctity of the contract. As a matter of fact, doing so is to respect the rights and status of the counterparty of the contract. A contract is binding on both parties who participate in the transaction. The government as a party of a contract should by no means supersede the counterparty of the contract. Unilaterally terminating, cancelling, or breaching a contract by the government is not allowed in the commodity economy. The government itself must strictly abide by the contract so as to serve as a model for society. In so doing, the government can gain the authority to deal with the contractual disputes in society.

Secondly, because several cases of violations of business contracts are related to abnormal property rights, the government as an institutional innovation sponsor must start the institutional innovation with normalizing property rights, reinforce the legislation with regard to property rights, and strictly execute the laws during the establishment of the order of the commodity economy so as to potentially eliminate violations of contracts. Just as we have discussed repeatedly, if property right is not normalized, it will be very hard to validate corporate legal identity, and it will be very hard for enterprises to take responsibility for their business transactions independently, which gives rises to various excuses for contractual violations in business transactions. Therefore, to reform property rights is one of the most important institutional innovations during the process of establishing the order of the commodity economy. Our analysis of contractual violations has supported this viewpoint from a different perspective.

Next, some violations of business contracts are intentional. One of the main reasons to do so is the possibility and practicality for the party who violates a contract to easily reap special interest. As for these types of violations, we cannot simply use moral persuasion as a solution. To a party of a binding contract, there should not only be moral constraints (or normally referred to as business ethics), but more importantly, there should also be legal and economic constraints. As one of the institutional innovation sponsors, the government must draw up laws and regulations to maintain order in the market and to ensure that a contract is executed according to binding terms and conditions. If the economic compensation and the penalty for the party who violates the contract exceed the marginal benefit that the violator can receive from doing so, every party of the transaction who intends to violate the contract in the first place will have to reconsider the costs and benefits of such action. As a result, there will be fewer violations of contracts.

Lastly, as the institutional innovation sponsor, the government should use legislation to minimize or lower the interference by a third party in the behavior of the two parties of a contract during a business transaction. The interference of a third party during the execution of a contract has often been one of the reasons for contractual violations. It should be emphasized that the government has the responsibility to ensure that the process of contract execution is free from interference by any third party as long as the contract is legal. The responsibility of the government is to protect the public interest, support fair competition in the market, and stop or eliminate violations of the law or transactional fraud in businesses. If fraud does happen in business transactions or is included in a binding contract, we should follow the legal procedures instead of allowing a third party to handle it.

All the analysis of the roles of the government in protecting and supporting market-oriented and contract-based transactions is based on the viewpoint that the government is an institutional innovation sponsor. Of course, the government is not only an institutional innovation sponsor. It also plays the role of mediator in business disputes, which is almost as important as the role of institutional innovation sponsor.

10.1.3 The Government as Mediator of Business Disputes

As the dual-track economic system is being transformed into the new economic system, we will not see the government as a party in a business transaction as frequently as before. This is because of changing government functions, i.e., the role of the government as the owner of state assets will be separated from its role as the regulator of the economy, and the government will start regulating the economy indirectly rather than directly. Not only that, the government will standardize property rights so that certain state assets located at an enterprise will be separated from the overall state assets and that the legal person of an enterprise, not the government, will represent the assets of the enterprise. As a result, the representative of state assets in a lease or subcontract will no longer be a government institution, but a company or a specific economic unit who is the lessor (or lessee) or the contractor (or contractee). Moreover, an entity that signs various business contracts, such as a supply contract, a sales contract, and a credit facility contract, will no longer be a government institution, but a company or a specific economic unit who represents the interests of the state. We should admit that this situation is normal and it is consistent with the nature of the commodity economy as well as the economic development trend.

Under such a new economic system, the government as a mediator of business disputes will play an important role in maintaining market-oriented and contract-based business transactions. When a violation of contract or a contractual dispute arises, regardless of whether it is an intentional or unintentional violation, it needs to be resolved properly. As important as unofficial mediation may be, the government needs to step in to resolve contractual disputes impartially in accordance with the law, which has always been a powerful protection of the order of the commodity economy. Impartial resolution is a resolution based on the law, clearly specifying contractual responsibilities, imposing necessary punishment on the violator, minimizing contract execution costs, and lowering economic losses arising from a contractual dispute.

When the government acts as a judge in a contractual dispute and wins over the trust from all transaction participants, the commodity economy can run relatively smoothly. Before the government takes this role, it used to act as a direct transaction participant and interfered with business activities by giving direct orders. So when there was a business dispute, the government was blamed for it. For example, when a dispute between an enterprise and its workers arose, the workers would see the enterprise and the government as one entity. The dispute between the enterprise and its workers (such as disputes over wages or terminations) would become one between workers and the government. Here is another example. When a seller and a buyer had a dispute (in which the seller failed to deliver an agreed-upon quantity of goods or the buyer failed to pay the amount due), the party who incurred losses would normally regard the party in breach and the government as one entity and thus kept the government involved in the dispute. These situations were very difficult to avoid under the traditional economic system or the dual-track economic system.

After the establishment of the commodity economy, the situation has changed. When an enterprise and its workers have a dispute over wages or employment, the dispute is between the enterprise and its workers. When the enterprise and its workers fail to resolve the dispute appropriately, the government will step in as the judge of business disputes to resolve the issue. By the same token, when there is a dispute between enterprises or between enterprises and consumers, the government will not get involved unless the dispute cannot be resolved appropriately. In that case, the government will act as a mediator of business disputes and help find a resolution. We can see from these examples that the government can play the role as a mediator of business disputes to ensure that the commodity economy can operate normally.

10.1.4 Monopolies in the Socialist Commodity Economy and Government's Solutions

Even after the transition of the dual-track economic system into the new economic system, the market in China is still unlikely to become perfectly competitive. We have discussed this issue earlier. Since the market is not perfectly competitive, it means that monopolies in the commodity economy will still exist. We can only conclude that there will be fewer monopolies under the new economic system than under the traditional economic system or the dual-track economic system and that the damage to the economy caused by monopolies under the new economic system will also be less severe than under the traditional economic system or the dual-track economic system.

Why can we draw this conclusion? Isn't the order of the commodity economy good enough to eliminate monopolies in the economy? Isn't there an institutional innovation that can prevent monopolies from emerging? We can fully understand why people ask these questions. Our analyses of disequilibrium economy and nonidealized government behavior have actually answered these questions. That is, the development of monopolies in the socialist commodity economy has its economic reasons. We cannot explain monopolies simply from the moral or political perspective, nor can we expect to get rid of monopolies simply by taking moral or political measures.

The root cause of monopolies in the socialist commodity economy is the scarcity of some resources and the consequent exclusivity arising from the scarcity. If resources were abundant, these resources would no longer be exclusive to anyone. As long as every market participant has equal access to these resources, nothing but open and perfect competition will happen, and the foundation of monopolies in the economy will naturally disappear. A monopoly in the socialist economy is after all related to the exclusive control over some resources or production factors. To a market participant, as long as he or she has exclusive control over some resources or production factors, he or she can monopolize the products made from these production factors and have full control over their selling prices. To monopolize the market is actually to monopolize resources. This is not only because any product on its own can be considered a resource, but also because all products are made from certain resources and we can also regard a product as a resource. Therefore, as long as a person monopolizes a resource, he or she can also monopolize any product made from the resource and therefore control the market of that product.

At time of the traditional economic system or the dual-track economic system, monopolies originating from scarce resources were common. Of course, there were some other factors leading to monopolies, e.g., the state granted special economic privileges to some sectors, enterprises, or even individuals and some sectors, enterprises, or even individuals gained monopolistic status in the economy due to their administrative powers. These situations were common. The exact purpose of establishing the order of the commodity economy and the institutional innovation that aims to create fair competition is to eliminate these monopolies. However, the efforts that we have made so far have at most eliminated the monopolies originating from these other factors discussed above. For example, the state will no longer grant special economic privileges to certain sectors, enterprises, or individuals. The state will also prohibit some sectors, enterprises, or individuals from gaining monopolistic status in the economy. Yet monopolies due to the scarcity of resources cannot be eliminated by establishing the order of the commodity economy or proposing relevant legislation. Monopolies originating from the scarcity of resources can still exist in the new economic system.

This explains why different degrees of monopoly will still exist in the market under the new economic system after the establishment of the order of the commodity economy. The degree of monopoly in various product markets varies. Some markets have a relatively high degree of monopoly (such as the mineral materials market, the heavy equipment market, and the raw chemical materials market), while other markets have a relatively low degree of monopoly (such as the market of some light industry products). Some markets have almost perfect competition (such as agricultural products market), while others are almost completely monopolistic (such as public utilities). The government should pay attention to different characteristics of these markets and do its utmost to minimize potential economic losses caused by the remaining monopolies in the economy.

Generally speaking, after the order of the commodity economy is established, the government can take action in the following four areas to minimize potential economic losses caused by monopolies that originate from scarce resources:

First of all, the government should understand that some monopolies in the economy arise due to resource scarcity. Therefore, it is necessary for the government to initiate laws and regulations to regulate the possession and utilization of scarce resources in accordance with the intensity of scarcity so that everyone can have an equal opportunity to compete for the possession and utilization of scarce resources. Doing so can prevent some enterprises or individuals from having advantageous opportunities to possess and utilize scarce resources and avoid the development of monopolies in the economy due to privileged possession and utilization of scarce resources.

That is to say, although the intensity of resource scarcity varies, the opportunity to possess and utilize resources should always be equally available for everyone. Except for the possession and utilization of resources for the purpose of national security, which needs special consideration, the possession and utilization of any scarce resource for economic purposes should generally be decided by the competition in the market so that the most suitable candidate can be selected. For instance, the process of public bidding can be used to select the most qualified enterprise to invest in a project or to produce a product.

It is necessary to point out that in several areas or industries, we may not necessarily see numerous participants compete for a project. This is because different areas and industries have different production or operation features. Competitors are subject to certain constraints. For example, the requirements of capital and technological skills can be some of the constraints that enterprises have in participating in competition, and only those who meet the requirements of capital funding and technological capabilities will be qualified. But this does not mean we reject the principle of equal opportunity. Keep in mind that if production factors can flow and combine freely, those enterprises who do not meet the requirements of capital funding and technological capabilities can form business alliances (such as a merger or a joint venture), which will allow them to gain access to new opportunities and raise the odds of winning a bid.

Secondly, even if an enterprise becomes a monopoly via fair competition because of its possession and utilization of scarce resources, we have to know that the price under monopoly and the "monopolistic profit ratio" will be higher compared to that under perfect competition. Therefore, it is necessary for the government to take action so that a portion of the "monopolistic profit" can be collected and used as public fund.

The way that the government treats the monopoly that originates from scarce resources is in accordance with the compensation principle of resource allocation.[1] Here is the reason. If the "monopolistic profit" comes from the possession and utilization of scarce resources, any tax that the government collects from the businesses with "monopolistic profit" because of their possession and utilization of scarce resources, such as resource tax or adjustment tax, will contribute to coordinated economic growth as well as increasing the efficiency of the utilization of scarce resources. The question is whether or not in this case the government should also allow the enterprises that possess and utilize scarce resources to retain a portion of their "monopolistic profit." That is, should the government collect only a portion of the "monopolistic profit" that is above normal profit or all of it? According to our discussions, as the possession and utilization of scarce resources is secured based on competition on a level field with everyone having equal opportunities, the government should only collect a portion of the "monopolistic profit" rather than all of it, especially for the enterprises who need to commit additional resources to organize production factors during their business operations. Otherwise, those

[1]Li Yining [1].

enterprises would lose the motivation to operate their businesses to compete in the market. Meanwhile, that will not help increase resource utilization efficiency continuously.

Thirdly, as there are various types of resources, the intensity of the scarcity of various resources varies, and the reasons why and the way how various resources became scarce are also different, the government should adopt different adjustment measures to regulate the "monopolistic profit" that originates from scarce resources by taking each specific situation into consideration, and the adjustment tax rates that the government applies should also vary accordingly.

We should not think that these resources we are talking about refer to natural resources only. It is relatively easy to understand that monopolies can originate from the possession and utilization of natural resources, because natural resources are scarce. However, besides natural resources, other types of resources can be scarce too. For example, technology and information are resources. New technologies and new information are all scarce resources. As another example, labor force can be a scarce resource in a specific area or industrial sector, or capital may be a scarce resource in a specific area during a certain time period. Therefore, if an enterprise has a new technology or a piece of new information that is inaccessible to others, it can be in a monopolistic position due to the scarcity of the resource and hence earns "monopolistic profit." If an enterprise located in a region that has shortages of labor or capital is able to secure the supply of labor or capital, it will also be able to earn "monopolistic profit." As for the "monopolistic profit" in this example, the government should have a different attitude, as the profit is different from that earned by possessing and utilizing scarce natural resources. When determining the tax rate or other adjustment measures, the government should adopt a relatively lenient way and allow such enterprises that earn "monopolistic profit" through the access to new technologies and new information, or through securing sufficient supplies of labor and capital, to retain a relatively large share of their "monopolistic profit." The government should take a relatively small portion or even waive the adjustment tax during a certain time period. It is obviously unfair if the government fails to do so, because it may hurt the motivation of those enterprises that have developed new technologies or secured new information as resources for their businesses or those enterprises that have made significant efforts to secure labor and capital as resources for their businesses in a tight supply environment.

Fourthly, a monopoly originating from scarce resources will experience a waning process. We should note that while one monopoly originating from one type of scarce resource is waning, another monopoly originating from a different type of scarce resource may develop. As a result, monopolies will always exist in the economy. Therefore, it is necessary for the government to understand the reason why monopolies come and go. Thus, the government can adopt the adjustment measures according to real economic situations, follow the trend of the ups and downs of different monopolies, and minimize potential losses caused by monopolies.

Why does a monopoly originating from a scarce resource gradually lose its power? This issue can be illustrated by the features of different resources. If developing a new technology or obtaining new information leads to a monopoly, sooner or later, the new technology and information will not be scarce any more when it becomes widely known and accessible. If that happens, the enterprises with exclusive access to the technology or information will lose their monopolistic status. If a monopoly formed due to access to sufficient labor or capital in an environment with tight labor or capital supply, it is also unlikely for the monopoly to exist forever, because labor and capital can flow freely in the commodity economy and the profit-seeking principle will direct the flow of labor and capital. Once labor and capital flow under the guidance of this principle, the value of labor and capital will diminish and the monopoly will gradually lose its power.

The most complicated case is the monopolies that originate from scarce natural resources. The constraints of the supply of natural resources, which are different from technology, information, labor, and capital, are likely to allow an entity who possesses and utilizes certain natural resources to maintain monopolistic power for a long time. However, keep in mind that as long as we can achieve breakthroughs in scientific research on substituting some natural resources in a competitive economic environment and apply these substitutes in our daily life, it is still possible for us to see a monopoly that originates from possessing and utilizing some scarce natural resources gradually lose its monopolistic power, and it is impossible for monopolistic price to rise continuously, as the price elasticity of demand will keep a lid on the price escalation and prevent price from being unilaterally determined by the seller. Even though it is a very slow process for the monopoly that originates from scarce natural resources to lose its power, this trend is unstoppable.

Based on these analyses, the government must adopt flexible measures. From the perspective of supporting fair competition, the government should encourage the development and distribution of new technologies and help disseminate new information to facilitate the demise of the monopolies that originate from technologies and information. The government should also apply economic adjustment measures to regulate the supply and demand of labor and capital and to create opportunities for the free flow of these two types of resources so as to facilitate the demise of the monopolies that originate from labor and capital. As for monopolies originating from natural resources, the government can adopt such measures as supporting the research, experiment, production, and distribution of natural resource substitutes, developing new resources and increasing the potential supplies of new resources. If the government adopts these measures, it will to some extent speed up the waning process of a monopoly that originates from scarce natural resources, which will benefit economic growth as well as consumers. Even those enterprises that secure a certain scarce resource via fair competition can benefit from these measures. As a result, the monopolies that still possess some scarce resources would realize that they are still under market competition and thus feel the urge to continue devoting themselves to increasing competitiveness, instead of simply relying on their existing monopolistic position and enjoying the monopolistic privilege.

As we have discussed before, while some monopolies gradually lose their power, others will emerge. Some of them emerge due to the scarcity of certain natural resources, some due to the development of new technologies or information. Thus the government should actually play the dual roles in dealing with monopolies.

That is, it should facilitate the trend that some monopolies lose their power, while appropriately regulating any emerging monopoly, including adjusting income. As long as the economy is in disequilibrium and constraints on resource supply still create monopolies, monopolies will remain. The strategies available to the government in response to monopolies should be two-pronged as we discussed above.

10.2 The Standardization of Institutional Variation and Institutional Innovation

10.2.1 Two Types of Institutional Variation in Institutional Innovation

During the process of establishing the order of the commodity economy, there is an issue related to institutional innovation, which is worth our attention. That is institutional variation. Institutional variation refers to the deviation of the actual institutional innovation from its original design during the development process or shortly after the completion of the development process. The deviation from its original design causes the new institution to fail to perform its expected functions. For instance, in terms of enterprise system innovation, the original design of the leasing system, the subcontracting system, or the shareholding system all took the interests of both owners and managers into consideration and were supposed to motivate enterprises during economic growth. But in reality, the leasing system, the subcontracting system, and the shareholding system all experienced certain variations, resulting in some deviations from their original designs. Another example is the institution innovation for the market, which was originally designed to achieve smooth circulation within distribution channels so as to ensure fair competition and to facilitate the circulation and recombination of production factors. Yet once in place, these institutions more or less changed. Some changes even hindered circulation and blocked fair competition as well as the circulation and recombination of production factors. These are the examples of the so-called institutional variation.

The variation of an institution can be in total or in part. It is hereby referred to as the total or partial variation of the institution that aims to establish the order of the commodity economy or referred to as the total or partial variation of the institution that occurs to different regions or sectors. Even though partial variation of an institution may occur in some regions or sectors, it is worth further research. People tend to think: Why does the institutional variation occur in that particular region or sector, while not in other regions or sectors? Why some institutions have variations while others don't? Why the variation of the same institution differs across different regions and sectors? Research on institutional variation can help deepen the study of institutional innovation.

With further analysis, it won't be difficult for us to find out that institutional variation is not necessarily a bad thing. It can be either good or bad. Now, the criterion of good or bad is whether it is helpful to the establishment of the order of the commodity economy. Since the institutional innovation we are discussing here refers to the type that aims to establish the order of the commodity economy, the criterion for evaluating the effectiveness of the institutional innovation obviously is whether it meets the needs of the establishment of the order of the commodity economy. Whether the design of a specific new institution by an institutional innovation sponsor can meet its anticipated needs must be determined by its performance. In this case, the following scenario may arise: During or after an institutional innovation, the original design of the institution innovation performs differently in reality, and hence variation arises during the execution. The variation can turn out to be even better than the original design and can better satisfy the needs of the establishment of the order of the commodity economy. In addition, it can be conducive to revising the original design and improving and completing the new institution. This type of institutional variation, regardless of whether it is a total or partial variation, should be considered a good thing. However, what we should pay more attention to is a different type of institutional variation, one that prevents the order of the commodity economy from being established, or a bad institutional variation, so to speak. This type of institutional variation, if we use a derogative term to describe it, can be called "institutional distortion" or "institutional deformation." If we use a colloquial sentence to describe it, it is what people normally say: "These rules are very good, but they are simply off when executed at the grass-root level." Why are they "off?" What do we do when they are "off?" These issues are exactly what we need to resolve in our research on institutional innovation. In the following analysis of institutional variation, we specifically refer to bad institutional variation, or "institutional distortion."

10.2.2 The Primary Cause of Institutional Variation

The primary cause of institutional variation can be analyzed from the following four perspectives: government behavior, enterprise behavior, personal behavior, and market mechanism.

1. Analysis from the Perspective of Government Behavior

Nonidealized government behavior is one of the main causes of institutional variation. As we discussed earlier, we can set aside nonidealized government behavior during the design of an institutional innovation in our analysis and assume that the original design is fairly good, but it has gone off the track during execution. This type of institutional variation is likely to occur in the following three scenarios from the perspective of government behavior:

First, improperly organized government institutions and concomitant ambiguously defined government agencies' responsibilities and functions bring obstruction or even drive them to take action to counter the performance of other agencies with rights and responsibilities endowed by the old institution during an institutional innovation. As a result, even if an institutional innovation is well designed in the beginning, it may be difficult to meet the anticipated requirements during execution. To resolve the issues in this scenario, we should start with political reforms and streamlining government institutions as well as simplifying and clarifying the rights and responsibilities of each government agency. As long as government institutions remain improperly organized, government agencies will continue to obstruct each other, and institutional variation will be inevitable during an institutional innovation.

Second, the quality and capability of government officials cannot meet the requirements of the institutional innovation. It is relatively easy to understand this point. Many examples have demonstrated that the cause of institutional variation was the relatively poor quality and capability of government officials. Some of them misunderstood the meaning of the institutional innovation, some tackled issues using certain measures that were detrimental to the institutional innovation out of habit, some failed to stick to the original plan due to incapability, and some even pursued undue personal benefit from the institutional innovation, all of which would cause institutional variation. Therefore, it is very important to continuously improve the quality and capability of government officials so as to eliminate institutional variation during the institutional innovation.

Third, there are no complementary measures. Any new institutional innovation must have some complementary measures in place if we are to avoid institutional variation. They are put in place to ensure that the institutional innovation can be completed. However, it is not always necessary to have a complete set of complementary measures in place before we can proceed with new institutional innovations. As a result, institutional variation arises. In this case, can government prepare various complementary measures during the planning of an institutional innovation and then introduce new institution only after these measures take effect? In theory, this is possible. If the government did do that, institutional variation would likely be avoided, at least from this perspective. In reality, however, the situation will be much more complicated than our theoretical assumptions. This is because either the government is unable to precisely predict social and economic changes and the changes of personal behavior after a new institution is implemented or it is impossible for the government to take all contingencies into consideration. Therefore, the government will always feel that there are not enough complementary measures during an institutional innovation. As a result, it is still possible to see institutional variation.

2. Analysis from the Perspective of Enterprise Behavior

Various institutional innovations brought to the economy are traced to the changing interests of enterprises. In response to an institutional innovation, enterprises normally adopt certain strategies to maximize profits or minimize losses from the new institution. If we assume that enterprises are real goods producers who make their own decisions and are responsible for their profits and losses, they will follow the profitability principle as well as their operating budgets and take action by balancing the profits and losses therefrom. In this case, even though some of the action they take may cross the legal boundary, the profitability principle will direct them to consider the consequences of breaking the law. It is for this reason that they have concerns and are forced to behave to some extent. An enterprise that makes its own business decisions, takes responsibility for its profits and losses, and operates under the guidance of the profitability principle will likely take action pursuant to the existing laws and regulations. Generally speaking, such enterprise behavior will not lead to institutional variation, because they are within the boundary of the existing laws and regulations.

Now, let us analyze the scenario where enterprises have not severed their affiliation with administrative institutions. As enterprises are not responsible for profits and losses, or only responsible for profits but not losses, the profitability principle will have limited impact on their behavior or even fail to work, causing enterprise behavioral shortsightedness and driving some enterprises to potentially ignore the consequences of breaking the law. The results will facilitate or foster institutional variation. In other words, the variation of the proposed institution is closely related to imperfect enterprise operation mechanism as well as enterprise behavioral shortsightedness. Nevertheless, this does not mean that every enterprise that has not been able to make its own business decisions or take responsibility for profits and losses will break the law. If these enterprises act according to the law, institutional variation will be avoided.

Here, we have to answer two questions. The first one: Why won't the actions of the enterprises that make their own business decisions and are responsible for profits and losses cause institutional variation if such actions are permitted by the law? The second one, why are the enterprises that are not responsible for their profits and losses more prone to violate the law than those who are responsible for their profits and losses?

The first question can be answered as follows: Per our earlier assumptions, institutional variation specifically refers to "institutional distortion," excluding any necessary revisions or additions to the original design of an institutional innovation during the execution process. If enterprises act according to the law, it is likely that they have provided the government with some information that will help improve the institutional innovation. With such information, the government can revise and improve the institution. In this sense, we shall conclude that any action that microeconomic units take within the boundary of the law will help the macroeconomic departments of the government improve and revise their decision-making. This scenario, however, does not fall into the institutional variation that we are discussing here.

The second question can be answered in this way: The question is raised based on the premise that the government regular checks, monitors, and punishes all enterprises for any violation of the law. If the government does not check or monitor any violation of the law regularly nor severely punish lawbreaking activities, any enterprise, even those that are responsible for their own profits and losses, may take action beyond the boundary of the law, which contributes to institutional variation. On the contrary, if the government effectively checks and monitors enterprises for any violation of the law and severely punishes them for any criminal activity, such as confiscating assets, levying financial penalties, revoking business licenses, and sending enterprise management to jail if necessary, we will likely see far fewer lawbreaking activities of those enterprises that are responsible for their own profits and losses. The enterprises that continue to break the law are those that are not responsible for their profits and losses and that are still controlled by government administrative institutions or quasi-government entities. The lawbreaking activities of these entities will to a large extent account for institutional variation.

3. Analysis from the Perspective of Personal Behavior

Basically, individuals should not be blamed for institutional variation. The reason is quite straightforward. Although everyone may have an opinion about an institutional innovation and take action to maximize profits or minimize losses according to his or her own interests, one person has limited power and his or her actions are not powerful enough to cause institutional variation. Compared to government behavior or enterprise behavior, personal behavior plays a much smaller role in institutional variation.

Yet this is what happens in a normal situation. In any one of the following two situations, personal behavior can still play a relatively significant part in institutional variation:

First, when the behavior of a person is no longer representative of that of an individual person but that of a group of individuals, it will exert a much more significant impact on institutional variation. In this case, the individual, be it a consumer, a provider of production factors, or a resident in a community, will likely act collectively according to their own interests, which will lead to institutional variation.

Second, significant changes of personal expectations or extremely unstable or chaotic personal expectations, despite being personal behavior, may have relatively substantial influences on institutional variation. In this case, changing personal expectations and extremely unstable or chaotic personal expectations will be reflected by personal consumption behavior or personal saving behavior. Abnormal changes in personal consumption or saving behavior will cause institutional variation. Keep in mind that even if a single person's behavior has limited influence, we cannot ignore the power of demonstration effects. Under such influence, abnormal changes of personal consumption and saving behavior will influence society and potentially create disorder in the economy, which will cause institutional variation.

4. Analysis from the Perspective of Market Mechanism

Imperfect market mechanism is another important reason for institutional variation. We have to keep in mind that the implementation of institutional innovation in the commodity economy is linked to market mechanism in every way. For example, the way in which profits and losses of different institutional innovation sponsors are adjusted is always reflected by market activities. To adjust the various economic relations that an institutional innovation requires is actually to adjust the relations among the various market participants in the marketplace. Resource recombination, or the recombination of production factors, that the institutional innovation aims to achieve, cannot come true without the market playing its role in the commodity economy. All these examples have fully demonstrated that the more perfect the market mechanism, the more likely the institutional innovation will meet its anticipated goals. On the contrary, the more imperfect the market mechanism, the more likely an institutional variation will occur.

In view of the current economic realities in China, it is especially important that we pay attention to the impact of the imperfect market mechanism on institutional variation. Because if the market mechanism is not perfect, the market may fail to accurately reflect all information that market participants need, nor will the market be able to quickly deliver economic information in its entirety to every participant. As a result, even if the government may have fully considered the redistribution of economic interests after institutional innovation before its proposition and implementation and have made all necessary arrangements, market participants may react in various ways and disrupt the government's arrangements, as they are unable to collect accurate economic information from the market to make right decisions. The reason why variation occurs during the process of institutional innovation is often traced to the imperfection of the market mechanism as well as the consequences therefrom.

In addition, the imperfection of the market mechanism can also be revealed by transactions that are nonpublic, noncontractual, and nonmonetary. Nonpublic, noncontractual, and nonmonetary transactions can bring two outcomes that are detrimental to institutional innovation:

First, such phenomena prevent the government who initiates the institutional innovation from collecting accurate market information, leading the government to some superficial signs that divert the government away from various nonpublic, noncontractual, and nonmonetary transactions that significantly impact the economy. As a result, institutional variation may arise during the implementation of the new institution.

Second, because transactions are done on a nonpublic, noncontractual, and nonmonetary basis, market participants may feel the market lacks transparency and become more uncertain about market prospect, which causes behavioral shortsightedness and leads to some unintended precautionary measures, such as purchasing extra raw materials, storing excess cash, and accelerating the purchases of consumer goods. All of these play a part in causing institutional variation.

The above analysis of government behavior, enterprise behavior, personal behavior, and market mechanism allows us to understand why we cannot simply rely on the original correct design of an institution initiated by institutional innovation sponsors to eliminate institutional variation during the process of institutional innovation. To minimize and eliminate institutional variation, we need to simultaneously work on government behavior, enterprise behavior, personal behavior, and market mechanism. We should not only improve government institutions, enhance the quality and capability of government officials, and implement complementary measures so that enterprises can be goods producers who are responsible for their own profits and losses but also gradually optimize the market mechanism so that market participants can develop stable expectations of their future.

10.2.3 The Possibility of Standardizing Institutional Innovation

In earlier discussions, we have explained the main reasons for institutional variation and pointed out in theory that we must start with multiple areas to minimize or prevent institutional variation, that is, to standardize institutional innovation. Next, let us analyze these two questions:

First, assuming that an institutional variation has occurred during the process of an institutional innovation, is it possible for us to restore the original design in a certain way after the institution is introduced? Restoring a distorted institutional innovation to its original design is called institutional innovation restoration, or institutional innovation standardization.

Second, assuming that we have restored the original design of the institutional innovation by making some adjustments to the variation of the institution, does this mean that the institutional innovation is back on track?

These two questions are worth our attention. They tell us that it is necessary to conduct more in-depth research on the institutional innovation process.

We need to recognize the possibility of institutional innovation restoration, which is to change nonstandardized institutional innovation back to standardized institutional innovation. Institutional innovation restoration is dependent upon how the interests of various groups are adjusted. In the aftermath of institutional variation, the interests of the sponsor and every other stakeholder of the institutional innovation are somewhat changed. It is the changing interests that make it possible to restore the institutional innovation. To what degree can institutional innovation be restored is contingent upon the actual situation.

Now, let us first look at three possible scenarios of institutional innovation restoration.

1. Let us assume that a new institution to be introduced incurs a variation due to improper government organizational structure, lack of capable or quality government officials, and lack of government complementary measures. When institution variation takes place, the government serving as the institutional innovation sponsor fails to realize its expected benefits. This situation may force the government to take necessary action, such as carrying out government organizational reforms, enhancing the quality and capability of government officials, and initiating complementary measures. These measures will likely

restore the institutional innovation. Institutional innovation restoration does not mean the self-adjustment of an institution, but the adjustment to an institution initiated by the government.

2. If the variation of a new institution following its implementation is caused by the fact that enterprises violate the law or that personal expectations are chaotic or extremely unstable, the government will take necessary measures upon seeing institutional variation, because it has not received its expected benefits as the institutional innovation sponsor. These measures include reinforcing legislation and law enforcement, banning various lawbreaking activities, and stabilizing personal expectations. On the other hand, if the government realizes that the main cause of institutional variation is that government administrative institutions are still in control of enterprises, it will initiate enterprise system reform to turn enterprises into economic entities that make their own business decisions and take responsibility for their profits and losses as early as possible. All of these measures will help restore the institutional innovation. Next, let us look at enterprises and individuals. They may or may not react to a new institution and take action that causes the institutional variation. However, as long as their benefits are still likely to increase under the new institution, they will support the new institution. Especially when the government takes necessary measures to prevent enterprises from breaking the law and to stabilize personal expectations, enterprises and individuals for the sake of their own benefits will gradually avoid the behavior that may cause institutional variation, which supports institutional innovation restoration.
3. If the main cause of institutional variation is the imperfect market mechanism, whether the institutional innovation can be restored or not in this case is dependent on how perfect the market mechanism can be. During the development of the commodity economy, perfecting the market mechanism becomes an inevitable trend driven by market participants' common interests. Therefore, we can come to the belief that the interaction between various interests will likely lead to institutional innovation restoration after an institutional variation occurs.

We need to further point out here that institutional innovation restoration is meant in relation to institutional variation. If institutional variation refers to the degree of deviation of an institutional innovation, institutional innovation restoration will refer to the correction to the degree of the institutional variation or restoring the institutional innovation to its original track to a certain degree. To what degree can an institutional innovation be restored is of course dependent upon the efforts of the government as the institutional innovation sponsor and the corrective action of enterprises and individuals in response to the institutional innovation according to the profitability principle and is also closely related to the degree of the institutional variation. That is, if the degree of the institutional variation upon the implementation of the new institution is relatively low, it will be relatively easy to restore the institutional innovation. On the contrary, the higher the degree of the institutional variation, i.e., the institutional innovation undergoes significant variations, the more difficult the institutional innovation restoration. In other words, not every institutional variation can be restored to its original design. Sometimes, after going through multiple variations, an institutional innovation cannot be restored to its original design. In that case, it is necessary to carry out a different institutional innovation, namely, to give up restoring the institutional innovation and to start the implementation of a new institution from scratch.

In addition, even if an institutional innovation is restored, it may not necessarily return to its original track. Institutional innovation restoration only means making corrections to an institutional variation to a certain degree. We can explain this by using pendulum as an example. When a pendulum swings back and forth, it may not necessarily swing exactly back to its original position. It may deviate slightly from its original position. Why can't it always return to its original position? Why can't institutional innovation restoration completely eliminate the deviation arising from institutional variation? This exactly illustrates the features of market activities and enterprise and individual behavior.

Keep in mind that it is common that the market mechanism is imperfect from the perspective of market activities. What we see is varying degrees of market imperfection. When we say that the market is becoming perfect, we only mean that the degree of market imperfection is abating. Therefore, regardless of how an institutional innovation sponsor or each stakeholder of the institutional innovation adjusts its behavior according to its own interests in response to an institutional variation, institutional innovation restoration will always be constrained by market imperfection and hence unable to completely eliminate institutional variation. This also reflects the limitation of institutional innovation restoration.

From the perspective of enterprise behavior as well as personal behavior, we cannot ignore the power of behavioral habit. When institutional variation occurs after enterprises and individuals take their own profits and losses into consideration out of their interests, they will likely develop certain behavioral pattern. For example, some enterprises tend to build excess inventories of raw materials, while some consumers tend to change their consumption and saving habits. These habits, once established, can hardly be changed in a short period of time, they will continue influencing economic activities over some periods of time, that is, the influence tends to persist for some time before disappearing, which also restricts the degree to which the institutional innovation can be restored.

In summary, the study on institutional innovation restoration and its likelihood helps us further understand the features of institutional innovation. Our research on the institutional innovation associated with the establishment of order in the commodity economy as well as on the phenomena where some new institutions or measures underwent significant variations at the beginning while experiencing waning variations later is all related to the issue of institutional innovation restoration. Therefore, our discussions are meaningful. Nonetheless, they are still preliminary. If we want to clarify the relationship between institutional variation and institutional innovation restoration, we will have to analyze every new institution or measure on a case-by-case basis. The overall trend is always straightforward: During the transition from the product economy to the commodity economy, institutional variation and institutional innovation restoration of varying degrees will exist side by side as long as the government functions properly as the institutional innovation sponsor, and they are not contradictory.

10.2.4 Relative Stability Following Institutional Innovation

After an institutional innovation is implemented, the institution will remain relatively stable for a period of time. The relative stability following an institutional innovation can be called "institutional equilibrium." Institutional equilibrium means that the institutional innovation sponsor has achieved its goal of adjusting the interests of various stakeholders through institutional innovation and there will be no additional benefits for the institutional innovation sponsor if it continues to reform the institution or propose a new one. As a result, all market participants have reached the consensus that there is no need to pursue further institutional innovation, which leads to relative stability after the institutional innovation.

Now, how long can the relative stability following an institutional innovation last? What kind of situations will break the relative stability and drive another round of institutional innovation? It all depends on whether the objective and subjective conditions have changed and how probable the interests of each stakeholder can be readjusted subsequently. In terms of objective conditions, any change in economic conditions, production technologies, and market environment can bring about the prospect of a new institution and allows a market participant to have an opportunity to realize additional benefits. In terms of subjective conditions, if a market participant as an institutional innovation sponsor has gathered sufficient information about the changes in objective conditions, understood the potential changes of various stakeholders' interests due to the new institutional innovation, the benefits to the economy and to the institutional innovation itself as result of such changes, and developed a realistic plan for the institutional innovation, the subjective conditions for the institutional innovation have become mature. When both subjective and objective conditions are met, the relative stability following the original institutional innovation will fall apart, and a new round of institutional innovation will begin.[2]

From a purely theoretical perspective, the abovementioned process of "institutional innovation—the relative stability following institutional innovation—new institutional innovation" is well grounded and consistent with the overall trend of institutional innovation. The problem is that objective conditions changed fairly quickly during the transition from the product economy to the commodity economy. Thus after the institutional innovation was implemented, it was hard to maintain the relative stability for a relatively long period of time. Sometimes, no sooner was

[2]Li Yining [2].

an institutional innovation implemented than the request for a new institutional innovation was raised. On the other hand, during the transition from the product economy to the commodity economy, more than one institution needed innovation in order to establish the order of the commodity economy. There were several institutions that underwent innovation at the same time, such as the enterprise system, the financial system, fiscal policies, the employment and wage system, and the social security system. The institutional innovation in these areas impacted each other. Even though an institutional innovation in one area had been implemented at a certain time, it was very difficult to maintain the relative stability for a relatively long time as long as institutional innovations in other areas were still in progress. In other words, even if the relative stability had been realized, it would break apart fairly quickly. The reason is simple: Every institutional innovation is one part of a complete system. An institutional innovation in one area is only a component of the systemic institutional innovation. Therefore, after an individual institutional innovation, it is very difficult to see the relative stability that comes with the implementation of the systemic institutional innovation, and the relative stability after the implementation of the individual institutional innovation is also temporary. If we also take into consideration institutional variation and institutional innovation restoration that we discussed earlier, it will be much easier to understand the transience of the relative stability following an institutional innovation.

Of course, we do not deny the possibility of realizing relative stability after an institutional innovation, nor do we mean that we have to undertake institutional innovation continuously in one specific area, i.e., immediately starting the preparation for another round of institutional innovation right after an institutional innovation in one area is completed. This is not only impossible but also unnecessary. If we force ourselves to do so, more institutional variations will likely occur, which will not benefit the institutional innovation sponsors as well as each market participant. The reason why we mention the transience of the relative stability following institutional innovation is based on two considerations:

First of all, understanding the transience of the relative stability helps us further understand the significance of coordinating and balancing various institutional innovations in different areas. We cannot think that an institutional innovation in one area will remain for the long term once implemented. The understanding of institutional innovation as a systematic and coordinated project helps us understand that an institutional innovation in one specific area cannot work without a series of other institutional innovations. The transition from the product economy to the commodity economy is dependent upon how well the systematic institutional innovation performs, not simply upon one component or a few components of the systematic institutional innovation. The institutional innovation during the establishment of the order of the commodity economy should be viewed dynamically rather than statically.

Secondly, having understood the transience of the relative stability, we should hold the belief that it is applicable to each particular institutional innovation. To be specific, we cannot require that everything be perfect right from the start or even wait for the perfect condition by postponing the implementation of an institutional innovation, nor can we hope, on the other hand, that a new institution can be launched once and for all, thinking it will last forever with no need for further revision, addition, or improvement after being implemented. The scientific attitude should be as follows: When the time is right, an institutional innovation shall be launched, and there is no need to wait for the new institution to become flawless; after the new institution is implemented, we should understand that it will be relatively stable over a short period of time and that it will need to be revised, added, or improved according to how well other relevant institutional innovations proceed during economic reforms.

As a result, our understanding of the relative stability following institutional innovation is comprehensive and beneficial to the establishment of the order of the commodity economy.

References

1. Li, Yining. (1986). *Socialist political economics* (pp. 365–371). The Commercial Press, Beijing, China.
2. Li, Yining. (1982). *The origin and development of institutional innovation theory, foreign economics review* (2nd ed., pp. 64–124). Shanghai People's Press, Shanghai, China.

Glossary

板块论 Thesis of infiltration
保值 Maintain value, capital preservation, preserve capital
边际成本 Marginal cost
边际收益 Marginal revenue
不完全竞争 Imperfect competition
不协调 Mismatch
财政支出 Government spending
差别税率 Differential tax rate
差别利率 Differential interest rate
产品经济体制 Product economy, product economic system
产权关系 Property rights
产出决策 Output decision
产业结构调整 Industrial restructuring
产值 Output value, output
超额需求 Excess demand
超额供给 Excess supply
承包制 Subcontracting system
存货 Inventory
单一市场定价机制 Single-market pricing mechanism
地区经济结构 Regional economy structure
动态均衡 Dynamic equilibrium
二元机制 Dual mechanism
房地产市场(房产市场) Real estate market
非均衡 Disequilibrium
非瓦尔拉均衡 Non-Walrasian equilibrium
福利 Welfare, benefit
个体户 Small business, small business owner
供给不足 Undersupply, supply gap, insufficient supply
供给结构 Supply structure
供求矛盾 Supply and demand mismatch

Y. Li, *Chinese Economy in Disequilibrium*, China Academic Library,
DOI 10.1007/978-3-642-39558-1, © Foreign Language Teaching and Research
Publishing Co., Ltd and Springer-Verlag Berlin Heidelberg 2014

固定价格 Fixed price
固定资产 Fixed assets
股份制 Shareholding system
过剩 Surplus
合同谈判成本 Contract negotiation cost
合同履行成本 Contract enforcement cost
红利率 Dividend rate
货币市场 Money market
汇率制度 Exchange rate system
机会成本 Opportunity cost
技术结构 Technology structure
价格改革 Price reform
价格刚性 Price rigidity
价格双轨制 Dual-price system
价格弹性 Price elasticity
价格调节 Price adjustment
价格信号 Price signal
价格预期 Price expectation
兼并 Merger
交易成本 Trading cost, transaction cost
交易活动 Trading activity, transactional activity
结构性失衡 Structural imbalance
紧缩 Deflation
警戒线 Warning line
经济的不平衡增长 Unbalanced economic growth
经济的平衡增长 Balanced economic growth
经济结构 Economic structure
经济体制改革 Reform of economic system
经济调节 Economic regulation
经济效率 Economic efficiency
经济运行机制 Mechanism of the operation of the economy
经济增长 Economic growth
经济增长主体 Agents of economic growth
经济资源 Economic resources
经济纠纷 Economic dispute
净收益 Net return
纠偏 Rectification
就业结构 Employment structure
绝对价格水平 Absolute price level
决策权 Decision rights
均衡价格 Equilibrium price
均衡利息率 Equilibrium interest rate
亏损 Economic loss, loss
可支配收入 Disposable income

凯恩斯经济学派 Keynesian theorists
控股制 Controlling shareholder system
劳动生产率 Labor productivity
劳务 Labor services
劳务市场 Labor services market
劳务支出 Labor expenditure
累进制个人所得税 Progressive income tax
历史比例原则 Principle of historical ratios, the history principle
利息率预期 Expected interest rate
利益刚性 Rigidity of interests
利益分配 Interest distribution
利益机制 Interest mechanism
利益原则 Profitability principle
利益约束 Constrained by self-interest
利益主体 Master of one's own interests
联产承包责任制 Household responsibility system
零短缺度 No shortage
零失业率 Zero unemployment
零通货膨胀率 Zero inflation
流通 Circulation
垄断 Monopoly
垄断价格 Monopoly price
垄断利润率 Monopoly profit margin
摩擦 Friction
目标机制 Goals mechanism
目标吸引 Lure of goals
目标原则(优先照顾原则) Goal-priority principle (the priority principle)
内部经济 Internal economy
逆效应 Counter effect
农村产业结构 Rural economic structure
农业合作化 Movement of Agricultural Collectivization
农业生产率 Productivity in agriculture
农产品平准基金 Agricultural production stabilization fund
配额均衡 Rationing equilibrium
偏好 Preference
平衡增长 Balanced growth
平均成本 Average cost
平均分配原则 Equal distribution principle
平均国民收入 Per capita national income
平均技术熟练水平 Average skill proficiency/level
平均收益 Average revenue
企业行为 Enterprise behavior
企业体制 Enterprise system
企业运行机制 Enterprise operation mechanism

企业制度的改革 Corporate institutional reform, corporate reform
缺口 Gap
商品比价 Commodity price ratio, the ratio of the prices of comparable merchandise
商品供给缺口 Commodity supply gap
商品市场 Commodity market
商品需求缺口 Commodity demand shortfall
商品经济体制 Commodity economy
商品经济秩序 Commodity economy order
商品生产者 Goods producer
社会购买力 Societal purchasing power, purchasing power
生产成本 Production cost
生产过剩 Overproduction
生产力水平 Productivity
生产能力 Production capacity
生产要素 Production factor
生产要素的流动 Flow of production factors
生产资料 Means of production
渗透论 Penetration theory
剩余 Surplus
市场单一定价制 Sole market price
市场的优先原则、垄断原则 The priority principle, the monopoly principle
市场不完善 Market imperfection, underdeveloped market
市场化 Market orientation, market-oriented
市场结构 Market structure
市场配额 Market quota
市场调节 Market regulation
市场机制 Market mechanism
市场经济体制 Market economy system
市场缺口 Demand shortfall
市场选择 Market selection
市场引导 Market leading
适度规模经营 Optimal scale management
失业 Unemployment
收入分配 Income distribution
收入决策 Income decision
数量配额 Quantity rationing
数量限制 Quantity constraint
双轨价格 Dual-track price system
双轨经济体制 Dual-track economic system
生产规模 Production scale
生产资料 Production materials
数量-价格调节措施 Quantity–price adjustment measures
数量调节 Quantity adjustment

税后利润 After-tax profit
税率 Tax rate
私营户 Private enterprises, small business owners
所有制改革 Ownership reform
所有制体系 Ownership structure
体制改革 Institutional reform
贴现 Discount
贴现率 Discounting factor
通货膨胀 Inflation
投入决策 Input decision
投资主体 Investment principal
土地所有权 Land ownership
瓦尔拉均衡 Walrasian equilibrium
外部经济 External economy
外汇收入 Foreign exchange earnings, foreign exchange proceeds
外汇市场 Foreign exchange market
完全竞争 Perfect competition
微观经济单位 Microeconomic unit
无效供给 Ineffective supply
无效投资 Ineffective investment
物质生产部门 Material production sector
物质生产领域 Material production
物质资源 Material resources
现金持有定额 Cash holding quota
相对价格水平 Relative price level
消费结构 Consumption composition
消费品市场 Consumer goods market
消费信贷 Consumption credit
销售收入 Sales income
销路 Market potential
小生产者 Small-scale producer, small producer
效力递减 Diminishing effectiveness
效率标准 Efficiency criteria
效率判断 Efficiency judgment
效率增长潜力 Potential in efficiency growth
信贷量 Credit amount
信贷支出 Credit expenditure
信贷规模控制 Credit scale control
信贷配额制 Credit rationing
信贷平衡 Credit market equilibrium
信贷条件 Credit condition
信贷制度 Credit system
信息不完备 Incomplete information
信息成本 Information cost

新经济体制 New economic system
行政改革 Administrative reform
行政机构附属物 Affiliation with administrative institution
行为的长期化 Long-term oriented (behavior), long-term orientation
需求价格弹性 Price elasticity in demand
需求约束 Demand constraint
需求主体 Buyer, purchaser
需求不足 Lack of demand
需求结构 Demand structure
预防性措施 Precautionary measures
预期 Expectation
预期纯利益 Expected net interest
预算约束 Budget constraint
运行机制 Operational mechanism
政府调节 Government regulation
再投资 Reinvestment
增值 Appreciation
政府调节 Government regulation
政府计划 Government plans
指标 Indicator
指导性计划 Nonmandatory planning;
滞后 Lag
滞销 Poor sales
滞涨 Stagflation
制度创新理论 Theory of institutional innovation
制度创新主体 Sponsoring entities of institutional innovation
制度创新复归 Institutional innovation restoration
制度均衡 Institutional equilibrium
制度变型 Institutional variation
转让 Transfer
资金市场 Capital market
资金周转 Fund turnover rate
资源存量 Stock of resources
资源短缺 Resource shortage
资源分配比例 Resource distribution ratio
资源利用效率标准 Efficiency principle of resource utilization
资源浪费 Resource waste
资源配置 Resource allocation
资源配置不当 Resource misallocation
资源配置机制 Resource allocation mechanism
资源投入和组合 Resource input and combination
自主权 Right(s)
指令性经济 Mandatory economy
总量失衡 Aggregate imbalance

自负盈亏 Liable/responsible for one's own profits and losses
自行调节功能 Self-regulatory function
自主经营 Make one's own business decisions
自主经营权 Decision-making right(s)
总供给 Aggregate supply
总需求 Aggregate demand
租赁 Lease
自主经营 Independent management, independent operation

MIX
Papier aus verantwortungsvollen Quellen
Paper from responsible sources
FSC® C105338

If you have any concerns about our products,
you can contact us on
ProductSafety@springernature.com

In case Publisher is established outside the EU,
the EU authorized representative is:
Springer Nature Customer Service Center GmbH
Europaplatz 3, 69115 Heidelberg, Germany

Printed by Libri Plureos GmbH
in Hamburg, Germany